GARCIA

Also by Jerry Garcia

Harrington Street
Jerry Garcia's Amazing Grace

Also by Charles Reich

The Greening of America
Opposing the System

Also by Jann Wenner

Lennon Remembers

GARCIA

A SIGNPOST TO NEW SPACE

The *Rolling Stone* Interview by Charles Reich and Jann Wenner, plus a Stoned Sunday Rap with Jerry, Charles and Mountain Girl

DA CAPO PRESS
A Member of the Perseus Books Group

Designed by Reginald Thompson
Set in 11-point Bell MT by The Perseus Books Group

Cataloging-in-Publication data for this book is available from the Library of Con-
gress.

First Da Capo Press edition 2003
Originally published by Straight Arrow Books
Reprinted by arrangement with Rolling Stone, LLC
ISBN 978-0-306-81253-8

Published by Da Capo Press
A Member of the Perseus Books Group
http://www.dacapopress.com

Da Capo Press books are available at special discounts for bulk purchases in the U.S.
by corporations, institutions, and other organizations. For more information, please
contact the Special Markets Department at the Perseus Books Group, 11 Cambridge Center, Cambridge, MA 02142, or call (800) 255-1514 or (617) 252-5298, or
e-mail special.markets@perseusbooks.com.

CONTENTS

FOREWORD

"The Interview with Garcia" was always one of the things I put off into some indefinite future. Jerry was always around and of course, we'd do it sooner or later. But five years later? Garcia was one of the earliest and most enthusiastic admirers of the interview segments in *Rolling Stone*. He told me that after issue four.

What finally brought on the interview, at long last, was meeting Charles Reich, the Professor of Law from Yale who wrote *The Greening of America*. I had never read that book and was skeptical about him or about *anyone*—who hadn't been around from the *beginning* explaining the new culture—"consciousness III" as he called it.

Reich visited our offices in San Francisco in 1970. He said he had been turned on in 1967, during a summer in Berkeley, listening to a Jefferson Airplane album from a window as he was walking down Telegraph Avenue. After reading an interview with him that we published in *Rolling Stone*, I was amazed at how deep his understanding of rock and roll was and how solidly based his musical knowledge was. Reich knew what he was talking about. And it turned out he was a Grateful Dead freak.

He, too, hit me with the question: How come you haven't done an interview with Garcia?

No one else ever popped up who wanted to do the interview and it always waited on me. Perhaps the true reason was that I had lost touch with the Dead. When Charles Reich asked me the question, I hadn't really listened to a Grateful Dead album since their first one and only recently had "Casey Jones" slipped into my ears. After their first album, I was running some insane rock and roll newspaper and got into Otis Redding like mad. The Dead, as far as I could pick up, had gone psychedelic, which had begun to lose interest for me. I would see Jerry Garcia around in various scenes, we'd yak, but . . . different places.

The truth of the matter is that I knew the Dead from when they were the Warlocks, I had known Jerry Garcia from the beginning of our careers in the San Francisco Scene. "The first time I saw them" . . . San Jose, after a Rolling Stones concert. I wandered into a Kesey scene there that turned out to be their first Acid Test. I remember asking someone (who turned out to be Phil Lesh) who they were. "We're the Grateful Dead" he said, and the impact, in my state of mind at that point, was severe.

Anyway, it took a professor from Yale to turn me on to the Dead again. He suggested that, together, we do an interview with Jerry: I'd do the major portions myself and he'd come along and ask one or two questions of his own. Reich knew the lyrics and spoke intelligently about them; I knew their history. It would be a good combination, and God knows, Charles "Conscious III" Reich Meets Jerry "Captain Trips" Garcia might turn into something of its own. I called Garcia in the spring and told him what the shot was. Open and always amiable, he agreed.

In July, Reich was at our offices raring to go and to settle who was going to be certain the tape recorder was operating correctly (me). I gave Charles our files on the Dead, and ordered *Anthem of the Sun* through *American Beauty* for myself from the local distributor that day. The next Saturday, I met Charles in his Avis sedan at a stopsign in one of Marin County's oceanside towns on the edge of Mount Tamalpais.

Garcia lives a suburban life with his old lady, Mountain Girl (once of the Merry Pranksters and a close friend of Kesey's in those days) and their two little girls. Their house is surrounded by sea-swept eucalyptus trees, five-foot hedges and large rose bushes, beyond which is a magnificent view of the Pacific Ocean and the Far East, as far as the imagination can take you.

On the lawn that looks onto that magnificent view, Charles Reich, myself, Jerry Garcia and Mountain Girl sat on a sunny afternoon with the tape recorder turned on. Five hours later, I packed up the machine and headed back to the city, not entirely sure I could drive too well and not entirely sure at all what had just gone down. Charles Reich was wandering around somewhere in back of the house remarking on the vibrancy of the trees and Jerry had to be in Berkeley at 7:00 for a gig.

I had the transcripts of the tapes three weeks later. What happened was one interview that I did with Jerry, based in an old familiarity and best described as the good old Grateful Dead trip; and a whole other statement that Reich was looking for: Jerry Garcia as spokesman, teacher and philosopher. To be honest, there came a point in that afternoon where I sank into my chair with my hands over my face, wanting out of the whole proposition: Reich was asking questions I thought either achingly obvious or obviously unanswerable But Garcia had done his best to explain.

After reading the transcript of that session, Garcia's intricate and compassionate replies to Reich's questions and his easy reminiscences of scenes where I just prompted the memories, I felt we had come up with the remarkable. Reich asked what no hip sophisticate would ever have asked, and Jerry—without hesitation or pretension—tried to answer it all.

A few weeks later, Reich went back to do another two hours on tape. A few months later I also returned to talk with Jerry for another four hours.

Charles Reich put it all into a rough chronological order and I edited it for publication. (He is identified as the interviewer in several passages where I felt it important to indicate the dialogue between the professor and the professional.) Almost half a year after the interview was published in *Rolling Stone*, Charles went back again, as he describes in his Introduction, for what turned out to be the Stoned Sunday Rap, published here for the first time. And thus we did, at long last, "The Interview with Garcia."

Jann Wenner
May 1972

INTRODUCTION

Jerry Garcia is a symbol of everything that is new and changing and rebellious in America. Yet when we read his story, we find that he is the very essence of the old American dream, the poor boy who makes good, who follows in the footsteps of his dead Spanish musician father, and who, while still a very young man, achieves wide recognition for his art as well as a house on a bluff overlooking the Pacific. How is it possible that both of these statements are true? What is the real nature of the new directions in which his life and his work have been heading?

Talking with Jerry on his front lawn, the sun bright and hot, flowers on all sides, a feeling of serene remoteness from radical political demonstrations, crowded concerts, the exotic world of the Haight-Ashbury, I felt a bit like a groupie, sitting uneasily with legendary characters like Jerry and Mountain Girl. But I tried to keep after the question of evolution, the idea of man and the cosmos that slowly grew out of the good times and acid tests and all the other amazing occurrences of which the Dead have been a part. I think Jann Wenner and I did get some answers, some genuine illumination. And that illumination makes a document that has real value for the history of our times, a guide to understanding some of the profound cultural changes of the Sixties. I believe it has value for people who are trying to find themselves in a new and almost unrecognizable America. Jerry Garcia says that the Grateful Dead try to be a signpost to new space. I think this interview can help some readers both to recognize what is happening around them and to find new space in their own lives. At least I can say it has done those things for me.

Jerry left the straight world at fifteen. Can any straight person comprehend the incredible meaning of that fact? From then on he no longer cared about getting good grades in school, or getting approval from authority figures, or entering college, or having a "career." He got off the escalator. He pursued good times, whether they were sanctioned by society or not. He was a street kid, a hoodlum, a dropout, a drug user. How did he spend his time? "Doing nothing." But it was that very "nothing"—hanging out with friends, learning to play the guitar, listening to rock and roll, getting high on marijuana, that formed his art. Suppose Jerry Garcia had been doing "something" instead—studying diligently in high school or looking for a job—what would he be today? The assistant manager of a company branch office? The owner of a short-order stand franchise on El Camino? A high school music teacher: "The whole senior class wants to thank Mr. Garcia for his help with our production of *Carousel*? All very worthy occupations—except that they do not seem to fit the Jerry Garcia that we know.

I believe that in America today if a young man or woman follows the prescribed route to education or a career, the chances are overwhelming that his or her real talents, abilities and genius will never see the light of day. School was ridiculous, Jerry says. Because it wasn't helping him to discover his own genius. It was trying to make him into something pedestrian, ordinary, and mass-produced. So the first explanation of the paradox is this: America today is so rigid, so overorganized that for many people the only way to achieve anything different is to drop out. Doing what society asks may mean a whole life in a job that for the person in question is in fact "doing nothing." But what society calls "doing nothing" may actually take you somewhere. Jerry makes it sound easy, but it isn't. Leaving the straight world is frightening and lonely. There are no parental models to follow, no paper stars from the principal. That is one reason the Beatles were so important to Jerry: they showed that "you can be young, you can be far-out, and you can still make it."

The "experts" have described the Sixties as a time of protest movements: civil rights, university rebellions, the peace movement, the radical new left, black power and women's lib. These were vitally important of course, but they dealt with issues at political or intellectual levels, they tended toward being against evils rather than for something new, and they involved only a small but articulate segment of the population. The story of the Grateful Dead is part of a very different history that happened at the same time and was, I believe, even more important. It is the story, not of political concern, but of a wholly inarticulate, almost instinctive, search for an alternative and better way of life.

Below the level of the media, below the level of students' intellectual abstractions, in the youthful white middle class, there was a desire for freedom and good times. It was a search for something positive, not a protest against anything specific. If it ran up against the law, it was simply because the law was so pigheaded and puritanical about the simple matter of enjoying life. If you never had a political thought in your life, but were simply an imaginative enjoyer, your whole way of life might be "illegal." That gave it the misleading appearance of something programmatic or political. But it was still only the search for good times. "I never was around in that world where you had to read about it. For me, it came in the form of dope. You got a joint, you didn't get a lecture; and you got a cap, you didn't get a treatise or any of that shit."

In the straight world, you might found a musical group in order to realize an ambition, or to make money to support yourself, or to advance yourself in the world, or for any number of other reasons to do with success and not with pleasure. But the Dead just wanted to "get together and get high and get loose—and have some fun—it was the good times." They had no money, no furniture, no place to sleep. They were unconcerned. They were just happy freaks. They did it out of loving being high, not to achieve some pre-set goal.

I spent a number of evenings down at the studio with the Grateful Dead, watching them work on the double album that was released in the fall of 1971. It was hard and exacting work. They got to the studio soon after 7 P.M., and stayed for five or six or seven hours, keeping going with coffee and sandwiches. Most straight people I know don't work that hard. Mixing a tune means combining and recombining sounds, playing them over and over again, getting it just right. There was no room for carelessness, sloppiness, or lack of craftsmanship. But I could see that it was fun, it was what they wanted to do. They were relaxed, they enjoyed each other, they dug the music, they stayed high. This was a second explanation of the paradox: the Grateful Dead were rebels because they insisted that work could be fun, that business need not be mercenary and that—heresy of heresies—the reason for working is not to "make a contribution" but purely and simply, good times—"that happy thing."

Jerry says it again and again: "We were definitely not serious; we were definitely not doing anything for a reason; we were just goofing and freaking out." "It was good times . . . unselfconscious and totally free." "No, I don't think sacrifice is contribution. I think that contributing is contributing your own positive energy, not forcing yourself or any of that stuff." "I don't think of my work as being full time work. What I'm doing is my work, but I'm playing! When I left the straight world at fifteen, when I got my first guitar and left everything I was doing, I was taking a vacation; I was going out to play and I'm still playing."

And the Grateful Dead have never allowed money or business to take them over. They ran up huge debts, they got cheated and robbed, they made every imaginable business mistake, but they remained happy freaks. They just didn't care that much. They wanted to stay together and to keep themselves and their friends alive. They formed their band because they were already friends, not the other way around. And in 1971, that fact was still paramount. One night I went to hear Jerry play a gig with Merle Saunders at a small place in Berkeley and one by one, for "no reason," the rest of the Dead showed up too, and eventually they got up on the stage and started playing. As Jerry says, they just liked to hang out together. Even as a big business, Jerry puts it this way: "The question is, can we do it and stay high? Can we make it so our organization is composed of people who are like pretty high, who are not being controlled by their gig, but who are actively interested in what they're doing?"

This is a point that has been misunderstood not only by the media but by so many of the kids themselves. Standing on Telegraph Avenue begging for spare change, or sleeping all day, or sitting in a trance all day, may be a way to survive while a person tries to find a scene, but these don't make up a way of life. The point is to find a scene where you can put out energy and have your work, high and happy. To the straight world, there's a choice: unpleasant work, or no work at all. Many of the kids accept this lie, and choose the latter alternative. But as Jerry points out, the "freedom lie" is as big a lie as the unpleasant-work-and-sacrifice lie. There's got to be responsibility, he says. He talks approvingly of "solid, together, hard-working people" he knows. He criticizes "drag energy." He himself is a prodigious worker. That image of the hippie lying in his pad all day, living off his parents, not temporarily, but as a permanent "occupation," that's the straight world's fantasy of what it's like if you stop doing work you hate. Too many people have tried to live that fantasy. The real idea is to be a functioning human being, but in a way that is not alienated, not servile, one that is fulfilling of one's human needs. The Grateful Dead did not sit in the library reading about the theory of non-alienated work. They felt the need, and they were out doing it.

Jerry Garcia is considered by the media as a high priest of the so-called "counter culture." Is part of his radicalism to be found in his art itself? If so, what elements of the music of the Grateful Dead can properly be termed a rebellion? I think the first step toward an explanation is to clear away the myth that there is any such thing as a separate "counter culture." "I don't see the rock and roll scene as being the new culture. I think the rock and roll scene is just the rock and roll scene. Basically it's a professional trip." Haight-Ashbury? It really was just a small neighborhood scene, Jerry says. When I was writing this introduction I took a couple of walks in the Haight-Ashbury of today, and I felt the truth of what Jerry says. There never was a separate "counter culture," and there is none now. Bell bottoms, handmade leather belts, light shows, drugs, may be the elements of something fresh and new, or they may be elements of a culture that is phony or dead. So many people have mistaken one artifact or another for the living principle which eludes them. But as Jerry says, the new culture was always in danger of dying from "the thing of doing it too long. Doing it too long and too continually. It's just like anything once it gets old. Once the enthusiasm from anything as intangible as having a party or having a good time goes, then the substance is not there. As soon as you're having a thing without that substance, what the hell."

The point is so vital, so misunderstood, so misrepresented by the media, that it needs to be said in many different ways. Like drugs: should you take them or not? Jerry says some people he respects super-highly take them, some do not. "There are people doing everything, and I just don't think that *anything's* it." I got him to say it still another way, by asking him where are the "magic people" now? And he said they're out leading productive lives, and raising the kids. So much for the media image of the "counter culture"!

Nevertheless, the music of the Grateful Dead *is* profoundly new and radical. One reason for this comes out very clearly in the interview. Although the Grateful Dead took old forms like blues and country music as their base, they were incredibly open to new influences and new forms which came their way. They had experiences with drugs and that went into their music, they entered into the fantasies of the Acid Tests and put that in their music, they played at spiritual happenings and their music developed a spiritual side, they used every element of a marvelous new technology, experimented with Owsley's weird equipment, used 8-tracks and 16-tracks, and simply opened their art to what was happening around them without regard to previous forms. The tin pan alley writers, the composers of Hollywood musicals and night club pop music, were never so open, so spontaneous, so much fun, so free.

I think a further explanation lies in the sources of energy which the Dead tapped. At an Acid Test, everybody was creating, everyone was doing something. In the Haight there was an exchange of high energy, with fewer free rides, drag energy, and merely passive listening than was common in Spectator-America. Our music had been too elitist, too much something imposed from above, too much a manufactured product for passive consumption, like pro football or television. The Grateful Dead brought it up from the people. "The new stuff, which has real energy, real vitality, and really talks to people on the level of what's going on in their lives, on the level of what their personal images are and so forth, works." Or as Jerry says at another point, "Rock and roll was the background music for my life."

I think there is more truth in rock than in the old tin pan alley hit tunes. Rock is more like the blues, which have been telling the truth for so many years, but for so long spoke only to blacks. Rock deals with sadness, bummers, fear, despair, adversity, desperation, as well as sex, sensuality, highs and super-highs. The straight world tends to like escapist entertainment, the hip world accepts more pain and thus more reality. If the "new culture" is anything, it is a movement toward greater personal reality.

With its roots in so much that was newly happening in America, from drugs to protest marches, with its sources of energy in ordinary lives, the music of the Grateful Dead was able to achieve a depth of meaning and a distance into new space that I consider to be one of the supreme achievements in American music. In a song like "Trucking," or "Going Down the Road Feeling Bad," or "Bobbie McGee," the Dead give expression to the whole unbelievable trip so many of us have been on. In "Dark Star" or "The Other One," they take us to places more far-out in the true sense of that term, than most of us have yet imagined.

Before I had ever seen the Grateful Dead in concert, or met any of them in person, I felt this in their music, as do so many of their listeners today. For that reason, I felt that maybe Jerry could shed some light for the rest of us on the real meaning of the new consciousness, which some people confuse with long hair, and others with ripping off a supermarket, and others with some political trip. That, and my desire to meet someone I thought of as a truly spiritual figure, led me to ask Jann Wenner to arrange this interview. It was difficult and funny and awkward to try to bridge the gap between different worlds and I made Jann and maybe some readers uncomfortable by my efforts to get Jerry to talk about what he himself called untalkaboutable things. There was some weirdness and some irony about it all. But I had a chance on my second visit, with the tape recorder turned off and a roast beef sandwich in hand, to explain my real goal, and Jerry and Mountain Girl dug it. I think that's what made it possible to get it all together in those last few minutes on the afternoon of the second visit when I finally started him talking about getting high.

I think, to put it most directly, that the art of the Grateful Dead has helped us with the process of human evolution, helped us in a profound way at a time of utmost stagnation and fear of change, helped us to see more and under-of organization, or business, or technology, if they are used to advance human consciousness. Technology can still be "knobs and dials and lights and things gleaming." We have discovered a new possibility of freedom. There are new forms, more like the way it is. We are all the agents of change, and we *can* change, and change is what we are meant to be doing. We can be optimistic because there is infinite space, and we can trust each other because the very existence of that space gives us room to be together and still be ourselves.

I think we can see that the most profound meaning of Jerry Garcia's life and art so far is the commitment to growth and new possibilities, personal and artistic. Life is a progressive thing, there are no true setbacks, he says. He likes anarchy, improvisation, chaos, because they lead on to new forms, and the new forms are more like the way it really is. It is this commitment to growth that is Jerry's true rebellion. It is a rebellion because he came of age at a time of fear of change, political and personal. One way to fight that condition was to seek a new politics. Another way is to seek a new life and a new spiritual vision. The former has proved incredibly difficult for even well-organized groups. The latter is open to any individual. The former is still a demand that someone else or something else change. The latter is an assertion of power over one's own life.

This is why Jerry says the revolution is over. It is over because we have learned that despite all the obstacles we can go out and do whatever we want with our lives. Not that change is ever fast or easy. We will not be saved by a new political leader, or a bunch of new laws, or anything so clear cut and simple. The revolution will proceed like the Grateful Dead: "We don't have any *real* plans, but we're committed to this thing; we're following it, we're not directing it. It's kinda like saying 'Okay, now I want to be here, now I want to get there,' in a way. Nobody's making any real central decisions or anything. Everything's just kinda hashed out. It stumbles. It stumbles, then it creeps, then it flies with one wing and then it flies with one wing and bumps into trees and shit."

I think that's what real revolutionary progress is like, in my experience at any rate, in a society or in a person. All you can promise yourself is to keep on trying to go farther. What we can learn from Jerry Garcia and the Grateful Dead is that they have been showing us places farther along: "There was suddenly this positive avenue and it was based on the premise that after you've been high you know that everything is possible. You know it's possible to do whatever your wildest dream is. It's just a matter of lining yourself along that line and doing it. That's what we were saying and that's what we were doing, and so we knew it to be so."

Long after the interview, when we were preparing to I it into book form, I went out to visit Jerry to see if he had anything to add or change. It was a Sunday morning, a foggy, quiet day in March. When I arrived, about eleven, Jerry and Mountain Girl were sitting at the table in a corner of the living room with a view over the Pacific. We all had some coffee, and Jerry read my introduction. Neither of us felt much like adding anything to the interview. But we did feel like talking. I had brought a tape recorder, and we let it run. We got high, and the talk developed its own energy. Sandwiches and tea came and went, and it was after four when we ran out of conversation and Jerry put on The New Riders.

Our Sunday rap is reprinted here, almost exactly as it took place, with just a few trivial cuts, and with very little editing of any kind. I think it brings to life much of what was mainly abstract in the interview. It is a three-character play about people getting to know each other, and how the barriers can be brought down when there is the real openness that new consciousness makes possible.

The rap goes beyond the interview in many ways. It has a down-home feeling, with jokes, peanut butter, and Annabel mixing in. It is only in the rap that we learn that Bertha—"Bertha don't come around here anymore"—was a big electric fan in the Grateful Dead office that used to hop along the ground because its motor was overpowered. ". . . if you left it for a minute, it would crash into the wall and chew a big piece out of it. It was like having a big airplane propeller, you know, live, you know, running around."

In the interview, Jerry dismissed the idea that music like "Dark Star" comes from any special place. It's the same as the blues, he says. But in the rap Jerry shows us a glimpse of that special, remote planet, off in space, where he says his most far-out music comes from: "like a planetoid and it's cold, but it's going extremely fast and it's kind of like the wind of space and there's infinite emptiness around it." The rap is full of personal imagery that is poetic and funny and cosmic at the same time: The Grateful Dead starting, waking up, "drying out the wings, wrrrrr"; danger: "the rapids are just ahead, the big rocks, the dragons, the end of the world . . . "; the vision of the Grateful Dead as space travelers temporarily on earth.

It is only in the rap that Jerry speaks directly of the thing that so deeply troubles most of us today—personal commitment. "I *just* decided to be . . . like two or three months ago . . . I've just been going along with it, I've been going with it all along but now I've decided that okay not only am I going with it but I'm fucking well you know like paddle and everything cuz I felt like I'd seen it long enough, I'd been watching it long enough and timing was right and given this lifetime in which to accomplish whatever and it's like there isn't anything else for me, I know it, you know what I mean, that's what I'm doing, so it's like that's been my decision. . . . Normally I would never make that commitment. In a normal lifetime, I don't think I would do it, but I think this time is special. . . . It's cool with me for life or death, either one is okay. And basically that's how I feel emotionally, but I've made my pitch, I've put my stand in for the life side of the cycle."

Most of all, the rap was a special, magical Sunday afternoon, something I want to share.

Charles Reich
San Francisco
Spring 1972

PART 1

THE
ROLLING STONE
INTERVIEW

*Y*ou'll be in our 100th issue.

Far out. We were in the first one, too, 'Grateful Dead Busted.'

I wrote that story.

I loved it. It's got some stunning pictures.

In one picture you can see Phil in dark glasses, holding a gun.

And there's a picture of Bobby handcuffed to Florence, coming down the stairs with a victorious grin. It was incredible.

REICH: *Start us at the beginning.*

Which beginning?

Your beginning—the day you were born.

My father was a musician. He played in jazz bands in the places that I play in San Francisco, the same ballrooms. I never knew too much about my father; he died when I was young. He played clarinet, saxophone, reeds, woodwinds. He was an immigrant, with his whole family, moved out in the Twenties or the Teens from Spain.

My mother was born in San Francisco. Her mother is a Swedish lady and father is Irish, Gold Rush Days people, who came to San

1

Francisco then. My mother met my father somewhere back then in the Thirties, something like that; he a musician, she a nurse.

Then the depression came along and my father couldn't get work as a musician. I understand there was some hassle: he was blackballed by the union or something cause he was working two jobs or something like that, some musician's union trip, so he wasn't able to remain a professional musician and he became a bartender, bought a bar, a little bar like a lot of guys do. He died when I was real young and my mother took over that business.

All through this time there was always instruments around the house because of my father and my mother played piano a little and I had lots and lots of abortive piano lessons, you know, . . . I can't read, I couldn't learn how to read music, but I could play by ear. My family was a singing family, on the Spanish side, every time there was a party everybody sang. My brother and my cousin and I when we were pretty young did a lot of street corner harmonizing . . . rock and roll . . . good old rhythm and blues, that kind of stuff, pop songs, all that. It was radio days, *Lucky Lager Dance Time* and all that.

And then my mother remarried when I was about 10 or 11 or so and she decided to get the kids out of the city, that thing, go down to the Peninsula, and we moved down to Menlo Park for about three years and I went to school down there.

Somewhere before that, when I was in the third grade in San Francisco, I had a lady teacher who was a bohemian, you know, she was colorful and pretty and energetic and vivacious and she wasn't like one of those dust-covered crones that characterize old-time public school people; she was really lively. She had everybody in the class, all the kids in this sort of homogeneous school, making things out of ceramics and papier maché. It was an art thing and that was more or less my guiding interest from that time on. I was going to be a painter and I really was taken with it. I got into art history and all of it. It was finally something for me to do.

When we went down to the Peninsula, I fell in with a teacher who turned me on to the intellectual world. He said, "Here, read this." It was *1984* when I was 11 or 12. And all of a sudden it was a whole new—that was like when I was turning on, so to speak, or became aware of a whole other world that was other than the thing you got in school, that you got in the movies and all that; something very different. And so right away I was really a long way from school at that point ... there was two or three of us that got into that because of this teacher, who ultimately got fired that same year because of being too controversial—got the kids stirred up and all that—all the classic things.

We moved back to the city when I was about 13 or so and I started going to Denman, a good old San Francisco rowdy roughneck school. I became a hoodlum, survival thing; you had to be a hoodlum, otherwise you walk down the street and somebody beat you up. I had my friends, and we were hoodlums and we went out on the weekends and did a lot of drinkin' and all that and meanwhile I was still reading and buying books and going to San Francisco Art Institute on the weekends and just sort of leading this whole secret life.

I was 15 when I got turned on to marijuana. Finally there was marijuana: Wow! Marijuana! Me and a friend of mine went up into the hills with two joints, the San Francisco foothills, and smoked these joints and just got so high and laughed and roared and went skipping down the streets doing funny things and just having a helluva time. It was great, it was just what I wanted, it was the perfect, it was—and that wine thing was so awful and this marijuana was so perfect.

So what's happening to music all this time?

Nothing much, I'm goofing around, I'm trying to play rock and roll piano and stuff like that, but I'm not settled in with my mother particularly, I'm sort of living with my grandmother and I don't really have any instruments. I want really badly a guitar during this time, about three years, I want a guitar so bad it hurts. I go down to the pawn shops on Market Street and Third Street and wander around the record stores, the music stores and look at the electric guitars and my mouth's watering. God, I want that so bad! And on my 15th birthday my mother gave me an accordion. I looked at this accordion and I said, "God, I don't want this accordion, I want an electric guitar."

So we took it down to a pawn shop and I got this little Danelectro, an electric guitar with a tiny little amplifier and man, I was just in heaven. Everything! I stopped everything I was doing at the time. I tuned it to an open tuning that sort of sounded right to me and I started picking at it and playing at it. I spent about six or eight months on it, just working things out. It was unknown at the time, there were no guitar players around. And I was getting pretty good and finally I ran into somebody at school that played guitar.

REICH: *Can I ask for the date?*

August 1st—let's see, I was born in '42—Christ, man, arithmetic, school, I was 15—'57. Yeah, '57, there you go, it was a good year, Chuck Berry, all that stuff.

I wanted to get an historic date like that.

Yeah, well that's what it was, August 1st, 1957, I got my first guitar. And that was it. Somebody showed me some chords on the guitar and that was the end of everything that I'd been doing until that time. We moved out of town up to Cazadero, which is up by the Russian River, and I went to a high school for about a year, did really badly, finally quit and joined the Army. I decided I was going to get away from everything. Yeah, 17. I joined the Army, smuggled my guitar in.

REICH: *In joining the Army, it was probably the time to leave home.*

Well, it was the time to leave it all. I wanted to just be some place completely different. Home wasn't working out really for me and school was ridiculous and, I just wasn't working out. I had to do something. At that time the only really available alternative was to join the Army, so I did that.

I broke off all my communication with my family when I went into the Army; and they didn't even know that I was out of the Army, in fact, and I . . . I just didn't want to say anything to anybody, I didn't want to have anything to do with that, I just wanted to be goofing out, goofing off, I didn't want to get a job or go to college or do any of that stuff. So there was nobody after me to do it. I would hear from people who had heard from them, you know. They knew I was OK.

Do you have any brothers and sisters?

I have an older brother. Circumstances made me a different guy from my brother, made it always—it was difficult for me to communicate with my brother. He was in the Marines for four years. All that's evened out now since he's gone kind of through a straight trip and . . . sort of fell out the other side of it and now he's a head, and living in the new world so to speak, so now we can communicate where as it used to be that we couldn't.

I lasted nine months in the Army. I was at Ft. Ord for basic training and then they transferred me to the Presidio in San Francisco, Ft. Winfield Scott, a beautiful, lovely spot in San Francisco, overlooking the water and the Golden Gate Bridge and all that, and these neat old barracks and almost nothing to do. It started me into the acoustic guitar; up until that time I had been mostly into electric guitar, rock and roll and stuff.

I was stuck because I just didn't know anybody that played guitar and that was probably the greatest hindrance of all to learning the guitar. I just didn't know anybody. I used to do things like look at pictures of guitar players and look at their hands and try to make the chords they were doing, anything, any little thing. I couldn't take lessons—I knew I couldn't take lessons for the piano—so I had to learn it by myself and I just worked with my ear.

When I got out of the Army, I went down to Palo Alto and rejoined some of my old friends down there who were kind of living off the fat of the land, so to speak, a sort of hand-to-mouth existence. Some were living off their parents; most of 'em, most people were living off people who were living off *their* parents. And there were a few like kindly—we were living in East Palo Alto which is the ghetto down there—and there would be various households that we could hang out at and get a little something to eat.

REICH: *This was the beginning of the dropout world?*

Yeah, yeah, well we were—well, like that's the period of time I met Hunter. Immediately after I got out of the Army, Hunter, who is like a really good friend of mine all this time, he'd just gotten out of the Army—he had an old car and I had an old car when I got out of the Army, and we were in East Palo Alto sort of coincidentally. There was a coffee house, 'cause of Stanford, university town and all that, and we were hanging out at the coffee house and ran into each other.

We had our two cars in an empty lot in East Palo Alto where they were both broken. Neither of them ran any more but we were living in them. Hunter had these big tins of crushed pineapple that he'd gotten from the Army, like five or six big tins, and I had this glove compartment full of plastic spoons and we had this little cooperative scene eating this crushed pineapple day after day and sleeping in the cars and walking around.

He played a little guitar, we started singin' and playin' together just for something to do. And then we played our first professional gig. We got five bucks apiece.

What did you and Hunter used to play?

Oh, folk songs, dippy folk songs. It was before I got into a purist trip and all that.

REICH: *You started playing because there was nothing else to do?*

Yeah, but also because it was what I was doin'. It was really, basically what I was doin'. And there was nothing else to do. There was a certain amount of hanging out to be done. Stanford was a rich place to hang out, there was all this stuff goin' on there. You could always hustle the girls to get you something from the dining room.

We played around, mostly at Kepler's Book Store—it was not professional or anything like that. We played at Peninsula schools and we played all these arty scenes and intellectual scenes down there, still the coffee houses—that coffee house beatnik consciousness was still what was happening.

What happened was I kept going farther and farther into music and Hunter was farther and farther into writing and so finally we just stopped playing together. But we hung out together. He's a poet, essentially. And the direction I went into music was Folkways Records, field recordings, that sort of thing, and old-time blues and old-time country music and got very serious about it for a long time although I was still in that same position of essentially being on the street, going around from place to place.

Who are some of the people you met on the coffee house circuit?

I didn't get into playing the coffee houses until a little bit later than that, really playing coffee houses—most of that time before that I was learning to play well enough to play anywhere—'61 or '62, I started playing coffee houses and the guys who were playing around then up in San Francisco at the Fox and Hounds, Nick Gravenites was around then, Nick the Greek they called him; Pete Stampfel from the Holy Modal Rounders, he was playing around there then. A real nice San Francisco guitar player named Tom Hobson that nobody knows about, he was one of those guys that was sort of lost in the folk shuffle, but he's still around and he's still great.

Let's see . . . in Berkeley there was Jorma playing coffee houses about the same time that I was, and Janis. In fact, Jorma and Janis and I met at the same time. They played at the place in Palo Alto I played at a lot called the Tangent. They came in one night and I just flipped out. Janis was fantastic, she sounded like old Bessie Smith records, and she was really good. And Paul Kantner was playing around; David Freiberg was playing around, David and Nikelah they called themselves, him and his chick played lefthanded guitar, they did these rowdy Israeli folk songs. Michael Cunney was around then too. He's a guy that's kind of like Pete Seeger's junior version, he's very good, he still plays around, banjo and some. Let's see . . . a lot of the people that are around now, that are still doing stuff now.

Did you begin hanging out with Jorma and Janis?

Well, I wasn't really hanging out with them but our paths would be crossing, playing at the same place the same night and pretty soon after two or three years of running into them you're friends. You never planned it or anything like that, it's just what's happening.

Were you making enough money to support yourself?

Nah . . . I was either not making money and mostly living off my wits, which was pretty easy to do in Palo Alto—things are very well fed—or else I was teaching guitar lessons in record stores.

What did you turn the kids on to who came for lessons?

I tried to teach them how to hear. My whole trip with teaching kids, was teaching them how to play by ear, teaching them how to learn stuff off of records, because kids were always coming in saying, "Here's this record, I'd love to be able to learn to play this guitar part on it." And so mostly it was learn how to associate the guitar with what you hear. I couldn't follow the notes myself; it would've been really ridiculous of me to try to get *them* to follow the notes, man.

Sometimes they would have some knowledge, sometimes they would be pretty good as a matter of fact, it was all different ones, different kinds, because in a guitar store you get people who don't know anything about music, let alone anything about the guitar and so it was my whole trip to try to teach them something about music first. I could relate to them stuff by making a tape of a whole bunch of kinds of music that would include the guitar that would all be technically pretty easy but attractive to the ear, like the Carter Family for example, is a real good thing to learn because it's all first position, simple chords, rhythmically very easy, technically it's easy and at the same time your ear can dig it, you can get into it.

I would play something for them and either there's a flash, a spark there, either you can turn somebody on by saying, "Listen, isn't that neat," or if the music doesn't communicate, you have to forget about teaching. That was my basis; that's what it finally came down to.

Hunter and I were still more or less together; at this time we're mostly living at this place called The Chateau in Palo Alto and me and Hunter and Phil is there a lot, Phil Lesh and Pigpen and all these . . . my fellow freaks.

Where did they turn up?

The old Palo Alto Peace Center was a great place for social trips. The Peace Center was the place where the sons and daughters of the Stanford professors would hang out and discuss things. And we, the opportunist wolf pack, the beatnik hordes, you know, would be there preying on their young minds and their refrigerators. And there would be all of these various people turning up in these scenes and it just got to be very good, really high.

How did they come along?

Phil was from Berkeley and he had spent . . . his reason for being anywhere on the Peninsula was that he had done some time at San Mateo Jr. College playing in their jazz band. Now, Phil, who I met down there at the Peace Center, was at that time composing 12-tone and serial things. He'd also been a jazz trumpet player. We were in two totally different worlds, musically. But somehow he was working at KPFA as an engineer, and I was up there at a folk music thing or something like that and Burt Corena who ran the folk music show there wanted me to do a show for KPFA as a folk singer, so Phil and I got together at a party. He put together a tape of me playing in the kitchen and it sounded pretty good to us. He took it up there and played it for them, they dug it, so I went up to the studio and he engineered my little performance.

Phil and I had always gotten along together real good. So that's me and Phil. That's one stream as part of the Grateful Dead—the oldest, probably. We met this other guy named Bobby Peterson who is like an old-time wine-drinkin' convict post criminal scene, a great guy, and he, Phil Lesh, a guy named John Winters and Bob Peterson all hung out together when Phil was going to San Mateo. OK, that's one little unit there.

Now, Phil had a girl friend from Palo Alto who he had met at
San Mateo, that's what brought him to Palo Alto. And when in Palo
Alto he'd hang out at St. Michael's Alley, which was where I and
Hunter and these various other people were hanging out. It was a
local coffee house where you could sit over a cup of coffee all night.
And we met like we always met, in the course of some apocalyptic
conversation from those old days.

Whose idea was it to have a band?

See, what happened was, I got into old-time country music, old-
time string band music, and in order to play string band music you
have to have a band, you can't play it by yourself. So I would be out
recruiting musicians. One of the musicians I used to play with in
those days was Dave Nelson, who plays guitar for the New Riders,
so that's another germ, and me and Nelson were playing old-time
music and we got into bluegrass music, playing around at coffee
houses. And Bobby Weir was really a young kid at that time, learning how to play the guitar, and he used to hang around in the music
store and he used to hang around at the coffee house.

Bob came from Atherton—he's from that really upperclass
trip, his folks are really wealthy and all that, he was like the Atherton kid who was just too weird for anybody. He didn't make it in
school and people were beatin' up on him and he was getting
kicked out of schools all over the place. His trip was he wanted to
learn to play the guitar and have a good old time, and so he'd hang
around the music store. I met him when I was working at a music
store—I was one of the kingpin pickers on the town. I always
played at the coffee house and Weir would come and hear me play
and so it was that kind of thing.

At that time he was like 15 or something, really young. He's
the kid guitar player. And the band thing kept happening various
ways. Bluegrass bands are hard to put together because you have
to have good bluegrass musicians to play and in Palo Alto there
wasn't really very many of them—not enough to keep a band
going all the time.

Now Bill Kreutzman was working at the music store at the same time I was. My first encounter with Kreutzman was when I bought a banjo from him way back in '61 or '62. He was just a kid then playing rock and roll. He was in high school. I may have even played a gig with him once when I was playing electric bass in a rock & roll band weekends.

Since I always liked playing whether it was bluegrass music or not, I decided to put together a jug band, because you could have a jug band with guys that could hardly play at all or play very well or anything like that. So we put together the jug band and Weir finally had his chance to play because Weir had this uncanny ability to really play the jug and play it really well, and he was the only guy around and so he of course was the natural candidate. And Pigpen, who was mostly into playin' Lightnin' Hopkins stuff and harmonica . . .

Where'd he come from?

He was another one of the kids from around there, he was like the Elvis Presley soul and hoodlum kid. His father was a disc jockey; he heard the blues, he wanted to play the blues and I was like the guitar player in town who could play the blues, so he used to hang around, that's how I got to know him. He took up harmonica and got pretty good at it for those days when nobody could play any of that stuff.

So we had the jug band with Pigpen and Weir and Bob Matthews who's the head guy at Alembic Studios now, and Marmaduke [of New Riders] even played with the jug band for a while, I believe.

The jug band we're talking about is pretty recent, that's like '63 . . . '63 or '64 . . . Phil's back from '61 or '60 . . . '60 and '61 from when I just got out of the Army. I met Phil almost the same time I met Hunter. Phil was doin' a straight thing, he was goin' to Cal, he was livin' in Berkeley, he was born in Berkeley. I think he was goin' to Mills College for awhile, he was studying music seriously . . . you'd go over to his house and find orchestra charting paper and incredible symphonies, man, all meticulously rapidographed. God— Phil, you know, has absolute pitch and this incredible vast store of musical knowledge, just the complete classical music education. And he'd been a trumpet player, that's what he played. So, anytime I did anything musical, he was always turned on by the music, because he loves any kind of music . . .

How did he get lured away from the classical world?

He just ran out of it . . . he ran out of it. I didn't really fall back in with Phil until after we'd had our electric rock and roll band started.

And you ran around and played the . . .

Played any place that would hire a jug band, which was almost no place and that's the whole reason we finally got into electric stuff.

Whose idea was that?

Well Pigpen, as a matter of fact, it was Pigpen's idea. He'd been pestering me for awhile, he wanted me to start up an electric blues band. That was his trip . . . because in the jug band scene we used to do blues numbers like Jimmy Reed tunes and even played a couple of rock and roll tunes and it was just the next step.

And the Beatles . . . and all of a sudden there were the Beatles, and that, wow, the Beatles, you know. *Hard Day's Night*, the movie and everything. Hey great, that really looks like fun.

REICH: *Well, that's something . . . when you say funny, well, say some more about that . . .*

JERRY: Well, funny is a good thing, I mean, what can I say about it?

REICH: *Yeah, but you made . . . you were the kind of band that was funny.*

JERRY: Well, It was funny because it was fun, you know what I mean, it was funny in that you could . . .

MOUNTAIN GIRL: Jug Band was a gas.

JERRY: It was funny in the same way the Grateful Dead is funny now and I can't really describe that, but if you're around for a little while you can see right away that it is funny, it's more funny than not.

REICH: *But it started way back there with the jug band with something that was fun and everybody knew was . . .*

JERRY: Well, good times is the key to all this.

And the Beatles were good times, that's what was in the movie.

Right, exactly.

So Pig fronts the blues band . . .

Yeah, well . . . theoretically it's a blues band, but the minute we get electric instruments it's a rock and roll band. Because, wow, playin' rock and roll, it's fun. Pigpen, because he could play some blues piano and stuff like that, we put him on organ immediately and the harmonica was a natural and he was doin' most of the lead vocals at the time. We had a really rough sound and the bass player was the guy who owned this music store that I had been workin' in, which was convenient because he gave us all the equipment; we didn't have to go out and hassle to raise money to buy equipment.

But then, we were playing at this pizza parlor, this is like our first gig, we were the Warlocks, with the music store owner playing bass and Bobby and me and Pigpen and Bill. And so we went and played. We played three gigs at that pizza parlor.

What was your repertoire?

We did . . . we stole a lot of . . . well at that time, the Kinks, and the Rolling Stones' "King Bee," "Red Rooster," "Walking The Dog" and all that shit, we were just doing hard simple rock and roll stuff, old Chuck Berry stuff, "Promised Land," "Johnny B. Goode," a couple of songs that I sort of adapted from jug band material. "Stealin'" was one of those and that tune called "Don't Ease Me In" was our first single, an old ragtime pop Texas song. I don't remember a lot of the other stuff.

REICH: *Nowhere near Dylan or something like that?*

Oh, yeah, we did "It's All Over Now Baby Blue." We did that from the very beginning because it was such a pretty song. Weir used to do "She's got everything she needs, she don't look back" . . .

REICH: *How much were the Beatles important to you?*

They were real important to everybody. They were a little model, especially the movies—the movies were a big turn-on. Just because it was a little model of good times. The Fifties were sure hurting for good times. And the early Sixties were very serious too—Kennedy and everything. And the Beatles were light and having a good time and they were good too, so it was a combination that was very satisfying on the artistic level, which is part of the scene that I was into—the art school thing and all that. The conscious thing of the artistic world, the Beatles were accomplished in all that stuff. It was like saying, "You can be young, you can be far-out, and you can still make it." They were making people happy. That happy thing—that's the stuff that counts—something that we could all see right away.

REICH: *What about Dylan, who was so unhappy for such a long time?*

Dylan was able to tell you the truth about that other thing. He was able to talk about the changes that you'd go through, the bummers and stuff like that, and say it, and say it in a good way, the right way. I dug his stuff really from *Bringing It All Back Home.* Back in the folk music days I couldn't really dig this stuff but on *Bringing It All Back Home* he was really saying something that I could dig, that was relevant to what was going on in my life at the time. Whether he intended it that way or not is completely unimportant.

That first gig . . .

The first night at the pizza place nobody was there. The next week, when we played there again it was on a Wednesday night, there was a lot of kids there and then the third night there was three or four hundred people all up from the high schools, and in there, man, in there was this rock and roll band. We were playing, people were freaking out.

Phil came down from San Francisco with some friends because they heard we had a rock and roll band and he wanted to hear what our rock and roll band was like and it was a flash to see Phil because he had a Beatle haircut, and he'd been working for the post office and livin' in the Haight Ashbury. He wasn't playin' any music, though, and he wasn't writing or composing or anything and I said, "Hey, listen man, why don't you play bass with us because I know how musical you are, I know you've got absolute pitch and it wouldn't take you too long and I could show you some stuff to get you started." He said, "Yeah, well, that'd be far-out." So we got him an old guitar to practice on and borrowed a bass for him, and about two weeks later we rehearsed for a week, and we went out and started playing together.

We never *decided* to be the Grateful Dead. What happened was the Grateful Dead came up as a suggestion because we were at Phil's house one day, he had a big Oxford Dictionary. I opened it up and the first thing I saw was "The Grateful Dead." It said that on the page and it was so astonishing. It was truly weird, a truly weird moment.

I didn't like it really, I just found it to be really powerful. Weir didn't like it, Kreutzman didn't like it and nobody really wanted to hear about it. But then people started calling us that and it just started, it just got out, Grateful Dead, Grateful Dead . . .

We sort of became the Grateful Dead because we heard there was another band called Warlocks. We had about two or three months of no name and we were trying things out, different names, and nothing quite fit.

Like what?

Oh, the Emergency Crew, uh . . . the Mythical Ethical Icicle Tricycle . . . ha, ha . . . we had a million funny names, man, really, millions of 'em, huge sheets of 'em.

What were the others?

Oh, God, man I can't remember, really you don't want to hear 'em, they're all really bad.

REICH: *I'd like to know about your life outside of playing. What kind of scene was that?*

Well, I got married back there somewhere and it was one of those things where she got into trouble, you know, in the classic way, "I want to have the baby," "Well, OK, let's get married." We got married, and the parents thing and all that and it was like I was tryin' to be straight, kinda. I was working in the music store, you know, in earnest now, and our baby was born and it was OK and all that, but it wasn't really workin'. I was really playin' music, I was playin' music during the day at the music store practicing and at nights I would go out and gig.

REICH: *Were you interested in anything besides music?*

Yeah, I was interested in everything besides music.

REICH: *I want to hear about that, too.*

Well, name something. I mean I've never had any hobbies, but music; I was never doin' anything, but anything that came up would interest me.

REICH: *Well . . .*

Drugs, of course.

REICH: *OK, let's talk for a minute about that, how they came in at that time . . . it was an old story.*

I'd been getting high for a long time, but marijuana turned up on the folk music world and there was speed. The thing about speed in those days was that you stayed up and raved all night or played. The *Doors of Perception* and stuff like that, we were talking about. And there was mescaline; we couldn't find mescaline, but we could find peyote. That was the only psychedelic around at that time.

REICH: *Religion?*

Religion, yeah, Martin Buber and that whole existential thing.

REICH: *Philosophy?*

Philosophy, right.

REICH: *Reading?*

Right, reading . . . films, films. My wife was at the Communications Department at Stanford and she was into film and I spent a lot of time working on sound tracks for people's films, and I got really interested in it and I spent a lot of time there, just hangin' out, watchin', seein' how they do it . . . There was a lot of stuff happening because it was a university town, good concerts and so forth . . .

REICH: *What about the Kerouac, Ginsberg world?*

Well in my travels around the Bay Area there was like Berkeley, San Francisco, Marin County and down the Peninsula. You'd go to North Beach and there would be sort of the remnants of that beatnik scene, but see I'd been into that scene as a young kid back when I was livin' in San Francisco going to art school down there in North Beach when that was all happening, the Bagel Shop was even going on then.

REICH: *Poetry, literature, stuff like that?*

All that, all of that, and on all levels. That was like a continuing thing, but then along came LSD and that was the end of that whole world. The whole world just went kablooey.

REICH: *What's the date of that?*

Let's see, LSD came around to our scene I guess around . . . it all was sort of happening at the same time, around '64, I guess. We started hearing about it in '63 and started getting it about in '64.

When we were living at The Chateau, even earlier, like '61, '62 I guess, or '63, the government was running a series of drug tests over at Stanford and Hunter was one of the participants in these. They gave him mescaline and psilocybin and LSD and a whole bunch of others and put him in a little white room and watched him. And there were other people on the scene that were into that. Kesey. And as soon as those people had had those drugs they were immediately trying to get them, trying to find some way to cop 'em or anything, but there was no illicit drug market at that time like there is now . . .

REICH: *Two questions together, how did it change your life and how did it change your music?*

Well, it just changed everything you know, it was just—ah, first of all, for me personally, it freed me, you know, the effect was that it freed me because I suddenly realized that my little attempt at having a straight life and doing that was really a fiction and just wasn't going to work out. Luckily I wasn't far enough into it for it to be shattering or anything, it was like a realization that just made me feel immensely relieved, I just felt good and it was the same with my wife; at that time it sort of freed us to be able to go ahead and live our lives rather than having to live out an unfortunate social circumstance, which is what the whole thing is about.

REICH: *In what sense did it free you?*

In making it all right to have or not have. That is, I think the first lesson that LSD taught me in sort of a graphic way, was . . . just . . . it's OK to have something and it's also OK to not have it.

REICH: *I don't understand yet.*

That's it, there isn't anything to understand.

REICH: *No, it's just a question of saying it another way.*

Well, let's see, let me think about it.

Accepting things the way they are.

Yeah, right.

REICH: *You mean it taught a religious idea of acceptance or a philosophical idea of . . .*

No, no, it was the truth; it's the truth just like these flowers are the truth, or the tape recorder there, or us sitting here or that sound we're hearing or the trees. It's the truth so you know it absolutely, you don't have to wonder whether it is. It's not in the form of an idea, it's in the form of a whole complete reality. I'm not saying that it does that for everybody, I don't mean that, I'm just saying that that's what the effect was on me. It meant that everything is possible; for one thing, it meant that everything else just took a step toward becoming more real and for me being able to do it without any reservations, that's what it did.

REICH: *And the straight life became less real.*

Well, I knew it for what it was and . . . it was me trying to make, trying to tell a lie that I didn't decide on. And I could no longer . . . and I was never good at it anyway, it was just like my most recent attempt at that time, that was my attempt because of the child, of having a child and having to support a wife and all that, it was like, all these things were like problems but then I . . . the thing about LSD was, that particular trip was . . . it was just not important, that was not the important thing.

REICH: *Did you have the feeling that like you'd known it all along? Inside?*

Sure, sure. Right, and it was like it made me immensely happy because like suddenly I knew that what I thought I knew all along I really did know and it was really, it really was the way I hoped it might be. That was the effect. And it was groovy because like for that first trip it was all, all of us people who'd been takin' various kinds of drugs together, a whole lot of us, we got this LSD, we all took it, glop, glop, you know, here in Palo Alto and we just wandered round and round the streets bumping into each other and having these incredible revelations and flashes, it was just dynamite; it was just everything I could hope for it to be for me.

REICH: *It was the thing you'd been looking for.*

It was like another release, yet another opening. The first one was that hip teacher when I was in the third grade; and the next one was marijuana and the next one was music and the next one was—it was like a series of continually opening doors, that's the way I see that.

REICH: *You've talked about continually opening doors. Is that like a philosophy you have, in other words, is that the way you want to keep on going?*

Well, I think that what doors have been opened for me now are enough to occupy my time forever.

REICH: *I was trying to ask you about a sense of direction. . . .*

Well, I don't have a personal philosophy . . . all I have is an ability to perceive cycles . . . and I think that things happen in a more or less cyclical way and the thing is being able to maintain your equilibrium while the cycles are in their most disadvantageous places and that seems a function of time.

What were you doing when you were dropping acid, listening to music or just wandering around?

Wandering around . . . We were playing around in this house, we had a couple of super balls, hard rubber dayglo balls, and we bounced them around and we were just reading comic books, doodling, strumming guitars, just doing stuff. We weren't really doing anything. All of a sudden you remember that you are free to play. Wow, we can play with all this stuff and do things! We were rediscovering the world and playing with all these wonderful things.

Our scene was totally anarchic, you know, we had no plans, we had nothing to prove or anything like that. Kesey, from what we could understand of what was going on up at his place at that time, was like into specific stuff apparently, although we didn't know.

REICH: *He seems to have had a definite idea of where he was headed toward.*

He was a writer, and writers always have the end of the book. Dig.

REICH: *Yeah. And I asked you that because I wanted to see if you had the same kind of thing.*

No, because I've always been a musician and into improvising and it's like I consider life to be a continuous series of improvisations . . . I view it that way.

When was the first time you played music on LSD?

Uh, when we were, let's see . . . we . . . oh, we were the Warlocks and we were playing in a bar in Belmont, we were playing this straight bar and we would do five sets a night, 45 on and 15 off and we'd be sneaking out in the cars smoking joints between each set and so forth. One of those days we took it. We got high, and goofed around in the mountains and ran around and did all kinds of stuff and I remembered we had to work that night. We went to the gig and we were all a little high and it was all a little strange. It was so weird playing in a bar being high on acid, it was just too weird, it was not appropriate, definitely wasn't appropriate.

The first time that music and LSD interacted in a way that really came to life for us as a band was one day when we went out and got extremely high on some of that early dynamite LSD and we went that night to the Lovin' Spoonful . . . remember that thing, the Lovin' Spoonful whatever, the Charlatans and whoever else down at the

Family Dog, Longshoreman's Hall, it was one of the first ones and we went there and we were stoned on acid watching these bands play.

That day—the Grateful Dead guys—our scene—we went out, took acid and came up to Marin County and hung out somewhere around Fairfax or Lagunitas or one of those places up in the woods and just went crazy. We ended up going into that rock and roll dance and it was just really fine to see that whole scene—where there was just nobody there but heads and this strange rock and roll music playing in this weird building. It was just what we wanted to see.

It was just truly fantastic. We began to see that vision of a truly fantastic thing. It became clear to us that working in bars was not going to be right for us to be able to expand into this new idea. And about that time the Acid Test was just starting to happen.

How did the music change? You're still playing country music and you're playing blues and . . .

Well, we got more into wanting to go . . . to take it farther. In the night clubs, in bars, mostly what they want to hear is short fast stuff, uhm . . . and we were always trying to play a little, stretch out a little . . .

MOUNTAIN GIRL: More . . . loud.

JERRY: So our trip with the Acid Test was to be able to play long and loud. Man, we can play long and loud, as long and loud as we wanted and nobody would stop us.

MOUNTAIN GIRL: Oh, God . . .

REICH: *So like would you take something you'd played before and just make it longer and longer and louder and louder? And you were improvising?*

Of course, we were improvising cosmically, too. Because being high, each note, you know, is like a whole universe. And each silence. And the quality of the sound and the degree of emotional . . . when you're playing and you're high on acid in these scenes it is like the most important thing in the world. It's truly, pshew, cosmic . . .

Our consciousness concerning music is opening up more, so the music is becoming, . . . is having more facets than it seemed to, having more dimensions . . . and we've also seen the effect of all of a sudden we find a certain kind of feeling or a certain kind of rhythm and the whole place is like a sea and it goes boom . . . boom . . . boom, it's like magic and it's like that something you discover on LSD and you discover that another kind of sound will like create a whole other . . .

We're just playing what's there, is finally what it comes down to, because we're not in a position to be deciding.

When did you meet Kesey, and how?

The Chateau, where we were all livin' several years earlier, was situated physically about two or three blocks from Kesey's place and there were people from Kesey's, that were over at our scene and so on. We didn't hang out down there too much because at the time it was a college trip, you know, they were college people kind of and it was, it made us self-conscious to be there, we were so, you know . . . undesirable, they didn't really want us, nobody really wanted us hangin' out.

When I first got into that scene, they reminded me of college people. They were all bright and clean and their whole scene was bright and clean. They were colorful, snappy and quick—college stuff.

But then, years later, here we are a rock and roll band. They were hearin' about us up at Kesey's place from our friends who are stayin' up there and gettin' high and comin' down and gettin' high with us.

There was this interaction goin' on. Just like there was interaction between our scene down on the Peninsula and the San Francisco scene . . . the San Francisco scene, all these little networks of one or two guys that go back and forth, sometimes it's dealers, sometimes it's musicians, you know, that was like the old line of communication.

So, it became obvious since you guys are a band and we're right up here in La Honda, and we're having these parties, we want to move the parties out into the world a little bit and just see what hap-

pens. So they had this first one down in San Jose, we took our stuff
down there and . . .

Had you met Kesey?

No, I had never met Kesey. It was Page, John Page Browning, he
was sort of the messenger. I don't think there was ever any real decision, just sort of a loose thing.

It was in a house, right, after the Stones concert, the same
night, the same night. We went there and played but, you know,
shit, our equipment filled the room, damn near, and we were like
really loud and people were just, ah . . . there were guys freakin'
out and stuff and there were hundreds and hundreds of people all
around, in this residential neighborhood, swarming out of this
guy's house.

REICH: *When did you get into all this fabulous equipment thing?*

It's always been kind of our trip. What it comes from is bein'
high, being high at these old Acid Test scenes and looking out on
the stage at this equipment, and this equipment is like squat and
functional with knobs and dials and lights and things gleaming . . .

REICH: *It felt like science fiction, right?*

Right, it's right in that world, right in that science fiction world
with the dayglo shit painted around and black lights.

REICH: *And you're at the controls of the rocket ship, right?*

Well, yeah, something like that, it's definitely that rocket ship
flash . . . yeah, science fiction, horror movies.

What happened at the meeting between you and Kesey?

After that first one we all got together, us and Kesey and everybody, and had a meeting about it, and thought, well, you know, that
first one there was all those people there, but it was too weird 'cause
it was somebody's house, you know and . . . it just didn't make it.

We just decided to keep on doing it, that was the gist of it. We
had all these people at this house that wasn't adequate, but the idea
was then to move it to a different location and then the idea was to
move it to a different location *each week.*

They had film and endless kinds of weird tape recorder hook ups and mystery speaker trips and all . . . just all sorts of really strange . . . it always seemed as though the equipment was able to respond in its own way, I mean it . . . there were always magical things happening. Voices coming out of things that weren't plugged in and, God . . . it was just totally mind boggling to wander around this maze of wires and stuff like that. Sometimes they were like writhing and squirming. Truly amazing.

That was the Acid Test and the Acid Test was the prototype for our whole basic trip. But nothing has ever come up to the level of the way the Acid Test was. It's just never been equalled, really, or the basic hit of it never developed out. What happened was light shows and rock and roll came out of it, and that's like the thing that we've seen go out.

REICH: *But what was it when it was at its greatest?*

Well, something much more incredible than just a rock and roll show with a light show; it was just a million more times incredible. It was incredible because of the formlessness, because of the thing of people wandering around wondering what was going on and . . . and stuff happening spontaneously and everybody bein' prepared to accept any kind of a thing that was happening and to add to it, it was like . . . uh . . .

MOUNTAIN GIRL: Everybody felt pretty much responsible for each other.

REICH: *You mean you were all creating, everybody was creating.*

There you go, everybody was creating.

REICH: *Everybody was doing something.*

Everybody was doing everything. That's about the simplest explanation.

REICH: *And it was magical besides.*

Truly, it was magical because there was that willingness for everybody to be constantly on the lookout for something new.

The scene now is watching television or going to a movie. That's essentially what's happening, you go into the show, there's a proscenium arch, there's the speakers, visually you're focused right at the center of things, the sound is coming at you from that direction; there might as well not be any back of your head, there's nothing happening back there and so it's that same old experience, . . . the very flaw that we were trying to eliminate with that Acid Test. The Acid Test was going in a whole other direction, something completely weird.

The Acid Test was a buck, but everybody paid it. The musicians paid it, the electricians paid it, the guy that collected tickets paid it, everybody paid it, and if there was only one buck we'd all pay it over and over again. It was always an exchange, it cost you a buck and you stayed there all night.

What do you think stopped it?

The fact that LSD became illegal was the thing that really stopped it. That's the thing that stopped it the hardest.

You don't think perhaps because too many people were coming . . .

MOUNTAIN GIRL: No, no, not enough people came, as a matter of fact.

JERRY: In San Francisco they were getting larger and larger. Had we not had to run for it, period, had Kesey not been busted and had LSD not been made illegal, perhaps a whole something other than what we're experiencing now would've evolved.

Where was the second Acid Test?

The second Acid Test was that at Muir Beach? Or was it at the Big Beat?

MOUNTAIN GIRL: It was at the Big Beat, I think.

JERRY: It was at the Big Beat, a plushy little nightclub in Palo Alto. That was a real nice one. There was the stage with the Grateful Dead setup on it over here . . . The Dead's on stage and on the other side there's a kind of a long sort of a runway affair. It's sort of an L-shaped room, and on the point of the L is the Grateful Dead and down here is where the Pranksters have their setup, which is like . . . it kinda looked like a cockpit, there was like these tables up on this runner with tape . . .

MOUNTAIN GIRL: . . . that weird table organ.

JERRY: Yeah, yeah, the dayglo organ and all these weird tape recorders and stuff and microphones and Babbs, who had on one of his quasi-uniforms.

MOUNTAIN GIRL: That was the first week of the Pranksters shirts.

JERRY: The Prankster shirts were quasi-uniforms, almost like uniforms but not quite, and Babbs looked kind of like a superhero.

MOUNTAIN GIRL: Except they were bright green and orange and white stripes and shit like that, so they were pretty loud.

JERRY: Yeah, they were real bright, everything was getting real bright; that was what we were all starting to flash on then.

MOUNTAIN GIRL: Oh, there was the two straight ladies who owned the place or something.

JERRY: Oh, right, right. They were hanging around behind the bar the whole time . . .

MOUNTAIN GIRL: . . . worrying what was going on.

JERRY: Middle-aged ladies.

MOUNTAIN GIRL: We had rented this place from them for $50 or $100 or something like that. They were just freaking out. Nobody could believe that Page had gotten this place—when we actually did come we were sort of surprised about it—because nobody ever took Page seriously; it was the first real thing he ever did. Oh man, we just got in there and set up our shit and everybody shows up and . . .

Who came?

Well, all the other psychedelic scenes at that time: There was Dick Alpert and his scene, Leary and that, Leary wasn't there, Dick Alpert may have been to that one; and there was the Berkeley psychedelic scene which was pretty well developed by that time because of the Cabale coffee house in the old days, the mescaline scene and all that.

MOUNTAIN GIRL: A lot of drifter Palo Alto types . . . and speed freaks, lots of speed freaks.

JERRY: And weirdos. There was always weirdos at the Acid Test. There were always a lot of people that didn't know from LSD; they were like bums and hobos and strange truck driver types and shit like that who would always somehow turn up there and find themselves in this weird other world.

MOUNTAIN GIRL: Oh, and Neal Cassady and Ann Murphy were there.

JERRY: Neal was really good. There was a strobe light in between our two set-ups. Just one small strobe light hanging out, but it was real bright, enough to flash the whole place because it was a fairly small room. We'd play stuff and the Pranksters would be doin' stuff and there was this incredible cross interference and weirdness. Stewart Brand was there with his Indian stuff.

MOUNTAIN GIRL: He had this little side show and recorded music, taped music and he'd just show all these beautiful slides of Indian trips and Indian homes.

JERRY: All kinds of Indian trips, things like neon arrowhead signs and highways, long expanses of highways that were really lovely images, each one a jam.

REICH: *How did you get into the idea of playing and having this visual thing?*

It was just the idea of everybody having their various stuff and doing it all at once.

What sort of clothes did you wear?

Just Goodwill junk—old clothes. I had some striped shirts—I think that was the hippest thing I owned. We had some Acid Test pants that were painted dayglo but you couldn't call it hippie stuff. There never was any hippie stuff really.

Let us ask you more about the Acid Test. What were some of the other things. What happened at the end of the evening?

This one ended up with Neal Cassady under the strobe light tearing up paper.

MOUNTAIN GIRL: Tearing up his shirt! He was ripping up that beautiful fluorescent polka dot shirt that Marge Barge made him, tearing it into little pieces. And then he got onto the paper after the shirt. He was ripping up anything he could get his hands on.

JERRY: It was going very very fast and then it was very quiet; there was almost nothing else happening.

MOUNTAIN GIRL: Right, except all the equipment was on and it was humming and any noise was sort of weirdly echoed around.

JERRY: And amplified around . . .

MOUNTAIN GIRL: And so it was sort of strange in there. A lot of people were drifting in and out of the spotlight and the strobe light was stopped and sort of the falling dance was going on, you know, people were still on their feet and meandering around.

JERRY: And it's getting to be about dawn.

MOUNTAIN GIRL: Yeah, people start to step outside to check the air, you know . . .

JERRY: Real cold in the morning . . .

MOUNTAIN GIRL: After an Acid Test was always morning. You start to pack up and step outside and it would be cold there and, ohhhh, really clear and everybody looking about eight inches shorter than they had been when they walked in, and about 20 pounds lighter. Not particularly haggard looking, but just a lot littler and packed down.

JERRY: Well used.

MOUNTAIN GIRL: And everybody would creep off home. Driving back was a really far-out experience because we always had to drive over this mountain route to La Honda.

JERRY: It always seemed really remarkable that . . .

MOUNTAIN GIRL: . . . that we were still alive.

JERRY: . . . That actually another day went by . . . there's the sun again another day, God, isn't it incredible it had been a long, long night.

What were some of the others? There was Muir Beach.

MOUNTAIN GIRL: That was a particularly nice one. One of the highlights of that one was—dare I, shall I breathe his name?— Owsley pushing a chair along this wooden floor, this old wooden chair, running it along the floor making this noise, the most horrible screeching and scraping. It went on for hours, I'm not exaggerating, it just drove everybody completely up the wall. That was really an incredible exhibition of making yourself . . . uncomfortable . . . making other people uncomfortable.

JERRY: No, man, it was just the guy completely freaked out with his body running around . . . that's what that was, I mean he was completely freaked out.

MOUNTAIN GIRL: He was scraping that chair and listening to the noise and lovin' it, I guess that was what was happening.

JERRY: How do you know?

MOUNTAIN GIRL: Oh, I watched him for a really long time.

JERRY: That wasn't it. I talked to him about that a lot and he just . . . his mind was completely shot, he thought they'd come and taken it from him.

Owsley was part of the Berkeley psychedelic scene.

Right. He didn't get along too good with our more wilder version, because, well, the big straight psychedelic scene always called our scene too high-energy you see, "Too high-energy, you can freak out in there, you know." That was what they always used to say.

MOUNTAIN GIRL: Hardly anybody did.

JERRY: Owsley did.

What was accomplished between the Pranksters and the Dead at that time?

We were even looser than they were. They became a sort of semi-fascist organization as soon as Kesey had to go to Mexico. And Babbs was kind of at the helm and at the time he was very much into keeping everything clean.

MOUNTAIN GIRL: He was into one of these big security trips.

JERRY: . . . and straight and "We don't want any strangers," and security. We were just really pretty loose, the Grateful Dead, we were real loose.

MOUNTAIN GIRL: Well, you guys were also doing up a lot of DMT and we were going on a number of not smoking any grass and not taking anything but acid and only on Acid Test night. We were really trying to clean up and you guys were really . . . ohhh, God . . . really weird.

JERRY: We were definitely not making ends meet, we were living solely off of Owsley's good graces at that time.

The free park thing started later after we moved back from L.A., after the L.A. Acid Tests, we moved back up to San Francisco.

The Pranksters were on their way to Mexico and we were at that time living at a house that Owsley had rented. We had no money, of course, no furniture, no place to sleep, or anything like that. Owsley's trip was he wanted to design equipment for us and we were going to have to be in sort of a lab situation for him to do it. He was really serious about it and so it was like the long wait for components and stuff while he was working on it, he and his partner.

What happened when Owsley's equipment finally came?

It got there piece by piece but it never really quite worked. We went on for about a year or so with it, but it never quite worked and we always had to spend five hours dragging it into a gig and five hours dragging it out afterwards and it was really bringing us down.

After going through a million weird changes about it and screaming at poor Owsley and everything and getting just crazy behind it, we finally parted ways, parted company with Owsley. He agreed to turn some of the equipment back into just regular money and bought us some regular standard simple-minded plain old equipment so we could go out and work. And you know . . .

That's when you became a working band.

REICH: *Kesey and the Pranksters are known to most people through the Tom Wolfe book that's made them into legend, and the legend is that Kesey's super-hero and the Pranksters are these unreal people.*

I think there was this weird emphasis placed there. There were similar scenes happening all over that just had no emphasis. The situation as it came into history was that Tom Wolfe was basically a writer who was writing about a writer and his emphasis was on that writer. When I was experiencing that scene it seemed to me that Babbs was the central figure and that Neal Cassady was the powerhouse. He was the guy that everyone was learning from. Kesey had a good situation happening because he knew what to do with the money he made from his book: He wanted to have a good time with it, and so he opened some space for his friends so they didn't have to be drudging and working and they could be going out and having a good time. That and the fact that he participated in the government psychedelic experiments. It was just timing.

REICH: *Did you feel it was a put-on?*

No, because we were all doing stuff together. When the Acid Tests were going on, everyone was getting real high, everyone knew that it was far-out. Everyone knew that it was at least cosmic. Whether it was or not is not even important, but we were definitely all together in that. We all found ourselves into it.

The Pranksters are essentially a lot more rural and down-home in a sort of way. Take a look at the difference in our scenes: their scene is up in Oregon, out in the country and Kesey mainly deals with the people right in the town around him. I think of us as being kinda like storm troopers 'cause we go out to places nobody else goes—Kansas and stuff like that. We're all really doing basically the same thing and we work together basically in the same way. We are basically structureless and leaderless—both our scenes. When the right situation happens, we work together as one scene.

On that certain literal level, Kesey was the leader, he was the spokesman. He talked a lot and because he talks a lot, a writer can listen. Whereas a guy like Neal Cassady would leave writers or speakers or literal thinkers or rationalists really crazy and they would say, "He's crazy"—they would dismiss him as crazy.

In my mind, Neal Cassady was the complete communicator—he was the 100 percent communicator. The guy always had it, always had a stream going and you could always jump right on it and be right in it. And he would always take into account that you were there. He was a model of a completely far-out guy.

MOUNTAIN GIRL: And he was personally responsible for a lot of people getting high, and ripping girls out of their suburban homes—boldly going in and plucking them off of the street and putting them in his car and taking them off and completely blowing their minds, changing their minds totally, and from that day on they'd be different people. He had a fantastic power over people, and it was all benign.

JERRY: We had more or less separate kinds of loose scenes that sorta had spillovers. There were people in Kesey's scene, Page, who was an old friend of mine and an old friend of Phil's. At one time our headquarters were very close together so to speak. Kesey used to live on Perry Lane, which is just down from Stanford, and we lived over at the Chateau, which was maybe two or three blocks away, and there would be a lot of spillover so that we would stumble over to their parties and some of them would spill over to our parties.

But we really were different scenes because we were much younger. And because we were younger we were basically undesirable to their scene. We were all just dropouts and they were college people. They were serious. This is going way back and Kesey at that stage was not, in the old days of Kesey the writer. And that's going way back.

In our scene, which was not the Grateful Dead at that time, and was not even the Warlocks and was not anything but a loose collection of freaks, we were definitely not serious—we were definitely not doing anything for a reason—we were just goofing and freaking out.

REICH: *Tell us about the Haight-Ashbury. Where did you live and who did you live with and what was the scene like?*

We came back from L.A. and moved into Danny Rifkin's house on 710 Ashbury. Actually we hung out there for about a week, we didn't actually move in because we were looking for a place in the country.

We ended up with a ranch—Rancho Olompalli—which is the site of the only Indian battle ever fought in California. It's up in Novato. It was a great place. It had a swimming pool and barns and that sort of thing.

The parties are well-remembered!

We didn't have that place very long, only about eight weeks. It was incredibly intense for everybody ... the parties were like really ... it's hard for me to tell, 'cause I'm seeing all this stuff from a really weird angle. So some things seem more important than others. I don't have any real central spot to be judging this stuff from, in terms of what it was. But those parties ... Novato was completely comfortable, wide open, high as you wanted to get, run around naked if you wanted to, fall in the pool, completely open scenes. And I think it was the *way* they went down and the way the people *responded* to that kind of situation. Everything was just super-groovy. It was a model of how things could really be good. If they really wanted to be. All that was a firming up of the whole social world of rock and roll around here, because all the musicians in the Bay Area—most of them are from around here, they've known each other for really a long time in one scene or another—and that whole thing was like shored up, so to speak, at those parties. The guys in Jefferson Airplane would get together with Quicksilver and different guys, 81 different players, would get together and get high and get loose and have some fun.

What other bands were there?

At that time there were some bands that are no longer in existence, like Clover or Wildflower or something like that. Good guys, all good guys—from the P.H. Factor Jug Band, and the Charlatans—that was when we started getting tight with Quicksilver. I've known David Freiberg from back in folk music days. They came and hung out at our place in Novato when we had our parties. And a lot of people like the various filmmakers, and writers and dope dealers. All the people who were into doing stuff. People who had seen each other at rock and roll shows and all that shit, in that first year. Those parties were like a chance to move the whole thing closer, so to speak. It was good times—unself-conscious and totally free.

After that we moved back into San Francisco.

Who lived at 710 Ashbury?

Danny Rifkin did and a whole bunch of other people. We had just one room there and we were kinda in and out. We were mostly just catching as catch can. We were all on our own, going around staying at different places and hanging out with people.

Then we got another place out in Marin. Camp Lagunitas it was called, it used to be a summer camp. We had our office in San Francisco at Ashbury because there was only one room there that was legitimately ours. Our business was done in the city and we were living out at Camp Lagunitas. Finally, we messed that up and got kicked out and we ended up back in San Francisco at 710. By this time most of the other boarders had moved out so we got the house and a whole lot of us moved in. Not everybody lived there. Bobby and I and Pigpen of the band lived there, and Danny and Rock, who were our managers at the time, Tangerine, who was Rock's old lady and a really good chick, and just various other assorted people hanging out at various times.

REICH: *Was it like a commune?*

Well, our whole scene had been completely cooperative and entirely shared. We never structured our situation where anybody was getting any money. What we were doing was buying food, paying rent, stuff like that. That was our basic scene and that's basically how we still operate.

REICH: *How many people came drifting in off the streets?*

Our place got to be a center of energy and people were in there organizing stuff. The Diggers would hang out there. The people that were trying to start various spiritual movements would be in and out; our friends trying to get various benefits on for various trips would be in and out. There would be a lot of motion, a lot of energy exchanged, and it was all real high in those days because at that time the Haight-Ashbury was a community. We had The Psychedelic Shop—the very first one—down in the Haight-Ashbury, and that was news, and other people were starting to open stores and starting to get under way. They were looking real good. It was just about that same time that people started to come to town to find out about the hippie scene, and that's about what the hippie scene was—it was just a very small neighborhood affair when we were all working for each other's benefit.

Most of the people of the Haight-Ashbury scene were people who had been at San Francisco State and gotten into drugs and acid and stuff like that and were living out there experimenting with all the new things that they'd discovered. It was a very high, healthy kind of thing—there were no hard drugs, only pot and LSD.

REICH: *No rip-offs? No paranoia?*

No rip-offs—none of that kind of stuff. No shootings, no knifings, no bombings, no explosions.

MOUNTAIN GIRL: No hassles with spades.

JERRY: None of that kind of stuff. Nothing that we weren't working on or handling or taking care of pretty good.

Then when the big media flash came out—when the *Time* magazine guys came out and interviewed everybody and took photographs and made it news, the feedback from that killed the whole scene. It was ridiculous. We could no longer support the tiny trickle that was really supporting everybody. The whole theory in hip economics is essentially that you can have a small amount of money and move it around very fast and it would work out, but when you have thousands and thousands of people, it's just too unwieldy. And all the attempts at free food and all that, certain people had to work too hard to justify it.

At the early stages we were operating completely purely without anybody looking on, without anybody looking through the big window. We were going along really well. And then the crowds came in. All the people who were looking for something.

MOUNTAIN GIRL: The Hollywood people came.

JERRY: San Francisco isn't really a super-wealthy city to begin with. Our scene was anything but wealthy, just supported by trickles, by grass and LSD and rock and roll music; that was essentially the income.

MOUNTAIN GIRL: Except for the occasional gift from a turned-on rich guy.

JERRY: The first really pure event was the Be-In, which was the first time that the whole head scene was actually out in force. It was

in Golden Gate Park. It was publicized through completely underground channels—posters and word of mouth and that sort of
thing—there wasn't much in the way of underground newspapers in
those days except the *Oracle*. Actually the *Oracle* started after that.

REICH: *Am I right in saying that the scene worked until it got invaded
by the mass media and it wasn't your scene that broke down as much as it
got destroyed from the outside?*

Right. We all had to do what we could to work on our own de-
velopment just to survive that. Everybody tried to deal seriously
with the problem. We all knew that the following summer there was
going to be a lot of people coming and we tried to prepare for that,
but there was no assistance coming from the officials. They weren't
going to believe it and so forth. It was just that same old thing. And
we knew that if we didn't do it ourselves, it wouldn't get done.

You were playing around San Francisco then.

Yes, and it was about the time we started playing free in the
parks too. It was in co-operation with the Diggers' trip and the Diggers were into free food and free everything and they were actually
doing that real well. They were making regular delivery once a
week—a big truck full of vegetables and chickens and all kinds of
food which they'd gone and gotten for free in various ways.

MOUNTAIN GIRL: They were just hustlers, in a mysterious way . . .

JERRY: They'd go down to the vegetable markets and scream . . .

REICH: *What began to spoil it?*

Too many people to take care of and not enough people willing
to do something. There were a lot of people there looking for a free
ride; that's the death of any scene when you have more drag energy
than you have forward-going energy.

REICH: *You were having to pull along more and more people?*

And it was getting harder and harder to do. For about a year or so
there was a regular thing you could see happen—people would come
into town, bounce around on the streets for about three or four
months, start to get hip to what was going on, they would start to find
themselves a scene and they would work into it and be assimilated

that way. That was working real well before there was the great big on-slaught.

And in that summer of 1967 the street was just packed with people—weirdos from out of town in on the weekend to get in on the free love and all the rest; Gray Line tours stopping in front of our house. People driving by behind locked windows and peering out.

Did you find your personal life was invaded?

Not really, because we've always been on the trip that if some-body isn't putting out the right vibes right now, then they get out real quick. That's the way we ran our house, in an effort to keep our own scene together.

REICH: *Did you tell them that they weren't putting out the right vibes?*

No, they knew it.

REICH: *One of the things with the communes that I have seen is that they're unable to do anything about a person like that and they simply keep him there and everything goes bad.*

That's the "freedom lie." There's been a lie about what freedom is and the big lie is that freedom means absolutely and utterly free, and it really doesn't mean anything of the sort. The case in point is when you have your own scene like that. Somebody comes in and they're free to move in, but likewise you're free to tell them to get out. Freedom is a premise that's been put forth that's been abused.

For any scene to work, along with that freedom there's implicit responsibility—you have to be doing something somewhere along the line—there is no free ride. And you have to know where you're going. It's helpful to have a scene that will indulge you long enough to let you find out. That's basically what our scene was doing and when people were coming into town and kicking around for a while, they'd learn the ropes, they'd learn how to work it on the street and how to do a little hustling during the day and just survive until they could find something they could really attach on to. That was the general story.

REICH: *So this was a model, but other people had to find their own scenes eventually for it to work?*

The idea at that time was to establish as many possible models as could be established.

MOUNTAIN GIRL: And they flowered fast, too, like the Diggers and the wonderful free store and all the leather shops and all that shit just blossomed overnight.

JERRY: Stuff was just happening. Finally, everybody who'd been concerned about anything had something to do with it. There was suddenly this positive avenue and it was based on the premise that after you've been high you know that everything is possible. You know that it's possible to do whatever your wildest dream is. It's just a matter of lining yourself along that line and doing it. That's what we were saying and that's what we were doing, and so we knew it to be so.

REICH: *Once you know it you never go back?*

Well, you don't need to—you can if you want to, but you don't need to—you can just keep pushing along.

But it wasn't the "media" which killed the Haight.

No. Do you want me to tell you the incident where I thought it started to get weird? I was walking down Haight Street, and all of a sudden in a window was a little notice. It said "Communications Company." And it was this horrible bummer of a depressing story about some 13-year old meth freak getting raped by nine spades and smack heads. It was just a *bummer.* Bad news. This guy took it upon himself to print up bad news and put it up.

Then he started putting out the whole "Free the Street" trip and he just brought in all this political, heavy-handed, East Coast, hard-edge shit, and painted it on Haight Street, where none of it was happening like that. It was still groovy. And *that* was the point where I thought, this scene cannot survive with that idea in there. It just goes all wrong.

At that point, Emmett Grogan began The Diggers and associated himself with those people, and they had a press conference . . .

Emmett made a lot of mistakes in those days. We all did because at the time a lot of that stuff seemed like it was right and good. But what happened was it turned out to be destructive and a drag. In fact all that stuff just turned into publicity. It didn't serve any purpose.

I was working at Ramparts *at the time, and I remember when Chester Anderson first came around the office and got them started on doing the first "hippie" article.*

He was the guy who did it. He was representative of the thinking which was not inimical to that scene of the people who had *already* gone to school, and heard speeches and heard all that shit. The peace movements and all that.

Everybody had already been through being disillusioned. It represented a step backward. I thought, "Aw, man, not this shit again." I thought we had already gone through it and now we're into the psychedelic era. There was a whole new consciousness starting to happen and it was really working nice, but then the flood came and that was it.

The "flower power" thing had its own inherent weaknesses.

Right, the inability of not being able to say, "Get out, go away." That tells us something about what innocence is. It's that which allows itself to become no longer innocent. There's some lesson in there. There was a thing about freedom which was very much in question all through that, with the Diggers and Free and all that. Emmett said a thing to me once which I thought was far out and I think it still applies. He was talking about being in his house and having somebody walk in, and the guy's rap was "Aren't I free to walk in?" And Grogan was on the trip of "Well, if there's freedom, then I'm free to kill you for entering my house. I'm free to do whatever I think I need to do."

What happened to move you out of that scene and then where did you go?

We didn't really move out of it; we didn't get up and leave. We hung around for a long time. We lived on Ashbury for a couple of years, anyway. Various of us were living in other parts of the Haight-Ashbury—up on the hill. Our scene has always been too big to be central and we've never really been able to get a really big place where everybody could stay together.

It just hadn't been working. We did ultimately get busted in the Haight-Ashbury and that was a good reason for everybody to leave. That was the point at which we all started to leave. We just started to find new places to be. I was the first one to move out to Marin County—to Larkspur. Then everybody else came out.

Do you miss not living together?

Well, we see each other all the time in our working scenes and at the office. We hang out together. That's really how we started—we were hanging out together and thought we might as well be doing something together. So we still hang out together and our scene still represents a place where other energy comes—it's just that now it's not in San Francisco, it's not in the Haight-Ashbury.

REICH: *Are the girls part of this, or do they get left at home like housewives?*

MOUNTAIN GIRL: It depends on the girls. I get left home a lot.

Do you like it?

MOUNTAIN GIRL: No. But it depends on what's happening. When these guys start to play, I don't play with them. I don't play with the band. There's nothing for me to do. I don't really go for the freakout dancing trip. They don't let me rave over the microphones very much. So I get really bored. Immediately, in fact. Frustrated, 'cause there's nothing for me to do, so I usually stay home. I'm still going through a transitional period, even though it's been going on for five years. I'm still working on the whole problem. It's still like a daily problem for me.

I try to have things going that I want to do more at home and not think about it—not thinking that I might be missing something. 'Cause usually when I get to their scenes I just get sleepy after a while.

JERRY: Either you're a person who really gets into the music and loves it for that reason, or you're a person who plays, or you're a person who works there, and if none of those things are happening for you, it's not what's happening for you.

MOUNTAIN GIRL: I love the music scene but still I want to be doing something while I'm listening. I'd have this urge to be doing something.

JERRY: The problem there is the form we've been stuck with. It's unfortunate. The most historical point, I suppose, would be the Trips Festival, when another form was starting to evolve. It was turned into the most obvious kind—you take a light show, you take a rock and roll band and that's your psychedelic experience. And that's not it. That wasn't it at the Trips Festival and that's not what we were doing either.

But in order to keep on playing, we had to go with whatever form was there. Because for one thing, the form that we liked always scared everybody. It scared the people that owned the building that we'd rent, so they'd never rent twice to us. It scared the people who came, a lot of times. It scared the cops. It scared everybody. Because it represented total and utter anarchy. Indoor anarchy. That's something that people haven't learned to get off with. But our experience with those scenes is that's where you get the highest, that's where people like Mountain Girl find stuff to do.

MOUNTAIN GIRL: And people are very protective about their equipment now.

JERRY: Our first free things were done sort of in conjunction with the Diggers who were now working on giving free food to people down in the Panhandle. It seemed like a good idea to go down there and play for them one weekend. We got a truck and a generator with the help of the Diggers and Emmett and all those guys and we just went down there and played. It was just great. It was easy. It was simple, and it was free in the sense that nobody had to do it, it was truly free. We were able to do that pretty comfortably for almost a year.

You don't do many free concerts now.

We haven't had the opportunity to do one that would be a good trip. Again, we're talking about the word "free." What does "free" mean? To me, "free" means free for us too, so that we're free to do it or not, is what it comes down to. The thing that was groovy about the Haight-Ashbury was that we could get up on a Sunday morning and say, "Let's play today down in the park," and we'd call a few people and the Diggers would have a truck and someone else would have gotten a generator and we'd be down there playing in an hour. That was free because we were free to decide to do that.

The kind of free that people are talking about now is, "Will you set up a free concert in Central Park on October 14th" or something like that. It's just the same as a gig for us—it's no different. Where is the free in that? That's another form that we haven't been able to get back to really comfortably, although we're always on the lookout to do something free. Spontaneous, open or fun, is what free means.

How do you remember a typical Avalon dance?

It's hard to say what's typical. I spent so much time high at those things, and wandering around, for various reasons, on various trips, that the whole experience to me is some completely subjective, kaleidoscopic scene, but definitely on the good side of the vibe scale. That's the only way I can explain it. I think there's a lot of that feeling on *Live Dead,* because it was recorded at the Avalon and it was a *good* time, when it was happening. It can raise a lot of the era, the way it seemed larger than life. I had some good times there. What can you do better than have parties? The Avalon at its finest was like a continual party. Everybody that was going to it was aware that the whole money thing—the way it was being distributed—was ultimately for the good of the community. That was in the days before there was a lot of capitalist accusations. Or before the great political consciousness consumed the whole city. It was a much freer time.

Why did it change?

I think just the thing of doing it too long. Doing it too long and too continually. It's just like anything once it gets old. Once the enthusiasm from anything as intangible as having a party or having a good time goes, then the substance is not there. As soon as you're having a thing without that substance, what the hell.

That's the thing we've become conscious of in our own trip, the Grateful Dead trip, because there were one or two years back there when we toured too much and we became mechanical. We began to see that there's a cycle that occurs: you're interested in what you're doing, and then you get disinterested in it. And then it changes and you get interested again. It's a matter of being able to leave space for those changes to happen; and to be in something which will provide you with an open end in which to change. That's the key. You have more of a flow happening, which can be a benefit in the sense of having a lot of people, various people whose energy will be working on a night when yours isn't.

The whole thing could happen, but I think the fact that it got desperate—in the sense that economics started to drive everything out, that it was the drawing power formula that worked, those kind of realities, business world realities—and the thing ultimately turned into a merchandising trip. A Show-Biz trip. That wrecked it. That wrecked it for me, anyway.

But you can have a commercial trip if the substance . . .

Right, if you keep the substance together, since that's the only thing there really is, in music or in anything else. It's the fact that it has *balls*, it has some intangible something which you can't pin down. And it has to do with the feelings of the people who are involved. In the Grateful Dead, our solution to it is to space ourselves out. So that we know it's gonna be good, because we haven't been doing it all along.

We touched on Owsley for a moment. Do you see him at all?

Yeah, we got to work with them [the inmates at Terminal Island Federal Prison] on their play and got to visit with him for the day. It was just great. Owsley is a hero. I didn't get a chance to get into a really in depth thing with him, which I was sorry about, but his head's together, he really feels good. And he's doing what he feels he has to do, I suppose. And I'm looking forward to having him out again. He's a tremendous asset when he's working.

When will he get out?

If everything goes at its absolute worst, I believe next October. But if there's any change or improvement, he could get out before then.

Owsley had a really weird role in the whole thing. You think he's mellowed quite a bit?

Right. I think that he still has the capacity to be what he is. But I think that there's an important lesson involved which took us a long time to snap to, which is this: Owsley is the guy who brought a really solid consciousness of what *quality* was, to our whole scene. And that's been the basis of our operations since then: being able to have our equipment in really good shape, our PA really good, stuff like that. We try to display as much quality as possible in the hopes of being able to refine pieces of what we do. And that's the thing that Owsley does like no other human being that I know can do or devote his attention to, and that is that thing of purification. It's a real thing with him. He's really really good at it. Owsley's a fine guy. He's just got an *amazing* mind.

He's got enough of *every* kind of experience, man! There's almost nothing the guy hasn't done. You know he's a licensed blacksmith? Not only that, but he's got a first class broadcaster's license, too. He worked for years in TV. He's also an *excellent* auto mechanic; he's obviously a chemist. There's almost nothing that he doesn't do, or at least have a good grasp of. He understands just about every level of organization. He's just incredible, he's got some incredible capacity for retaining information.

REICH: *You have a reputation that during the Haight-Ashbury time and later, that you were a sort of spiritual advisor to the whole rock scene.*

That's a crock of shit, quite frankly.

Jefferson Airplane says that on their first or second album.

I know. That's because at that time, they were making their second record and they were concerned about it—they didn't want it to be like their first record. And RCA had given them the producer, and he was like this straight producer who used to produce Andre Kostelanetz or somebody like that and he didn't really know what they wanted to do, how they wanted to sound or how they wanted their thing to be. The Airplane thought it would be helpful to have somebody there who could communicate to their producer who they could communicate to and since they all knew me and I understood their music and understood what they were doing pretty much at the time, it would be far out. I went down there and hung out and was a sort of go-between them and their producer and helped out with some arrangements and stuff like that—I just hung out.

REICH: *But that's a big difference from being the "guru" of the whole scene?*

Here's the thing—I would like to preface this whole interview by saying I'm one of those guys who's a compulsive question answerer. But that doesn't necessarily mean I'm right or anything. That's just one of the things I can do. It's kinda like having a trick memory. I can answer any question. I'm just the guy who found myself in the place of doing the talking every time there was an interview with the Grateful Dead.

How about among the musicians themselves?

I've played with nearly all the musicians around and we all get along okay. But the whole music scene is very groovy. Here there's very little competition, very few ego games. Everybody knows what it takes to make music pretty good around here. It's that thing of being high and playing. I think it's the scene this area has that makes it attractive for musicians and that's why a lot of them moved here. That freedom, that lack of competition, the fact that you aren't always having to battle and you can really get into what playing music is all about. But as for coming to me for advice and shit like that, that's ridiculous. That's like "Captain Trips." That's bullshit.

REICH: *Now, can I act like a professor, and ask you a long thing? People that write about rock say that it started as a rebellion, that it spoke to these needs in people to express their feelings. Tin Pan Alley was music that didn't tell the truth and rock did. The question is, do you think that rock began with that kind of revolt and has it changed?*

I don't know. I don't go for any of that stuff. If I were going to write about rock and roll music, I wouldn't write about it from that sociological standpoint and so forth because all that stuff really had to do with who you were. If you were wearing a black leather jacket and swinging a chain in the Fifties and listening to rock and roll, yeah, it was the music of rebellion. But if you were a musicologist following what music does, or a musician, it was something wholly different. It depends on who you were or who you are when they hit you.

REICH: *What I'm trying to get at is your idea of what rock meant.*

It was music I loved. That's what it meant. I mean it didn't mean anything—it meant have a good time, it meant rock and roll—whatever. I like the music, that was the thing. It was the background music for the events of my life. My theme music. Them rock and roll songs—that's what was happening.

The people that are writing about rock and roll are doing it as writers and they've got to create a situation to write about. Because if you don't create something to write about, you're left with no excuse for writing. That's not true of all writers. There are some writers that write for the flash and writers that write about the flash too. And it's easier for me to read the flash than it is for me to read about the sociology. I think you could make a better movie. *Rock Around The Clock* I think was a good movie about the source of what rock and roll was and *Rock Around The Clock* was the background music for 1958 and that was right on.

REICH: *Well, if knife fights and stuff like that was the background for the Fifties, what's the scene from which your music comes now?*

It's everything that I've ever experienced. It's everything that we—the Grateful Dead—has ever experienced as a group. It's a combination of every crowd we've ever seen, of every time we've ever played.

REICH: *In a way you're just a reflection of your times, wouldn't you say?*

Everything is, yes. But I don't know if I would go so far as to say *that's* what it was; that's the thing it *does*. I don't know that's what it *is*.

REICH: *People pointed out how angry the public got at rock. Remember how furious they were when it first began with Elvis. What was it that made them so mad?*

I really don't know. I always used to wonder, too. No one around me was ever that mad at it. I never experienced that. See, music was always a part of my life and no one was really around making big value judgments about one kind of music or another. My grandmother listened to country music; my mother listened to opera; my father was a musician. I was in the middle of music. And nobody was saying this kind of music is good and this kind of music is bad, nobody was telling me that rock and roll was out of tune. I didn't get that. Somebody must have because they always write about it, but I never did.

How did you avoid the music business taking over your lives? Because nobody wanted it?

Yeah, that's a good part of it. And with us, we've never really been successful in the music business; we've never had a super-big hit album or a hit single or anything like that. Grateful Dead freaks are our audience, you know. We're not mass market or anything like that, which I think is super great. I think that we've been really lucky because we haven't had to put up with all the celebrity stuff, or star stuff. At the same time it's been somewhat of a struggle to survive, but we're doing good, we're doing OK. So it worked out OK.

REICH: *You really are celebrities, though, aren't you, don't you feel that?*

Only in a certain world.

REICH: *But you couldn't walk around Yale without being mobbed.*

Possibly not, but I could walk around in downtown San Francisco without anybody even knowing who I am.

REICH: *In Berkeley, you'd be like surrounded by 2000 people . . .*

No, I don't think so. I move very freely around here. It's like the way it is with the people who know me, usually they're almost all hip enough to just let it go at "Hey, man, I really like your music." And that's always a turn-on, I can live with that. And almost nobody ever insists upon getting me to do weird shit or anything like that. It's been really cool, I think . . . I complain about it a lot though.

Do you think you could cope with a Crosby, Stills, Nash & Young type of success?

I might be able to cope with it, but I don't think that I could be really that comfortable with it, you know, because the place where I get strung out is . . . I'd like to be fair, you know, I want to be fair, so I don't like to pull the thing of having somebody at the door that says, "No, fuck you, you can't see Garcia, you know, you're not going in no matter what, no matter how good your rap is."

Our backstage scene and all that is real open, we try to let as much stuff possible come by, and I just've gotten into the thing of being able to move around pretty fast so I don't have to get hung up into anything, but I like to let it flow rather than stop it. I think that if there's more pressure along that line—it's getting now to where maybe 50 or 100 or 200 people backstage is getting kinda outrageous and if we were like super popular it would be that many more, and that (I'm thinking in purely physical terms) would start to get to be a problem somewhere in there, if we get much more famous.

That's why I feel pretty good about finishing up our Warner Brothers thing, stopping being part of that mainstream, and just kinda fallin' back so that we can continue to relate to our audience in a groovy intelligent way without having to be part of a thing that . . . really that other world of the higher up celebrity thing really doesn't seem to want us too badly, so, you know, we're able to avoid it. We're really not that good, I mean star kinda good, or big selling records good.

All we could hope to do, all we are really interested in doing is being able to keep doing what we do, but be able to have the energy come more directly back to us and be able to keep more of our friends alive, that kind of trip. Essentially that's what we're interested in doin'.

REICH: *So you'd rather play than not?*

I don't think of my work as being fulltime work. What I'm doing is my work, but I'm playing! When I left the straight world at 15, when I got my first guitar and left everything I was doing, I was taking a vacation—I was going out to play and I'm still playing.

REICH: *And is it still a vacation?*

Yes.

REICH: *But a while back you were saying that you couldn't have a good scene like the Haight-Ashbury unless people would contribute but it still shouldn't be the old-fashioned kind of work?*

No. I don't think sacrifice is contribution. I think that contributing is contributing your own positive energy, and not forcing yourself or any of that stuff.

Do you think it'll go on for a long time . . . the band?

Uh, I don't see why not. Barring everybody dying or complete disinterest or something like that. As long as it's groovy and the music is happening I don't see why it shouldn't just keep on going. We don't have any *real* plans, but we're committed to this thing; we're following it, we're not directing it. It's kinda like saying "Okay, now I want to be here, now I want to go there," in a way. Nobody's making any real central decisions or anything. Everything's just kinda hashed-out. It stumbles. It stumbles, then it creeps, then it flies with one wing and bumps into trees and shit. We're committed to it by now, after six years; what the fuck? It's still groovy for us. It's kinda like why break up the thing when it's working, when it seems to be working good and everybody's getting off

What happened to Mickey?

Mickey is still working on his record. He's still got his barn and all that. He's in a good place, I saw him last night, he was at the Crosby and Nash concert. Mickey is a very even dude. He's pretty together in his own way. He likes to walk on the edge of the cliff. But he stays cool behind it, he's able to do it. I like him.

What's the scene with Pigpen now?

He's pretty sick. But he's living. He was really, really *extremely* sick. I don't really know *how* sick, because I never hung out at the hospital that much, although I did give him a pint of blood. We all did. He was really fucked up; his liver was full of holes and then he had some kind of perforated ulcer—just all kinds of bum trips from juicing all these years. And he's a young dude, man, he's only 26. I think he might even be younger than that.

From juicing! It's incredible, but he survived it, and he isn't dead. He survived it and now he's got the option of being a juicer or not being a juicer. To be a juicer means to die, so now he's being able to choose whether to live or die. And if I know Pigpen, he'll choose to live. That's pretty much where he's at. For the time being he's too sick, too weak to go on the road, and I wouldn't want to expose him to that world. I don't think it's good for him at this point. It would be groovy if he could take as long as it takes to get him to feelin' right, and then to work on his solo album, and get himself together in terms of becoming. It's sorta like stepping out of the blues story, 'cause Pigpen is a sort of guy who's like been a victim of the whole blues trip. It's like Janis exactly, in which you must die. That's what the script says. So Pigpen went up to the line, and he's seen it now, so the question is how he's going to choose.

REICH: *You feel like it's on the prow of a ship up here, that's a very good way to think of it because you can see the Captain's stands.*

Right, it's kinda like a retired admiral's place, little brass telescope, cranky parrot.

REICH: *That's fine, Captain's cabin, that's what I've been thinking of you as, see, . . .*

I know, that's an attractive image and sometimes it seems like it, but I always thought that Kesey was. But he ain't either. Nobody is, man, there isn't anybody, it's just a convenience, it's just a place you can be, a way to express yourself.

The way it works is it doesn't depend on a leader, and I'm not the leader of the Grateful Dead or anything like that, there isn't any fuckin' leader. I mean, because I can bullshit you guys real easy, but I can't bullshit Phil and Pigpen and them guys watchin' me go through my changes all these years, and we've had so many weird times together. But it's that kind of thing. I know in front that the leader thing don't work, because you don't need it. Maybe it used to, but I don't think you need it any more because everybody is the leader, you know what I mean, all of a sudden, you're the guy that knows in that situation . . .

That's right.

You know, I think the Grateful Dead, the Grateful Dead is like one dumb guy, instead of five, you know . . . dumb guys, it's like one dumb guy and it seems like everything that we learn comes in the form of these big dumb, you know, take this, you know, the manager, krecccchhh, and we get hit over the head, oh yeah, manager, manager, yeah, it takes like a big one for us to notice it, man. That's kind of the way I see it.

. . . persevering . . .

Yeah, that's all we can do. I can't do anything else, hahahaha, and the Grateful Dead is still a good trip through all of it, through all of it it's been a good trip and I've dug every minute of it, man, it's just like I really love it, it's really a good trip, and that's the payoff, ultimately, you know, and that's the reason why we're all doing it, really, that's the one thing that still makes it. And you know, now actually for us everything is making it, everything is just going real good, it's going good enough where we can actually decide what the hell we want to do, which is—aw, fuck that's what.

What's the creative part of making your music—do you make it as you go along on the road or do you make it when you're settled back in San Francisco or do you make it all the time?

I'd say we make it all the time. Because we've all pretty much decided after a long time, that we're in fact musicians and it's just something you do, it's in your head, musical pieces and records and all that. As a band, for the last two years, our music has been evolving as we play it. We haven't been rehearsing because we haven't had a place to rehearse—like that's a whole other school of problems, rock and roll rehearsal spots.

REICH: *How does a song come into being and how does it grow from its beginnings into what you might hear eventually on the record?*

They're all different. Sometimes I'll start out with a set of chord changes that're just attractive to my ear. And then I'll hear a sketch of a melody over it. Then I'll just sort of let that be around my head, for however long it is there, for three or four weeks. I never try to work on stuff, you know, like sit down and labor it. But pretty soon there'll be more adjoining pieces to any one phrase, a melodic phrase, say. Then I hum it to myself for a long time and kind of play it on the guitar for everybody who's around and then I'll get together with Hunter who writes our lyrics and we'll go through what he's got. If he's got lyrics already written that he likes I'll see if anything fits or else we'll start working on something from scratch. But the whole thing is completely organic. I don't have any scheme.

REICH: *It comes from somewhere outside.*

For sure. And what happens is that you're lucky enough to remember a little of it as it's going by. And then what it turns into after it's become a song in your head is it turns into a piece of material for the band—everybody plays an equal role in that part of it—and that's the way it finally evolves as a song on a record or something like that. If it's one of my songs, it's never what I originally heard, it's always something that includes more than I might have conceived myself.

REICH: *And the words probably came by, too, is that right?*

Well, that's the way Hunter writes—he writes his words pretty much the same way. Things come to him, you know. An idea comes by, or a picture, an image, sort of floats by, it's all in the air kind of. It's a matter of being able to tune into it.

REICH: *One of the things about your music that everybody feels is how it just makes them happy. Do you have any thoughts about that?*

We've never been motivated by negative trips. We've never been into black magic or satanism or evil vibes or sex and sadism or . . .

MOUNTAIN GIRL: Or personal aggrandizement.

JERRY: . . . or any of those kinds of trips. We've just been into playing music. And it's kind of got positive roots, if you know what I mean.

Do you know bands that are into black magic?

Well, just stuff I've heard, you know. I don't really know. I mean, I don't know anything that I'd want anybody to print. You can never know what's in a cat's mind when he's doing that. I've looked into those things just out of interest—because of having been high and seeing things that seem to be intrinsically evil, say, something that has an evilness about it that's really archetypal—and because of a realization of that sort, you get curious, you wonder, "What's it about?" "What is it?" and you try and find things that are kind of like it, and say, "Oh, I see," and isolate the idea. But I've had that kind of interest in all those things, I've never felt that I wanted to be a part of it. It was never really my trip. I thought Altamont was like a perfect expression of that, you know, that particular whirlpool, whatever it is.

Who wrote "Casey Jones"?

Me and Hunter. He wrote the words, I wrote the music.

Did you start off to write the same thing or did you have the melody first and then the words?

No, he had the words, and the words were just so exquisite, they were just so perfect that I just sat down with the words, picked up a guitar and played the song. It just came out.

In one sitting?

Yeah, it just came out. It just triggered. Play it, here it is.

Do you alter the words when you write with Hunter?

Many times, yeah. Sometimes I use pieces of three or four of his different songs and put them together. I also adjust the phrasing, I sort of edit to make the things more *singable* usually. But he's gotten to be really a craftsman at it lately. In the last year or so, he's gotten to really understand what it is to sing words, and just the technique: that vowels sing a certain way and consonants sing a certain way and what you have to do. Certain things you can sing real gracefully and other things you can't sing to save your soul.

REICH: *Three or four songs I just want to talk about. The first is "Ripple" and it just makes everybody feel so good. And I guess what people, uh,*

*would want to know is how do you get it together so beautifully so that it
makes you happy and makes everybody else happy and . . .*

It's a thing of just watching real carefully what does what and
trying to keep as much of it in mind when you're doing what you're
doing. It's just taking into account everything you know about all
that stuff that you know about a thing like that. Most of it is pretty
conscious. Hunter wrote those words. "Ripple" is one of those things
of having two halves of a thing and having them come together just
perfectly. Bob Weir had a guitar custom-made for himself and I
picked it up and that song came out, it just came out.

REICH: *Came right out of the guitar?*

Right. Or at least that melody came out of the guitar and then
when I saw Hunter—Hunter was in England at the time—next
time I saw Hunter he says, "Here, I have a couple of songs I'd like
you to take a look at," and he had "Ripple" and it just . . . all of a sudden, just bam, there it was, it was just perfect.

The interesting thing about that is the little bridge in there is a
perfect Haiku. The little "Ripple in still water" part is a haiku, 17
syllables. There's a lot of those kinds of things in our music that
most people just never get. Hunter is just a fantastic craftsman. He
had lots of years of speed freaking, you know, to get really crazy
about language.

"Trucking" seems to be the story of the Dead.

When Hunter first started writing words for us originally, he was
on his own trip and he was a poet. He was into the magical thing of
words, definitely far out, definitely amazing. The early stuff he wrote
that we tried to set to music was stiff because it wasn't really meant to
be sung. After he got further and further into it, his craft improved
and then he started going out on the road with us, coming out to see
what life was like, to be able to have more of that viewpoint in the
music, for the words to be more Grateful Dead words. "Trucking" is
the result of that sort of thing. "Trucking" is a song that we assembled; it wasn't natural and it didn't flow and it wasn't easy and we
really labored over the bastard, all of us together.

REICH: *It comes out of somewhere in the past, doesn't it?*

It comes out of nothing specific but it's really a lot of like the way it is, the pace of it and the flow of it and the kinda like fast thoughts that you have as things are happening around you; the ideas in it are right-on in that sense. I like "Truckin'" a lot, "Truckin'"'s one of my favorites.

REICH: *You sing, "Sometimes the lights all shining on me and sometimes you can't even see." How does an idea like that just get into your music?*

Well, it's there. You can see it happen if you hang around backstage. If you go to a concert you see there's the on-stage part with the bright lights, the show, loud music, people screaming, all that stuff happening. And then you're backstage between sets and there's all kinds of milling crowds and people going, "Hey man, hey man," stuff coming at you and weird shit and you're having to duck and get out of the way and lie and talk fast—all these things to just be able to preserve a little composure, just so you don't have to be constantly putting out. That's just a way of saying that thing, I mean it's a beautiful way of saying it.

What about "Box of Rain"?

"Box of Rain" is a lyric that was written to a melody which Phil wrote. Phil had all the music that you hear in it all written out and Hunter got together with Phil and they went over it phrase for phrase.

It has that very worked-out feeling to it.

The way Hunter works is that you have a melody and you're sort of singing it at him, you're going da-da-dum, da-da-da-da-da-da, something like that, and he'll listen to the way you're singing it at him and he'll pick up the sounds that you're using as you're singing it at him and he'll try to construct his words along those lines. He'll listen over and over to you sing it and then he'll make a sentence out of what you've been singing at him.

We've all been doing it pretty long so that the craft is there and luckily sometimes, the flash is there, the brilliance to be able to . . .

for the craft to have something to hang on to, you know, a little shred, that's the thing that really counts.

In "New Speedway Boogie" you say "one way or another, this darkness has got to end." Have you seen that way yet?

Ummmm. . . . Ahhh. . . . I think that that song's an over-reaction, myself. I think that it's a little bit dire. Really, the thing that I've been seeing since Altamont is that periodically you have darkness and periodically you have light, like the way the universe is in the yin/yang symbol. There's darkness and light and it's the interplay that represents the game that we're allowed to play on this planet. Just the fact that there are two opposing elements in the universe is the grace of that cosmic game that we're allowed to dick around here, you know, on the planet.

That's an existential solution?

Well, it's just a vehicle through which to . . . it's a lens through which you can look at it but keep the integrity of your operating reality. You know, you get to be whole, as whole as you conceive yourself to be, but you have to be able to look at every event and not turn from any one. Most philosophy excludes some experience somewhere.

REICH: *In "Box of Rain" you're saying, "Just look anywhere, all the wonder in the world is right there."*

Well, I'm not saying that, though, that's Hunter and Phil. . . .

REICH: *Alright.*

. . . that are saying that. Hahaha, got you there.

REICH: *Yeah, that's true, but ah, well is it a . . .*

I go for it, I go for it.

REICH: *The thing I suppose that especially means something to me is "inch your way," because instead of telling people it's easy you tell them it's going to be hard and slow and painful . . .*

Yeah, "Speedway Boogie" is more or less that same thing, just go slowly so you can see what's happening. That's the thing that age has always told youth and that's what they used to tell me and I never believed it. But it's one of those pieces of information which a little age gives you perspective on. Suddenly, you see that, *yeah, that's really true.* To keep putting that out is just saying what's already been said, but maybe somebody will pick up on it; that's about the best you can hope for. But you can't *expect* anybody to really.

REICH: *Well plenty of people pick up on that song and pick up on the idea that when it's tough, you know, your experience has been that it gets tough, and then it gets easy, gets tough . . .*

Right, right. It goes a whole lot of different ways.

What if somebody came up to you and asked you "What's psychedelic music?"

Ohhhhhhh, God damn . . . Phil defined it pretty good once. He said ummmmm. Oh, somebody asked him once what acid rock was—which is psychedelic music, OK, whatever—we'll use those two as an equation—and he said, "Acid rock is music you listen to when you're high on acid." Psychedelic music is music you listen to when you're psychedelic. I think that's what its real definition should be because subjectively I don't think that there really is any *psychedelic music,* unless except in the classical sense of music which is designed to expand consciousness. If you use that as a definition of psychedelic music, then I would say that Indian music was definitely that, and that certain kinds of Tibetan music are too.

REICH: *No, the real meaning is where the music comes from. Psychedelic music comes from a different place than blues comes from.*

I don't think so. Really? I don't think so.

REICH: *Inside of a person.*

I just think that there are cultural differences in how that place is defined, but basically it's the same thing. I see a lot of similarities, but that's just me; I mean, this is for the sake of discussion. I'm not qualified really to answer that kind of a question; all I can do is say, "Well, my opinion is, yeah . . . "

REICH: *What I mean is that "Dark Star" comes from a place in the consciousness that's entirely different from the blues, which is an emotional place, a tearing, screaming emotional place, that's a whole different place than the place that "Dark Star" comes from which is a fantasy trip off into some fantastic world, that's what I'm trying to say.*

Well, there's a great big huge difference in form between "Dark Star" and the blues, but I think that its essence is the same. Also there's the blues and there's the blues: there's the blues that transcends the state of consciousness known as the blues, I mean the music. I think that the music is a step further than the emotional experience and I think that any musician who is a blues musician is not usually a person who is stricken with the emotional affliction known as the blues. I think that that consciousness is musician consciousness, which is where music comes from, and I think that that's the same.

REICH: *Alright.*

Go around it that way.

REICH: *Well then if we wanted to talk about "Dark Star," uh, could you say anything about where it comes from?*

You gotta remember that you and I are talking about two different "Dark Stars." You're talking about the "Dark Star" which you have heard formalized on a record, and I'm talking about the "Dark Star" which I have heard in each performance as a completely improvised piece over a long period of time. So I have a long continuum of "Dark Stars" which range in character from each other to real different extremes. "Dark Star" has meant, while I'm playing it, almost as many things as I can sit here and imagine, so all I can do is talk about "Dark Star" as a playing experience.

REICH: *Well, yeah, talk about it a little.*

I can't. It talks about itself.

REICH: *Each time it comes out in a different way?*

Yeah, pretty much. There are certain structural poles which we have kind of set up in it, and those periodically we do away with.

REICH: *So it's just whatever trip it is that particular night?*

That's why we came up with such a thing; there are a few things that we do which are vehicles for that openness and what I . . .

REICH: *Alright, now, let's see what I wanted to bring out . . . probably becoming less coherent with every . . .*

It's hard to talk about this kind of stuff.

REICH: *But anyway, what I wanted to say was . . .*

Goddamn, it's tricky, no shit.

REICH: . . . *"Dark Star" is different from "Trucking" because one feels that on "Dark Star" you're being taken into a person's inner world more than you've ever been taken into such a world before. Somebody's taking me into their whole world of wherever they are that night, and I've never been there before.*

Songs are a whole different form, songs are like . . . oh what . . . like epigrams. They are complete little statements and they are always appropriate once you have given them their form: they're just little statements. But a thing like "Dark Star" and some other things that we do, have done, do do—there's something on our new album that unfolds in the "Dark Star tradition," so to speak. This new one is even more amazing. It is really some of the best playing that we've ever done, or that I've ever heard us do.

If it were possible for us to be able to survive playing music that was as potentially free and open as "Dark Star," it's likely that we would do that or something along those lines. We're trying to guide ourselves into a place where we can become more music, where we can play more music and have it get to higher places and express finer and subtler things. And that has to do with being able to more or less control the circumstances in which we're playing. And you can only play so much high music in gyms and then you're squeezing it out of yourself and it's not really happening.

There are really severe limitations that we're having to deal with just because of the form; I've always thought that the Grateful Dead should be sponsored by the government or something. It should be a public service, you know, and they should set us up to play at places that need to get high. That's like the kind of thing we should be doing: we shouldn't be business—it shouldn't be any of that stuff—it should be a thing like that and that's the direction that I'm looking to go into.

If you wanted to play all the instruments on your own record, you would lose the whole group feel wouldn't you?

Yes, of course, except that that's the challenge. If it were possible for me to make a record where I could play by myself and sound like the whole group, I would consider it to be a successful record. In the context of this kind of experiment and in the nature of the kind of material I'm doing on my solo album, it'll be that kind of an experiment. I'll be able to make myself sound like a band. The reason, musically, I know I can do it is because it's all coming from my head, it's going to at least agree. But then you get this unified, too-much-agreement sort of sound, and you don't have that excitement of interchange.

Does the group have a producer?

No, we are our own producer. A producer is just one of those recording studio . . . The function that a producer sometimes fills is that he's the guy who sits in the recording studio while the band plays and tells them whether they're playing well or not, what's wrong with what they're playing, whether they're out of tune, in tune, whether it needs to be a little faster and so on. He's an ear. He translates the band's wishes to the engineer. That's essentially what the producer does.

When you're working at the studio night after night, after the recording is over, you're mixing. Whose responsibility is that?

That's whoever cares. Usually, if a band has a producer, the producer will be mixing and the guys from the band will be listening and say what they want to hear and what they don't want to hear. And that's kinda the way we work except any one of us can be the producer on any given tune. I'll mix a tune and Bobby and Bill will be in the room telling me what they like and what they don't like, whether it needs more this and more that. Generally the thing is that if you're doing everything, you lose track. There's only so much you can pay attention to at the same time. If it's your own music in front, you tend to listen to it through different sort of ears.

Mixing is really composing in a way.

The whole studio trip is composing. That's why I'm doing a solo record. It's as a composer, not a performer. I'm not going to try to be a band. I'm going to try to be a composer, because the 16-track is the perfect way to do it.

The old idea of a composer is a person who wrote notes on paper.

But now you can create any sound you want in a recording studio. So why not just go and do the sound that you hear in your head? It's like scratching an itch. The idea of having that complex code of writing music is so that you can get the sound in your head out and it's a very imperfect way to do it. There's huge, big flaws in the notation system because it only tells you about pitch and meter; it doesn't tell you about the shape of a note, except in the crudest way. It just doesn't cover the amount of sounds available. Most modern composers invent their own ways of writing music.

Our whole trip with making records has been to learn *how* to make records, to learn how to deal with a tune. To be a musician means to be a composer and to be a 16-track recording virtuoso and so forth—it's an expanded role. As well as being the guy who sits around here and bullshits like this hour after hour. It's obviously not what it once was.

REICH: *There's a common idea that the band plays, and then somebody else—some mysterious figure—comes in and does the mixing.*

There are bands that work that way, but not us. But there are mysterious personages between what leaves the recording studio and what comes out on the disc. If you don't follow the recording all the way down to actually cutting the master disc, and if there's not someone actually there supervising, some technician, some union employee or something, will compress the record, and it'll come out sounding way different than you remember it.

Do you usually pursue the master disc?

We've only started doing that in the last three records. Just because we didn't really know that much about it before. Our particular failures have been just because we didn't know what we were doing.

REICH: *How has your music changed from one record to another?*

The first one was called *The Grateful Dead*. At that time we had no real *record* consciousness. We were just going to go down to L.A. and make a record. We were completely naive about it. We had a producer whom we had chosen—Dave Hassinger—and we were impressed by him because he'd been the engineer on a couple of Rolling Stones records that we liked the sound of; that was as much as we were into record-making.

So we went down there and, what was it we had, Dexamyl? Some sort of diet-watchers speed, and pot and stuff like that. So in three nights we played some hyperactive music. That's what's embarrassing about that record now, the tempo was way too fast. We were all so speedy at the time. It has its sort of crude energy, but obviously it's difficult for me to listen to it; I can't enjoy it really. I just plain cannot enjoy it just because even as soon as we'd finish it there were things that we could hear. . . .

MOUNTAIN GIRL: Man, it's so fast, it's just blinding!

What music was it?

Just simply what we were doing onstage. Basically that. Just rock and roll. Plus we wanted to have one extended cut on it. But in reality, the way we played was not really too much the way that record was. Usually we played tunes that lasted a long time because we like to play a lot. And when you're playing for people who are dancing and getting high, you can dance easy to a half-hour tune and you can even wonder why it ended so soon. So for us the whole time thing was weird 'cause we went down there and turned out songs real fast—less than three minutes which is real short.

It was weird and we realized it. The first record was like a regular company record done in three nights, mixed in one day. It was done on three track, I believe—it wasn't even four track—Studio A in L.A., an imposing place, and we really didn't much care about it while we were doing it. So we weren't surprised when it didn't quite sound like we wanted it to.

It's hard for me to go back to the past in terms of the music because for me it's a continuum and to stop it at one of those points it's got . . . to me it always looks underdeveloped and not quite working. Which in fact it was.

What kind of places were you playing at then?

We were playing all the places that were trying to become the Fillmore or trying to become the Avalon as well as the Fillmore and the Avalon. And there were places down in L.A. that were trying to get started and places in San Diego, but all the rest of that stuff is stuff that's everywhere.

This is '66 by now, something like that.

Yeah, '66, right.

Then on the second record, we went the whole other way. We decided we'd spend time on our record: we're going to work on it, we're going to make sure it sounds good, we're really going to get into recording and go on some trips with it. So our second record turned out to be a monumental project. We started out by recording for a couple of weeks, experimentally, in L.A. where we accomplished absolutely nothing. Then we went to New York to try some studios there and we got our producer so excited that he quit. We got him uptight because we were being so weird and he was only human after all and didn't really have to go through all that, so he decided not to go through it and we decided, "Well, we can do it ourselves." So we just worked and worked and worked—mostly Phil and I—for months, maybe as long as six months—at least six months. It was an eight-track recording and we worked a lot in San Francisco. We assembled live tapes and we went through the most complex operations that you can go through in a recording studio.

Did Phil use his background or did you just learn it from scratch?

Phil used what he knew and I was learning from scratch. I had had some experience after working with the Jefferson Airplane, pretty nominal, but at least I had some idea. And we had an engineer, Dan Healy, who is like a real good fast-on-his-feet, able-to-come-up-with-crazy-things engineer. And we worked and we assembled an enormous amount of stuff, and since it was all multitrack, it all just piled up.

With *Anthem of the Sun*, after an enormously complex period of time, we actually assembled the material that was on the master tape. Then we went through the mixing thing, which really became a performance, so *Anthem of the Sun* is really the performance of an eight-track tape; Phil and I performed it and it would be like four hands and sometimes Healy would have a hand in. We'd be there hovering around the boards in these various places at Criteria Studio, Miami, and in New York. We selected, from various performances we did, the performance which seemed the most spaced and we did that all the way through. So that's a spaced record if there is one.

How was the music different from the first record?

We were thinking more in terms of a whole record and we were also interested in doing something that was far-out. For our own amusement—that thing of being able to do a record and really go away with it—really lose yourself.

What do you think of that second record, Anthem of the Sun?

There's parts of it that sound dated, but parts of it are far-out, even too far-out. I feel that that's one of those things . . . see, it's hard for me to be able to listen to any of that stuff objectively, 'cause I tend to hear a thing like *Anthem of the Sun* matching it up against what it was that we thought we were gonna do, intellectually speaking. So I have to think of it in terms of something we were trying to do but didn't succeed in doing. I listen to what's *wrong* with it. I tend to listen to it in the inverse way; but on the other hand, if I have the right kind of head, and I'm not on an ego involvement trip with it. . . .

You can get behind it . . .

Yeah, but in a different way. It's definitely weird. Phil just went on a trip of remixing it, and the remixed result is even weirder, or *as* weird as the original because, first of all, it was an eight-track tape, so we spent a lot of time crowding things down to one track. Mixing down and mixing down, and we had the tapes for *really* long, and a lot of stuff is dubbed off quarter track, little tiny half-inch or whatever, four-track stuff and all kinds of oddball stuff which we assembled in the hopes of producing what would be a sound collage symphonette or some damn thing. On one level it's successful, in terms of the form and structure of it. It's something which you can *dig*. But in terms of the way the individual things are performed, it's a drag.

Did the next record mark any kind of change?

No. The next record was really a continuation of the *Anthem of the Sun* trip—called *Aoxomoxoa*—a continuation in the style of having a complex record. When we started, *Aoxomoxoa* was an eight-track record and then all of a sudden there was a 16-track recorder in the studio, so we abandoned our entire eight-track version and went to 16-track to start all over again. Now at the time we were sipping STP during our session, which made it a little weird—in fact, very weird. We spent too much money and too much time on that record; we were trying to accomplish too much and I was being really stupid about a lot of it, because it was material, some new tunes that I had written, that I hadn't really bothered to teach anyone in the band and I was trying to record them from the ground up and everybody was coming in and doing over-dubs. It was weird—we went about it in a very fragmentary way. We didn't go about it as a group at all.

Some of the music is pretty strange.

Now I like that record personally, just for its weirdness really. There are certain feelings and a certain kind of looseness that I kinda dig; but it's been our most unsuccessful record. It was when Hunter and I were both being more or less obscure and there are lots of levels on the verbal plane in terms of the lyrics being very far out. Too far out, really, for most people.

That was one of my pet records 'cause it was the first stuff that I thought was starting to sound like how I wanted to hear songs sound. And the studio stuff was successful. I'm really happy with the remix. I hope you get a chance to hear 'em. All the new mixes that are coming out will say on them "Remixed."

How did that title come about, Aoxomoxoa?

Well, he insisted on calling it that . . .

Who did?

Rick Griffin. He was working in that whole palindrome scene, at that particular stage of his drawing, and he suggested that title to us. We were toying with the idea of calling it "Earthquake Country," a little bit. But Rick Griffin wanted to call it Aoxomoxoa.

What was it like doing that album?

It was great fun. *All* the music is on the tapes, the tapes were well recorded, and the music is well-played and everything on it is really *right*. It's just that it was our first adventure with 16-track and we tended to put *too* much on everything. We tended to use up *every* track, and then when we were mixing, we were all of us trying to mix. Well, *we* couldn't; somebody might be able to. Anyway, it came out mixed by committee. A lot of the music was just lost in the mix, a lot of what was really there on the tape. But I really had fun remixing it. The remixes are admittedly somewhat simpler and I left out a lot of what seemed unnecessary to the content of the stuff. I just got farther into trying to make it sound like what I hoped it would sound like in the first place.

There's some really pretty moments in it; "Mountains of the Moon" is really a lovely tune. It's still one of my favorites of the ones I've ever written. I thought it came off like a little gem. On the record as it is now, I've dropped a lot of the junk off it. It sounds more like what I hoped it would when we recorded it. "Dupree" is one of my favorite recorded ones too; it reminds me of a little cartoon strip, with cartoon characters. It has a banjo in it, a little 12-string and stuff like that. Texturally, it's really successful to my ears. It does what it's supposed to. It has a little sort of a calliope sound, where T.C. is playing a *perfect* organ part for it. All that stuff was *there*, it's just a matter of making it work. That record is one of my pets. I really like it. I was always sorry that it came out so fucked up and then didn't sell and all. It was one of our most expensive ones— it might've been *the* most expensive one.

How much? Eighty thousand?

An *easy* that.

What happened?

Well, you know, there were good intentions all over the place, whereas with *Anthem* we didn't really succeed in gettin' 'em onto the tape too successfully. In *Aoxomoxoa* we did, and then we blew it in the mix.

What makes you decide to do a record when? You just go along doing concerts . . .

And it comes to record time and at that time we knew in-front that we weren't going to be able to sound like we sounded on stage in the studio—we just couldn't do that. We haven't ever been able to do that.

REICH: *Why does record time come along?*

Because of a contractual thing. But that's only part of it. We're not so rigidly contracted that we're being moved around by the record company, but in reality, about a year—that's a good time to start to get your ideas together. I sorta see them as annual reports.

The next one is Live Dead.

It's good. It has "Dark Star" on it, a real good version of it. We'd only recorded a *few* gigs to get that album. We were after a certain sequence to the music. In the sense of it being a serious, long composition, musically, and then a recording of it, it's *our* music at one of its really good moments.

It has a picture on the inside of that concert on the truck-bed on Haight Street.

That was a special time. That was when the city agreed to close off Haight Street.

It was already too late by then. That was kinda like our swan song to Haight St. To the whole scene. It was the very height of the most highly publicized, highly energized moment. That's when we went down there and played. Which got everybody off real good. It was really a great day, but that was the end of it.

It wasn't like a happy performance, in the way the Speedway Meadow gigs were.

It was intense. It was real intense. It wasn't like a park scene back in the days when it really didn't matter. And that was when it was real gold, when things were really pure. You weren't posing for a picture in some magazine of the future. It was just like a regular thing, you go down there and play. None of the other stuff. Not to put any of that down, it's just that it was a different thing before . . . then it got that attention. And shit, I'm as much to blame as anybody for focusing that attention on it. We all are.

Live Dead was actually recorded about the same time we were working on *Aoxomoxoa*. If you take *Live Dead* and *Aoxomoxoa* together, you have a picture of what we were doing at that time. We were playing *Live Dead* and we were recording *Aoxomoxoa*. When *Live Dead* came out, it was about a year out of date.

After *Aoxomoxoa* we hadn't made a studio record for almost a year since *Live Dead* came out in its place. We were anxious to go to the studio but we didn't want to incur an enormous debt making the record like we had been. When you make a record, you pay for the studio time out of your own royalties. That costs plenty. *Live Dead* was not too expensive since it was recorded live. It ended up paying for the time on *Aoxomoxoa*, which was eight months or some really ridiculous amount of time. A hundred grand or even more than that—it was real expensive. And we ended up at our worst, in debt to Warner Brothers for around $180,000.

So, when record time came around and we were getting new material together, we thought, "Let's try to make it cheap this time." So we rehearsed for a month or so before we went in to make *Workingman's Dead*. We rehearsed and we were pretty far into the material and then we got busted in New Orleans. After we got busted, we went home to make our record. And while we were making our record, we had a big, bad scene with our manager. Actually making the record was the only cool thing happening—everything else was just sheer weirdness.

How had your music changed?

We were into a much more relaxed thing about that time. And we were also out of our pretentious thing. We weren't feeling so much like an experimental music group, but were feeling more like a good old band.

REICH: *Do you feel that's like giving something up?*

No. See, we never really gave it up, we just didn't put it out on that record. We still play that way, we still stretch out. It wasn't meant to indicate any trend whatsoever because we've never accepted any limitations. We don't think of ourselves as a rock and roll band, an experimental band, this band or that band. If anything, we think of ourselves as musicians, who have lots of possibilities. And *Workingman's Dead* is one of the possibilities and I expect in the course of a lifetime of music, we'll have thrown out lots of possibilities and that's the way I see each record. But it's never the total picture.

How did the scene with Lenny, your manager, taking the dough affect the making of the album?

The album was a tremendous joy. Being able to do that was *extremely* positive in the midst of all this adverse stuff that was happening. It definitely was an upper. We were getting far into our own thing, without really a gallery to play to, for example, or an audience to interact with. It's just us, bouncing off each other. It was the first record that we made together as a group, all of us. Everybody contributed beautifully and it came off really nicely. That was also our first really together effort at having our songs be groovy and everything. The whole thing.

That was the year we got turned onto singing, so, being turned onto singing, we would approach it in that particular way. I like the mixes on it—they aren't my mixes particularly, but they came off.

Does "Casey Jones" grate on you when you hear it sometimes?

Sometimes, but that's what it's supposed to do. (*laughs*)

It's such a sing-songy thing . . .

Right. And it's got a split-second little delay, which sounds very mechanical, like a typewriter almost, on the vocal, which is like a little bit jangly, and the whole thing is, well . . . I always thought it's a pretty good musical picture of what cocaine is like. A little bit evil.

And hard-edged. And also that sing-songy thing, because that's what it *is*, a sing-songy thing, a little melody that gets in your head.

What songs on Workingman's Dead *do you particularly like?*

I liked all those tunes. I loved them all, (*laughs*) to give you the absolute and unashamed truth. I felt that they were *all* good songs. They were successful in the sense you could sing 'em, and get off and enjoy singing 'em. "Uncle John's Band" was a *major* effort, as a musical piece. It's one we worked on for a really long time, to get it working right. "Cumberland Blues" was also difficult in that sense. The song that I think failed on that record is "High Time." It's a beautiful song, but I was just not able to sing it worth a shit. And I really can't do justice to that kind of song now. I'm not that good of a singer. But I wish someone who could really sing would do one of those songs sometime. I would *love* to hear some good singers do that stuff. I mean it would just tickle me. There are some people doing "Friend of the Devil," I understand. But other than that, we haven't heard of any people doing our songs at all.

That's a beautifully written song.

That was a rich, that particular album has some *really* beautiful songs on it. They came out like gold or something like that. "New Speedway Boogie" is one of those miracle songs. It's one of those "once-through" ones. The words were just *so* right, that it was immediately apparent, just bam! It came out right. Simple and straight-ahead.

Where was Workingman's Dead *made?*

It was made at P.H.R.—Pacific High Recording.

You still work there?

No, we work in Wally Heider's now, because the P.H.R. room has some oddly accented frequencies. It's very difficult for us to record the bass and any other instrument at the same time at P.H.R. There's "standing waves." It's a very big sort of clumsily-clover-leafed shaped room. It makes a great sound stage, but it's not very good as a studio. It was good enough with *Workingman's Dead* because the whole tone of the album was quiet, so we didn't play too loud on that album. A lot of it was live.

What stands out in your mind about American Beauty? *Each song sounds closer to the others.*

There isn't too much difference. And that's . . . well, I tried to block that whole trip out. You see, my mother died while we were making that record. And Phil's father died. It was raining down hard on us while that record was going on. They're good tunes, though. Every one of 'em's a gem. I modestly admit.

That had one of the few things Pigpen sings by himself.

One of his own tunes. He's come up with a lot of them lately.

What side of you does American Beauty *represent?*

Well, let's call *Workingman's Dead* a song record, a singing record because the emphasis is on the vocals and on the songs. And *American Beauty* is another record in that trend where the emphasis is on the vocals and the songs. And that's basically what we're doing, the music being more or less incidental—not incidental—but structural rather than the end product.

The records are not total indicators, they're just products. Out of the enormous amount of output that we create in the course of a year, they're that little piece that goes out to where everybody can get it.

The new album, the live double set, is like listening to the old Grateful Dead.

It's *us*, man. It's the prototype Grateful Dead. Basic unit. Each one of those tracks is the total picture, a good example of what the Grateful Dead really is, *musically*. Rather than *"This* record has sort of a country, light acoustics sound," and so on—like for a year we were a light acoustics band, in somebody's head. The new album is enough of an overview so people can see we're like a regular shoot-em-up saloon band. That's more what we are like. The tracks all illustrate that nicely. They're hot.

What places did you use most in that record?

The one we used most of was Fillmore East. And the one we used least was Winterland. At Winterland we used one track, "Johnny B. Goode."

The originals are so much better, of course, why did you do it?

Of course. There's really no hope in competing with it in any sense. It's nothin' at all like the original, it's just straight-ahead. We've had better "Johnny B. Goode"s. But that song for that year had been feeling good for us to play it. We have a lot of respect for Chuck Berry, what the fuck, it's traditional to do a guy's tune if you like his music.

Do you do "Down the Line" these days?

Sometimes we do. "Beat It on Down the Line" is one of the few from that era we still do. We still sometimes do "Sittin' on Top of the World." We still do "Morning Dew." We don't do "Viola Lee Blues." We've been known to do "Mingle-wood," too. And "Cold Rain and Snow" we still do. Actually, a lot of that shit we still do.

Have you ever thought of recording that stuff again?

Yeah . . . it'll happen in the future. That *could've* been this record here, because we recorded everything we did and we didn't have a "set" show or anything. We didn't have a decent recording of it or we would've taken "Cold Rain and Snow" or anything that was good, cause that's what we were after. We didn't care what song it was or whose it was or anything.

I heard those records made from tapes of early Avalon shows.

There's no point in going back to the past, for one thing, and for another thing, those performances weren't meant to stand around forever. They were for *that night*. And if you were stoned and there that night, that was probably *exactly* what was happening, but it's not what's happening *now*. It's just a source of embarrassment.

Why are you doing an album by yourself?

I'm doing it to be completely self-indulgent—musically. I'm just going on a trip. I have a curiosity to see what I can do and I've a desire to get into 16-track and go on trips which are too weird for me to want to put anybody else I know through. And also to pay for this house!

Are you doing it with anybody?

I'll probably end up doing it with a lot of people. So far I'm only working with Bill Kreutzman because I can't play drums. But everything else I'm going to try to play myself. Just for my own edification. What I'm going to do is what I would do if I had a 16-track at home, I'm just going to goof around with it. And I don't want anyone to think that it's me being serious or anything like that—it's really me goofing around. I'm not trying to have my own career or anything like that. There's a lot of stuff that I feel like doing and the Grateful Dead, just by fact that it's now a production for us to go out and play, we can't get as loose as we had been able to, so I'm not able to stay as busy as I was. It's just a way to keep my hand in so to speak, without having to turn on a whole big scene. In the world that I live in there's the Grateful Dead which is one unit which I'm a part of and then there's just me. And the me that's just me, I have to keep my end up in order to be able to take care of my part of the Grateful Dead. So rather than sit home and practice—scales and stuff—which I do when I'm together enough to do it—I go out and play because playing music is more enjoyable to me than sitting home and playing scales.

You've done some playing with Tom Fogerty.

The drummer in that band now plays with the Sons of Champlin and Merle Saunders has a small recording team of his own as well as composes and I'm going to gig with them. It's that kind of thing—a loose hangout.

Even though you tour a lot, you still do a lot of playing outside the band, like with Merle Saunders.

Yeah, I still do that. I hope to do a few gigs with Howard. It's just that I love music. I love an opportunity to go out and play. I'm a total junkie when it comes to playing. I just *have* to play. And when we're off the road I get itchy, and a bar's just like the perfect opportunity to get loose, and play all night or whatever's comfortable. With guys that are good players, Merle or Howard or anything, it's always a complete open jam scene.

Could you ever play with another group?

If I had another life to live, I could. Just like I could dig playing with Howard for a long time or Merle, all those guys. I enjoy playing and if I had more of me to go out and play those gigs, I'd do it immediately.

The Howard Wales record came out really nice.

It came out pretty successfully. It could have come out better. It could've come out *really* fine, in my opinion. I'm talking about the way it fell together, 'cause none of their material was written or anything. We either worked it out in the studio or it was totally improvised, like "South Side Strut" is just a jam, it's a thing which just happened, with all those changes and horn parts, we did it all live. It was very loose, but the results of it came out remarkably sophisticated.

You got into money, you got into business, you got into management duties, and you got into records and somehow you stayed yourselves.

Well, we didn't really get into any of those things is the reason. See, our managers were Rock Scully and Danny Rifkin who were really our friends and they were a couple of heads, old time organizers from the early Family Dog days and they agreed to sort of manage us. Which they did as well as they could. They investigated the music business and learned as much about it as they possibly could, but really they weren't too experienced at it and we weren't very experienced at it and so what we really managed to do in that whole world was get ourselves incredibly in debt, just amazingly in debt in just about two years.

MOUNTAIN GIRL: They never wrote anything down or anything like that.

JERRY: And we never cared, I mean it was just a . . . it was a . . . we were mostly interested in just keeping going.

Didn't anybody in the band think, "Hmm, we're getting more and more in debt and . . . "

Well, no, because we didn't know about it. But nobody knew about it, Rock didn't know, Danny didn't know about it. Really. We didn't know about it until we tried to get ourselves completely organized.

REICH: *Is this a different story from the other stories?*

It's similar, it's different but similar, every band has gone through trips kinda like it.

REICH: *So the real story is you just didn't . . .*

We didn't give a shit.

We were just happy freaks, man, we didn't know anything about money, or bills, or anything of the rest of that stuff. It wasn't bad, though. Don't get the idea it was bad because it just wasn't real, and because it wasn't real was the reason that it got to outrageously out of hand. And it wasn't until somebody started saying hey, listen, you guys are really in big trouble. And . . .

Who started saying that?

Lenny, who is Mickey's father. Now Lenny comes into the picture. And we had our office reorganized; Danny had gone off on a trip because he just felt like traveling, he didn't want to have to hang around, and we thought it was groovy that he do that. And Rock was trying to get our office back together with the help of Jonathan Reiser and John MacIntyre, all the guys that used to work at the Carousel. The Carousel had folded and they had to do something so they started working for us.

What happened to the Carousel?

The cat who owned the place was overcharging the rent from what I understand. At the time Ron Racow was running the Carousel Ballroom and he got called "mismanager" and all the rest of that stuff, but in reality there was no way to make it work. When Graham moved in he tore out a whole lot of stuff, put the stage in a different place and just made more room, he was able to make it work that way. But at the time we were sort of competing with Graham. It was a great scene, even though it failed; it was good and a lot of people worked there and it got a lot of things together and it was good energy, it was really fine.

How did you finally get the financial act together?

All of a sudden there was a concern there that was fictionalized in our minds by somebody else. It's entirely possible that we could have fixed it without ever knowing about it. But we were made conscious of it and we became paranoid: "You guys are really in big trouble, you're out of money and there's no money coming in and you're going broke and I think these guys have been ripping you off," and all. That is really a poisonous kind of thinking and we went for it, foolishly we went for it and said, "OK, you be our manager." So Lenny Hart said, "OK, boys, I'll take care of you," and we thought, "Ah, at least here's a manager that we don't have to worry about, he's an old business man and he's Mickey's father, well, we can trust him, of course we can trust him, you know, he's his father."

But along the way all the people who were our friends and people that we trusted to work for us began to leave. He was putting them uptight. It was really a classical manipulation trip and really creepy. Looking back on it, at the time we were just really not sure of what was happening and we were testing Lenny a lot, too, we were putting him on the line a lot, like "we don't want to do these kind of gigs; we don't want to do that or we don't want you to go out and talk to people, we want to talk to 'em ourselves, you just stay in the background as much as possible."

I'd been concerned about our management scene because I knew that Lenny didn't understand us and we didn't understand him and it really wasn't working out, but we had no way to replace him. But these old friends of mine, the Parkers, who had been having straight gigs for a long time, had just gotten back from a vacation. They had nothing to do and they were kinda looking for work and I said, "Wow, here's some people that can maybe help us out." At the same time, this was after Altamont, Sam Cutler had come back to the United States after having gone through that Altamont scene and he was looking for something to do—he came and hung out at my house for awhile. I thought because of this experience, in the music business, that maybe he could sort of look into our scene and see if maybe he could suggest some stuff.

Sam started looking into it and they discovered that Lenny had really been taking a lot of money and that the books were really weird and there were odd bank accounts and it came down to a real heavy scene. We were recording *Workingman's Dead* when we actually fired Lenny; we'd just been busted in New Orleans and things were really looking heavy, this New Orleans threat hanging over our heads and Lenny was our only contact with the New Orleans District Attorney. What happened, what finally sprung it, was Ramrod, who's our head equipment guy, who's been with us a long time, said, "Either you gotta get rid of that Lenny guy or I'm quitting." And that flashed us: "Wow, we can't work without Ramrod, we've gotta get rid of Lenny."

What did Mickey say about all this?

Well, Mickey was dismayed. He'd never expected anything like that of course. He knew his father had been into shady trips before but he thought he was reformed just like we all did. He was really shocked, and he was right with us about our decision to get rid of Lenny. In fact he was really good about working it out just 'cause it was so tacky.

As soon as we started to get closer and closer to finding out more and more of the truth and trying to get bills and old things from Lenny he just disappeared. A great deal has been lost and is missing and has never been filed or put anywhere . . . a lot of it . . . there's really no way of estimating how much money we've lost, as a result of that. There isn't. There's only sort of rough estimates. That was the weirdest ever; God, that was incredible.

When did you first meet Bill Graham?

Graham, well, we met Graham around that first Mime Troupe benefit. Phil knew him before that because Phil had done some music with the Mime Troupe I think. Graham used to be their business manager and so he was the guy in charge of the benefit and he'd heard about us I guess from someone and sort of asked us to come and do the benefit, that's where we first met.

And at the Trips Festival. Graham was there. The first time we saw Bill Graham as Bill Graham now, as the classical Bill Graham, was at the Trips Festival, that's the image that I remember: all this incredible color chaos going on, and there was one guy, you know,

Bill with his blue sweater, his little V-neck sweater and his shirt and his watch and his clip board, you know, with a schedule, and he's running around trying to make order in this incredible sea of chaos, it was fantastic, it was really fantastic. That was the first time that we really met Bill.

Have you ever gotten straightened out financially?

We *just* got straightened out financially.

What makes you think it's going to last?

Nothing. It won't. It can't last, you know, it's just that now at least we can decide to fuck up, we're at least free to decide to fuck up rather than bumping into it all the time.

The last time we talked about what you might do as a business by starting a small record company. Is that any more real now?

It's as real as it was then, that is to say, it still depends on whether or not . . . what it depends on is us getting out of our present contract, or it expiring. Then we're in a position where we can start to think about that. We've been planning to do it seriously and really, but it's still a question of how best to. . . . it's still an idea. See, Grunt Records is still RCA. There's no question about it. It's not *truly* independent. And our fantasy is to be *completely* independent if we can do it.

At this point it's open-ended. Obviously we want to be able to employ the people who are our friends. Who are talented and all that, and who are interested in what we're trying to do. That whole "Deadheads Unite" message was on that level. That's our story, like the basic groundwork, what we were gonna use.

Well, it's not a dislike for Warner Brothers, but an antipathy towards the current form of record company systems.

Right. I don't think that they're that bad; I just think that they're incompetent. That's probably the worst thing about them. I don't object to the idea of record companies at all, in fact, record companies are *good*.

But we're already getting reports—this is the kind of thing that really fries me—we're getting reports that our new album has a slight skip on every record. Goddamn, it makes me want to scream. We go to every length we can to insure quality all along the line, on our end of it. We even suggest a place to Warner Brothers where they can have 'em pressed, where they can receive the attention that we want to give it.

I'm gonna do it with my own record, my solo record. Insist that they be pressed at a place that uses quality vinyl and allows the proper drying time and all the rest of that. Think of the billions of records that a big pressing plant has to rush through. Then when you hear that your record has a side that nobody can play, especially a double record, which is expensive, it just burns me. I feel that we have a responsibility to the people who put out their money for our record, because they are the people who are allowing us to continue what we're doing.

Going totally outside the record companies is easily the heaviest new change of all.

I don't think it will be too difficult; I think it's a question of doing it right. I don't want to be put in a position of having to compete with them. I just want to be something else entirely. The fact that we put out records doesn't necessarily mean that we're just in the record business, or a threat to them. We wouldn't put out any records but our own. If they want to make it a toe to toe standoff, that will just illustrate what *they're* up to. All we're trying to do is survive and be independent. Other guys have tried it before, but I don't think they've had the opportunity to really do it right.

Well, they've never tried to avoid the basic distribution system, which is the basis of the thing.

That's what I want to avoid.

You got to have somebody really good on mailing labels and on the books.

We have a great guy on the books. Dave Parker is fantastic on books, he's really brilliant. He's brilliant on all the organizational levels.

The way we're looking to approach it initially is pretty modestly. The cost of production for the first two or 300,000 records would *more* than set us up. But we don't have to be a crashing huge success anyway. Not at all. The idea would be to keep it marginal so we didn't have to escalate our trip. I'm interested to see how it's going to turn out.

We're really serious about it too. We're gonna do everything we can to try to make it happen. It would be like a good affirmative little gesture. It wouldn't be any big beans or any shit like that, but, what the fuck? All it is is an illustration of the kind of thing that we've been trying to do all along: "Look man, here we are, we're on the edge, and we can make it. So can you, give it a try."

We're finding out the kind of stuff we need to know, talking to people and stuff like that, and it seems to be going pretty good. My main concern is being able to put out a fucking record that you can play a million times with a minimum of wear; and it's available, that kind of vinyl is around and you can get it. It's just doing a fair thing.

We've about got it covered people-wise. That's our main resource. That's why we're able to move through $400,000 a quarter, or whatever it is, but nobody gets rich, just everybody keeps going. Because that's our one energy, it's people. Same as your scene, I'm sure it must be like that.

Except we're more commercially oriented . . . I want it like that . . .

Well, we wouldn't object to it either, but we don't want to sacrifice that other thing.

Sometimes I become real impatient. . . .

Right, because somebody starts feeling bad. We have high water marks and low water marks and guys that'll . . . we have certain people in our organization that will freak out the minute it's not what it's supposed to be. It's like defined by all the people. That defines our movement, our rate of speed.

But when you get big, it gets much more difficult . . .

No shit. I think that there's an optimum number of people with whom you can communicate successfully and keep everything going. I'm sure it doesn't really go much past fifty.

We're at about the fifty level right now. Heading toward sixty.

Are you diversifying as you're going?

We haven't yet. With the books, it still all takes place within the office. The whole office is involved in the books.

I think that's probably good, 'cause that represents that there's the functional thing happening. That organic thing where it's not really so much ... I myself, in a situation where I'm having to do something, don't respond very well, even if it's something I want to do. But when there's stuff to do and the availability of being able to choose a different trip, I dig that, that kind of space seems very necessary ...

How many people do you have connected with the Dead now? How many people do you support?

Oh, I really don't know in exact numbers. I would say that there's probably about 40 pretty much solid, definitely, absolutely you gotta count on them to be there every morning. The band; then there's the whole office staff. The office staff is Dale and Annette, and Bonnie and David, and Ellen and Rock, and John MacIntyre. At least seven of them. And then there's like offshoots, like part-time people who do stuff.

That's a lot of people to support.

Yeah, but it's hard to do what we do, and it's worth it. See, our whole trip is to get farther along on the Grateful Dead trip, or whatever it is. And all the people that're involved are like in some way, in some sense or another, committed to that idea. And the thing that we're doing is something more than just *succeeding*, hopefully.

What is the 'California Book of the Dead'?

The *California Book of the Dead* is an idea in somebody's head. Something that's completely hypothetical. It has to do with how successful an experiment is. And the experiment is can you take a bunch of pieces and put them together and make 'em into something. That's what it's gonna hinge on. That's the whole thing. The idea of there being a Grateful Dead just like there being a rock scene is a complete fiction. It's like a little piece of reality which we've been able to gouge out. You've done it, you know how it is. It's

exactly the same for us. It's like we're existing on the border of this
other scene. We're just over the line and we're able to use its energy.
We just run it around real fast.

Transforming . . .

Right. Exactly. We're dealing with traditional problems of
structure, organization, people working together, human dynamics,
all that stuff. It's all stuff that people are concerned with on all levels
all the time.

The question is can we do it and stay high? Can we make it so our
organization is composed of people who are like pretty high, who are
not being controlled by their gig, but who are actively interested in
what they're doing? And the whole thing is making sense on a lotta
levels. That's one of the aspects of what it is we're trying to do. We
won't know whether it's successful until we're dead. Until we have
some historical place to stand at and look back on it. Get some perspective or something. But that's what we're trying to do.

How do you survive in New York, when you go on tour?

For me, it's lock yourself in the hotel room more or less, turn on
the TV, stay real high, and hang out with your friends. That's one of
the things about traveling with a band, like the Grateful Dead scene,
a big family, and all that. You have an insular situation that rein-
forces what you believe to be true, although in New York it looks as
though it maybe isn't.

I like to remain open to some extent, just in case there's anything to see. I don't like to turn people off, yet there are people calling up and they want to talk to me and stuff like that. It's only
because of being a rock and roll star and all that which makes it very
weird for me there. I think it would be groovy to go there and be
anonymous, walk around and see what the street scene is like, but
I've never been really able to do that.

*What good times have you seen in New York—that you left yourself
open for?*

Well, it's mostly people. There are like good people in New York
that are kind of bravely in the middle of it there fighting the good

battle. And, it's like year after year you go there you see these same few people that are hassling it out in New York and you see New York just staying the same and God, it's weird.

What'd you find when you went to England?

I enjoyed going to England. I liked the English people, they seemed to enjoy us, but we didn't play for shit. We only got to play once, at a thing called The Hollywood Festivals while we were there. So it was a drag, but I'd like to go and really spend some time playing and get to know some people. But it was really nice.

What was France like?

It was beautiful. We went there to do a big festival, a free festival that they were gonna have. Bill Hamm came over from France— these people had brought him over to get him to talk to us, to get us to go there on the following weekend. So we thought, wow—a week's notice—let's go to France for the weekend. And play this free festival. They were ready to take us over there and have us stay and everything, for nothing. So we would be going over and not charging anybody. We went over but the festival was rained out, it flooded.

We stayed at this little chateau which is owned by a French film-score composer who has a 16-track recording studio built into the chateau, and this is a chateau that Chopin once lived in, *really* old, just delightful, out in the country, near the town of Auvers, which is where Vincent Van Gogh is buried. The famous "Church of Auvers" painting, that's the town.

We were there with nothing to do: France, a 16-track recording studio upstairs, all our gear, ready to play, and nothing to do. So . . . we decided to play at the chateau itself, out in the back, in the grass, with a swimming pool, just play off into the hills. We didn't even play to hippies, we played to a handful of townspeople in Auvers. And the guy who owns the chateau, who's like a courtly gentleman, perfect host, beautiful French meals every day, and we played and the people came—the chief of police, the fire department, just everybody. It was an event, and everybody just had a hell of a time. Got drunk and fell in the pool. It was great. They have the tape. We made a lot of friends over there.

Do you find traveling on the road exhausting?

Yeah, yeah. The regular tour is exhausting, especially for us because we do a long show. We try and pace it so that we don't play every night but it hardly ever works out that way. The alternatives are that you can either go out on the road and play as often as you possibly can and get it over with as quickly as possible and come back—that's like one school of thought that you can space it out and pace yourself while you're out on the road, but it means that you'll have to live out there for awhile. We've tried a lot of different ways. This last tour [Spring 1971] was around the East Coast and it was shorter distances, 300–400 miles and that sort of thing, and we did a lot of traveling by bus, and that was really fun, we were just able to hang together all the time, we didn't have to go through a lot of airports and that. And we got to see some of the countryside. It was a little more like traveling and less like matter transmission.

But you play all night, that's what . . .

That's what makes it hard, that's what makes it really difficult. What we're doing now is working generally two or three nights in a town, in one spot, so that we have the advantage of being able to get into the room that we're playing so that it starts to sound good by about the second night and so that we don't have that oversold house and an uptight crowd that can't get in.

But really, it's getting trickier and trickier to do it, it's getting harder and harder. In Boston we played for two nights and even so there were still about three or four thousand people outside each night that weren't able to get in because the place was sold out and the police maced them and did all that, it was . . . I mean you wonder, you begin to wonder why you're doing it if what you're doing is leading people into a trap.

Right now we're in the process of stopping all our agency tours, stopping all our activities, and just . . . we're finally out of debt, and we're finally out of the past and after all this time, three or four years, we're at a place now where we can decide what to do instead of just working for something we already did. One of the things we decided was that we didn't want to do that kind of tour; want to try to pick our gigs carefully, if possible, put them on ourselves and generally determine what we're going to do rather than have that six months in advance plan—in December we're going to be going to Pittsburgh and Cincinnati and all those places—to be able to let stuff happen.

Did being busted in New Orleans make you more careful on the road?

Uhm, well, as more careful, as much more careful as it is possible for us to be, which is not very careful, . . . hahahaha . . . actually man, we're a bust and I think any rock and roll band is. They can walk in on you any time and get you and you're guilty and everything, you just have to . . . it's the lawyer trip, you know; it's one of the hazards of the job, the way I see it; it's like dogs and mailmen.

How many people go on the road?

This next time there's gonna be twenty-two going out; there's us and the New Riders, and our combined equipment guys, who are Jackson, Ramrod, our guys; and Sparky, who's one of the P.A. guys, and then there's this guy Gary, who's one of the New Riders' guys, and John Hagen, who's also one of the New Riders' guys. So there's those five guys, then there's Matthews, going out to mix, and then there's both bands so that's twenty-two. Then there's Rock, he's going along, and Hunter's going along to do the radio stuff; it's great to have Hunter on the road, he's got like the *perfect* viewpoint, to be able to keep you from getting *too* crazy out there. The *more* of us there are, the cooler we stay, you know what I mean? If we go out there in a small group we feel intimidated and get weird fast. If we go out there with a lot of us, it's much cooler. Going through airports and shit like that is much easier when there's twenty people straggling through. Fuck, they don't even want to mess with you. They don't want to know who you are or *nothing*. *(laughs)* Get 'em outa here! Get 'em outa here! At any rate, *that's* the show.

If anybody could see the way it really is, they would have to get there at 10 o'clock in the morning when the trucks pull in, and watch the equipment guys get the stuff off the truck with all the cussing and hollering and dropping shit and getting pissed off and moaning and hassling with the local hall guys, and doing all that stuff. And then us going in there in the afternoon to do the sound check. It's a total intense experience when you're on the road. There's nothing else happening. It's just straight ahead. It's an *incredible* scene, the whole thing. It's a lot like the circus, in a way, in terms of all that gear, and all that energy going on.

It's preparing the "elements" as Owsley might say, or preparing the ingredients for some alchemical trip. Everybody kind of views it that way, or approaches it that way. The whole Alembic [studio] trip is that way. In fact, Alembic is the word for the vessel that they seal stuff in when an alchemical action is taking place.

When you're on tour, you play with the New Riders and then do a set with the Dead?

Playing the pedal steel is not much physical exertion: you just sit down, and it's all very close work. It's more like working out with a sewing machine than it is standing up and playing ball, which is the way playing guitar is. It's not such a totally physical trip. It's little motions. So it's easy for me to sit down and play the pedal steel, I can play it for eight hours in a row without hardly noticing it. But the New Riders are trying to find another steel player, so they can tour more independently. Cause they're pretty much on their own, they're cooking along real nice. They sound *good* lately, too. It's been fun playing with them. The whole thing is starting to really get together in a neat way. It's really satisfying.

What happened at Altamont? Did you see what was coming?

No. God, no. It was completely unexpected. And that was the hard part—that was the hard lesson there—that you can have good people and good energy and work on a project and really want it to happen right and still have it all weird. It's the thing of knowing less than you should have. Youthful folly.

But the things you didn't know about had nothing to do with music, they had to do with logistics and they had to do with things commercial and economic . . .

Yeah, but it was the music that generated it. I think that the music knew, it was known in the music. I realized when the Rolling Stones were playing at the crowd and the fighting was going on and the Rolling Stones were playing "Sympathy for the Devil," then I knew that I should have known. You know, you can't put that out without it turning up on you somewhere.

I remember seeing that scene down at the Heliport, waiting to fly over to Altamont.

Going over to the big rock festival.

MOUNTAIN GIRL: And that girl was trying to get on the helicopter, oh, man, was she weird.

And there were the Stones, walking around, and the Dead.

Totally weird.

I saw you talk to Mick for a second or two.

MOUNTAIN GIRL: What did he ask? "What time is the helicopter coming?" he said. And his little entourage caught up with him and forced him away so he had to keep walking real fast to keep ahead of them.

When you look back on it, do you see anything in those moments leading up to it?

No, not really. I was completely unsuspecting. There was one thing beforehand that we all should have spotted. [Emmett] Grogan wrote up on the blackboard up at the Grateful Dead office, just as the site had been changed from whatever the first one was, he wrote a little slogan up on the blackboard which said something like "Charlie Manson Memorial Hippie Love Death Cult Festival." Something along those lines, something really funny, but ominous. And there had been the street, certain people—certain elements of the street had been saying . . . it was a very weird time on the street in San Francisco at that time if you recall. There was a lot of divisive hassling among all the various revolutionary scenes; the Red Guard was on one trip and Chicanos on some other trip and people were carrying guns and stuff, there was a lot of that kind of talk.

Originally the idea was that the Stones' thing was going to be a chance for all these various community elements to participate in a sort of a party for the Rolling Stones. That was the orignal concept, but then we couldn't have it in Golden Gate Park so that really was the end of the plan as it was supposed to have happened. That eliminated the possibility for any community scene in San Francisco because of the transportation problem—how many Chicanos, Chinese or blacks or anything like that are going to be able to get a bus out to wherever the fuck? That was really the end of the original plan. And then we began operating on just sheer kinetic energy . . . Rolling Stones was in the air, Rolling Stones, Rolling Stones, and thus it was just being swept along; but everybody was feeling—and it was all good people—everybody was feeling very good about it. Chet Helms was there doing stuff, and Emmett and Chip Monk and all these solid, together, hard-working people, but somehow the sense of it escaped everybody.

Whose idea was it to have the Stones to do the thing in the first place?

Rock and Sam originally conceived the idea although it was, again, it was the music, it was an idea that was in the air. It was like San Francisco had free stuff, the Rolling Stones hadn't been touring, they were suddenly going to be in the United States, somebody Rock used to know, Sam, and it just seemed as though it was an obvious step—and could have been under the right circumstances, I'm convinced—but it wasn't meant to be that.

Why do you think so?

I've thought about it a lot. A friend of mine, Steve Gaskin, capsulized it better than I ever could about "Why did it happen?" Just period, "Why did it happen?" He said, and this has been quoted somewhere else, "Altamont was the little bit of sadism in your sex life, that the Rolling Stones put out in their music, coming back. It was the karma of putting that out for all those years, it was that little bit of red and black." Just there. The Hell's Angels, it's that same image.

Do you accept the necessity of having that in life, that little bit of evil?

Well, it's there, whether you accept it or not. It just has to do with how you conceive your own destiny or your own journeys through life. I just think that it's there, I'm not into judging it really, it's not my game particularly—but I do know it's there.

Altamont was to be a thing to get the political people together and the minority groups and like that. How come that's never been able to work?

Because there isn't anybody out trying to make it work; there isn't anybody out who is in a central enough position to be able to command the respect of all those different scenes. There isn't that individual person. There used to be guys that were out doing stuff like that but most of 'em aren't out doin' it anymore, ah, for one reason or another. Each of those scenes has gotten to be more . . . and also, the texture is . . . the way most of those scenes are now, they're not so much into really *including* everybody as they are into providing a firm identity for themselves and the next stop after you have your firm identity is to be able to relate to everybody else who is on the same trip you are. I *think* that's what's going on, anyway.

I got a letter from Emmett, after Altamont, talking about what a ripoff everything was. The letter was one of the meanest, uptight, nastiest . . .

Are you sure it was really from Emmett Grogan? 'Cause it might've been a bullshitter. There're a lot of people who have used his name . . . Have you by any chance ever run into any of the articles Al Aronowitz did on Altamont? One of them contained this thing which Emmett Grogan said about Altamont which in my opinion summed it up more beautifully than anything else written. Emmett says, "I'm the guy who did it, blame me." And then he lays down all the reasons, all the fuck-ups, he tells just what happened. It's beautifully concise, it's lovely.

He wasn't around during the Wild West Festival, but those people that he spawned, that activity, people like Ronnie Davis . . .

People who misunderstood, misunderstood a lot of shit. All it takes is for that *doubt* to be there. It's the thing where *trust* falls through. All of a sudden there's no trust happening, so fuck, what's going on here? Back in the early days of our scene, and the Prankster scene, there was that expression "Never trust a Prankster," never trust *anybody*. There was a living pantomime of that thing trust, "I don't trust you, you're going to rip us off." The whole thing all of a sudden becomes a house of cards which immediately collapses. As

soon as a *feeling* turns into an intellectualization and conceptualiza-
tion then it's "I have something which you can take, therefore you
will take it." All those things are beside the point.

If Wild West had happened, hadn't been brought down by taking those
people seriously, then Altamont would've never happened the way it did.

Probably not, or at least we would've had an early chance of pre-
venting it. But we blew it. Altamont was interesting on another
level, because it involved a lot of the same people who were involved
in the Wild West show. The *working* on Altamont was a very good
trip for the people who were involved in it, but the reality of the
event was a horror.

These people used Altamont as an attack point on rock and roll, to
prove by it that rock and roll was no good.

That discussion is all gone now. I think that it's run its course
and it's all over. There's too much other shit that's happening that's
too important. We've seen a change of consciousness in the last
year-and-a-half traveling around the East Coast and places like that.
People are really thinking differently. At last. I think that the whole
negative thing has done what it's gonna do, it's killed a lot of people
and left a lot of them; it always does. All we can hope is that the next
cycle will be faster. We'll be able to say, "Ah, here it is. Zip! Here's
your hat, what's your hurry?" that kind of thing. Get it out, quick.
Run it through, run it through *fast.*

What happened to Janis?

I think it was a mistake; I think it was an accident, like driving
your car off the road. I don't think that there was any *why* to it,
really. She probably hadn't had smack for awhile or something like
that. She probably had a few drinks or something after a gig, coming
back to the hotel, take a hit and on out, go to sleep for the night, and
it was probably more than she expected and she just died. That's
how easy it can happen, it can happen to anybody if you don't know
what you're getting, and that's the way it is when you're having to
deal with things that are illegal.

I think that it's the law that killed Janis, if anything killed her, because she couldn't go and get exactly the right hit for herself of exactly the proper purity in a drug store and do herself up; she wouldn't be dead now. That's the thing that I think did it. In my opinion, Janis handled it pretty good, and she got a lot of weirdness, but she was more on top of it than a lot of people I've seen. I don't think that fame killed her, I don't think that being a celebrity killed her. She just accidentally, like cutting yourself with a razor or something, just accidentally died.

And Jim Morrison?

It's just everybody dies. He was a musician, and that's the only reason people are talking about him dying. If Jim Morrison had been anybody else, nobody would be talking about Jim Morrison dying. And that's the same with every other musician. Statistically people die and that's all. Every profession—people die in it.

What music do you listen to now?

I listen to all kinds of stuff, just all kinds of stuff.

Do you listen to the Band's records?

Some of them I do. At first I just wanta say, "Wow, they're getting into this repetitive bag," each time I hear the record for the first time. Then after a few weeks it starts creeping into the back of my mind and I start thinking, "Wow, what was that tune?" And I go and find the record and put it on. It's like scratching an itch. Some of them I really dig, others I probably will, and then other ones I think are halfway efforts; it's just like anybody. I dig their music more or less consistently, so I don't really know whether the record's good or not.

Which tunes on the new one do you like?

I love "Life is a Carnival"—that's beautiful. Shit, that's great. All the stuff in there, all those great parts. The Dylan song is great, too. I love that song. I'll probably sing that with the barroom band. I like to do those kinda tunes. They're good songs, and good songs are fun to sing.

You like Robbie Robertson?

Yeah, yeah, I went and visited with him one day, when we were on the East Coast. And I really dug being able to sit down and talk to him. It was just like that kinda stuff you do where you've never met anybody before, but you know what they do, and you respect them. We were both kinda there cause we'd been on that tour—we'd met before, actually—on that tour with Janis, that Canada thing. We got off on their music, of course, and they dug our music, 'cause really, they're kinda similar. We just have slightly different viewpoints of an almost similar trip.

When I got together with him, we were talking on pretty groovy grounds, in terms of mutual respect and understanding. It was good. We talked about guitars, and pianos, and music . . . and I went over and dug his studio. Just a friendly scene. It's one of those things that sometime in the future, I'd love to be able to spend some time and actually work with those guys, actually play music together with them, under some circumstances or another.

How would you describe his guitar playing?

He's one of those guys who descended from Roy Buchanan and those Fifties Fender-pickers. I can hear where he's picked up a lotta his stuff. His approach to it is more or less orchestral. The kinda stuff he plays and the music, is like punctuation, and structural. He's an extremely subtle and refined guitar player, that's the way I think of him. I really admire him.

How would you describe your own guitar playing?

I don't know. I would describe my own guitar playing as descended from barroom rock and roll, country guitar. Just 'cause that's where all my stuff comes from. It's like that blues instrumental stuff that was happening in the late Fifties and early Sixties, like Freddie King.

But your guitar playing also has to do with the harmonic and the structural role . . .

Right, and that has to do with the way I see myself in relation to the band that I'm playing in. It must be like much the same way

Robbie Robertson sees himself, in the sense that you write songs and you tend to think a certain way about how the music is supposed to work, what kind of background you're lining up. It depends on whether you're approaching it on the level of a texture or whatever. I tend to think of it in terms of punctuation and stuff. Same thing.

When I get ready to go on the road, I make up cassettes of all my favorite music. Country and Western stuff. Just whatever. Ali Akbar Khan. Crosby, Stills and Nash.

Any English groups?

Beatles.

They're not an English group....

I don't really like the English bands too much. A few of the older ones, yeah. Traffic is good, Stevie Winwood is great. Some of them I enjoy listening to, but I don't enjoy them in the sense of the soul. There's something that I listen to music for which ... Neil Young has it, but Elton John doesn't, for me. It's well-executed and everything, it's good music, but it just has to do with how it makes me *feel*. I love American music. I love Indian music, too. I even love English music. Actually, there's a lotta English stuff which I like a lot, but I'm just tending to be general. You know what I think of as being the English sound, the real sound, is like Pentangle. Pentangle, to my ears, is the English sound, because it's very much that sort of madrigal, Elizabethan thing, very crisp. Economical. But it's not in any of the trends. It's more *basic*.

Other rock and roll bands?

I like Crosby, Stills and Nash and all the various elements that they do, their solo trips. I like Neil Young's stuff a lot, it's real great. I like his sensibilities. The Band, I love the band, I really like the way they play and their idea of what music is, is really neat to me.

Crosby, Stills, Nash and Young are into a political bag, which I don't like that much. But their singing's so good, their whole thing is. They're entertainers. Crosby's such an incredible ham, a Show-Biz guy, but it's alright. Their singing is strong. Their whole musical scene is *so together*. It comes across really well. They're gonna be together again. They're gonna do a tour. I talked to Crosby today. It seems like they're pretty sure of it next year. They're Hollywood, sometimes even Neil. They all are, even Steven. Steven is an extreme dude. He's a guy who goes too far, *all* the time. Takes a lot of drugs, stretches his mind out a lot, he's into some kind of complex, competition scene with his father. Something which you and I couldn't know about, really. He's too far ahead. But he's a good dude, he's got a good head. I respect him and dig him. He's not any kind of asshole or anything, even when it seems like he *might* be. They're all real good guys. Graham Nash is a fine guy. Crosby's a good old happy California hippie, L.A. version.

When did you decide to stop doing the blues stuff, the harder rock and roll thing, and go into the stressed harmonies?

That was really the result of hanging out with Crosby and those guys just because they could sit down in any situation and pick up an acoustic guitar and it's instant music, these beautiful vocal harmonies.

I think that nothing really communicates like the human voice. It is really the ultimate instrument. I used to think of myself as a guitar player but hearing singing, and seeing it up close, has kinda made me want to sing a lot; it just makes me want to do it, I don't really know what it is . . . and it's real satisfying to sing. I've always gotten off on a good singer, and that's what I'm basin' it on.

Did the group called Planet Earth ever turn out anything?

No. Everybody is off on their own trips still. It'll probably happen one of these times, it's a question of timing. Everything that I've ever done on anybody else's record has been a matter of timing, we're both in the same town.

That's part of where our music wants to go, but it's record companies and the music business structure that's making it that difficult. It should be possible for everybody to do everything, especially in music, where music can only get better when people get together in different combinations. But record companies wanta be exclusive. They're getting looser and looser and hopefully the thing could get loose enough where everybody could do whatever they want. That would be ideal.

What guitarists have you learned the most from?

I think Freddie King is the guy that I learned the most volume of stuff from. When I started playing electric guitar the second time, with the Warlocks, it was a Freddie King album that I got almost all my ideas off of, his phrasing really. That first one, *Here's Freddie King*, later it came out as *Freddie King Plays Surfin' Music* or something like that, it has "San-Ho-Zay" on it and "Sensation" and all those instrumentals.

When did you begin playing pedal steel?

Pedal steel was an instrument that was on my mind since back in the days when I was a banjo player. I didn't think that I wanted to get that serious about it because I knew it was extremely difficult and that I'd have to spend a lot of time to actually get into it. It's so difficult, man, and my playing is so mediocre I can't begin to tell you how embarrassed I am about my playing on the damn thing, really it's lamentable. Oh, I get off on it's really fun, but that doesn't mean that I can do it well; it's kinda like standing up on a pair of skates, it makes you happy.

What new things have you heard, other groups, other sounds?

I'll tell you what I've heard lately that I really like a lot, these two kids in Stinson Beach, the Rowan Brothers, Chris and Loren Rowan. I love their music. Me and Kreutzman and Phil have been doing some sessions with them because Dave Grissman, who's one of their managers, is an old friend of ours from bluegrass days (he's the guy that plays mandolin on *American Beauty*, there's some nice mandolin on "Friend of the Devil" and that, a real good musician). And these two kids: one them's nineteen, and the other's twenty-two—from New England—just write some really really pretty music and soulful songs, really high. It's fantastic, their music is just sparkly, brand-new, shiny. That's like the latest turn-on for me. They're super, and they're right at that point of just starting out and nobody knows about them. I hate to see them go into the music business; I wish somebody could just say, "Here, man, here's $5000 so you can live for another six months without having to sell out." The music is too good for it. They could be, given the proper kind of exposure and stuff like that, they could be like the Beatles. They're that good, their music is that good.

REICH: *I have a question right off one of the evening talk shows and that is, "Dr. Garcia, how do you stay so high?"*

I smoke a lot of dope.

REICH: *Do you think that's . . .*

Would you like some?

REICH: *Do you think that that's it?*

Well, in reality I don't really stay that high, although I get high a lot, smoke a lot of pot, is what I'm trying to say. That's what it comes down to, but that doesn't necessarily mean that I'm high. A certain amount of seeming to be high has to do with my being more-or-less well-rehearsed in the role of Jerry Garcia, 'cause it's kinda laid on me. In reality I'm like lots more worthless than any of that would make it appear.

REICH: *Among the different things the kids say about you, one is "Mr. Good Vibes."*

Yeah, but that always is part-true bullshit, because my old lady can tell you about how often I'm on a bummer. Really, I'm just like everybody else and it's just that I really love those times when I'm high, so my trip has always been to make them count as much as possible.

REICH: *What I'm trying to get at is that you believe in being high and many other people not only don't believe in it but think it's dangerous and hateful.*

Well, you know, I . . . everybody's . . . one man's poison is another man's dope.

REICH: *For instance, I believe in being high but not as much as you believe in it. In other words I have more reservations about it than you do— or less experience with it, how about that?*

That's it right there. I don't have that many illusions about it because I was never around in that world where you had to read about it. For me, it came in the form of dope. You got a joint, you didn't get a lecture; and you got a cap, you didn't get a treatise or any of that shit. You just got high, you took the thing and found out what happened to you; that's the only evidence there is. Being programmed by dope talk or any of that stuff is like somebody trying to tell you what it's like to fuck if you've never fucked anybody.

You can't know it that way, that's all, and also it'll put weird ideas in your head, misinformation and shit. Misinformation is the root of all . . . uh . . . er . . . ah . . . ignorance—nah, that's not it—ineffectuality . . . nah, fuck it, well, nice try, maybe next time.

Really, I don't think that. I think that the whole discussion about drugs, whether to take them or not, is like, . . . well, I don't think that there's a *side* on that. I know a lot of people who I respect superhighly that don't take anything, and of course, I know people that get really high and I respect them as highly too; and I know far-out junkies. There are people doing everything, and I just don't think that *anything's* it.

REICH: *How do you manage to be so optimistic?*

Music is a thing that has optimism built into it. Optimism is another way of saying "space." Music has infinite space. You can go as far into music as you can fill millions of lifetimes. Music is an infinite cylinder, it's open-ended, it's space. The *form* of music has infinite space as a part of it and that, in itself, means that its momentum is essentially in that open place.

REICH: *You said you would only play on optimistic days or I said I would only write on optimistic days.*

That might be optimum, but my experience has been that a lot of times we've played sets that we didn't like or that I didn't like, or I didn't like what I was doing, but it got on and it sounded good on tape and the audience got on. There's lots of degrees. I don't like to try to paint everything in those real, specific cartoony figures because there's degrees all over the place. For example, if I'm super, super-depressed, I sometimes play the highest music I play.

REICH: *How do you do it?*

Because music can contain all of it. It can contain your bummers, it can contain your depressions, it can contain the black despair, man, it can contain the whole spectrum. The blues is a perfect example. The blues is that very effect, operating in a very sublime way. You hardly ever hear anybody say they're depressed because they've heard a lot of music. That's a pretty good example, right there. Even the worst music—the poorest, baddest, most ill-thought-of music on earth—doesn't hurt anybody.

REICH: *I know some people that are angry at Lennon's album with the screaming and crying, they call it self-pity. Does that bother you?*

No. I love the album myself.

REICH: *I love it too. It's very different from the kind of music the Dead plays.*

That's true, but we haven't been exposed to the really extreme pressure that John Lennon has.

REICH: *I read a book on rock and roll recently that said the real medium of rock and roll is records and that concerts are only repeats of records. I guess the Grateful Dead represents the opposite of that idea.*

Right. Our records are definitely not it or ever have been. The things we do depend so much upon the situation we're in and upon a sort of a magic thing. We aren't in such total control of our scene that we can say, "Tonight's the night, it's going to be magic tonight." We can only say we're going to try it tonight. And whether it's magic or not is something we can't predict and nobody else can predict; and even when it's over and done with, it's one of those things where nobody's really sure. It's subtle and it's elusive but it's real.

REICH: *And the magic comes not just from you but from the whole thing.*

The whole thing. The unfortunate thing about the concert situation for us is the stage; and the audience has either a dance floor where they all sit down or seats where they all stand up. It's too inflexible to allow something new to emerge. It's a box that we've been operating in; and we've been operating in it as a survival mechanism and yet hoping to get off when we can. But basically it's not set up to let us get off and it's not set up for the audience to get off either. The reason is that anarchy and chaos are things that scare everybody, or scare a lot of the people—except for the people that get into it.

REICH: *Why doesn't it scare you?*

Because I've had enough experience with it to where I like it. It's where new stuff happens. I have never understood exactly why people get scared but they do get scared for reasons, like to protect oneself, to protect one's own personal vision of oneself. They're all paranoid reasons. That's the thing you stimulate if you fight it. It's like any high energy experience; if you fight it, it hurts; if you go with it, it's like surfing, it's like catching a big wave.

REICH: *Do you think they don't believe in magic?*

I think that our audience definitely does. Or, rather than dwell on the idea of magic, they know that there's a certain phenomenon that *can* happen and if they come to see us enough, they've observed it, they've seen it, they've been part of it. And that's the pay off. That's the reason to keep on doing it. We know that it can happen and the problem has been in trying to figure out how can we make that happen and at the same time keep our whole scene together on a survival level. And that's essentially what we're doing.

REICH: *Who's the audience now? Who are the magic people?*

The magic people are out living productive lives, working on things, doing things—post-revolutionary activities, and women are out raising the kids. I think we have a whole range now for an audience and the reason we have the range is because of the popularity of our most recent records. We have grandmothers! and grandfathers! All kinds of people that come and get off and are happy to have been there.

REICH: *But they all believe in magic, wouldn't you say?*

That's a generalization I hate to make. It's too spotty. Some scenes we've played at that have been expressly for people to get high in; for example, the spiritual trips that haven't been advertised as rock and roll concerts bring the kind of people who know what it is to get high and are thus able to participate in that way and really get high. The times we've played at spiritual things have been our most hits, when people are there to get high. I think basically the Grateful Dead is not for cranking out rock and roll, it's not for going out and doing concerts or any of that stuff, I think it's to get high.

I can envisage a new world in which society has a way for there to be music whose function it is to get you high. Do you know what I mean? That's the sort of thing that we're hammering at, but now it's become difficult for us. The Grateful Dead has become cumbersome because now when we play at a place we can expect five or 10,000 people. They're of all ranges, and a lot of times people who just don't know how to get it on way outnumber the people who do know how to get it on. There's all kinds of other stuff entering in there.

REICH: *Why is it important to get high? Why is it important to stay high? What good does it do anybody—the world, the community or people themselves?*

To get really high is to forget yourself. And to forget yourself is to see everything else. And to see everything else is to become an understanding molecule in evolution, a conscious tool of the universe. And I think every human being should be a conscious tool of the universe. That's why I think it's important to get high.

REICH: *Getting zonked out or unconscious is a whole different thing.*

I'm not talking about unconscious or zonked out, I'm talking about being fully conscious. Also I'm not talking about the Grateful Dead as being an end in itself. I don't think of that highness as being an end in itself. I think of the Grateful Dead as being a crossroads or a pointer sign and what we're pointing to is that there's a lot of universe available, that there's a whole lot of experience available over here. We're kinda like a signpost, and we're *also* pointing to danger, to difficulty, we're pointing to bummers. We're pointing to whatever there is, when we're on—when it's really happening.

You're a signpost to new space?

Yes. That's the place where we should be—that's the function we should be filling in society. And in our own little society, that's the function we do fill. But in the popular world—the media world and so forth—we're just a rock and roll band.

We play rock and roll music and it's part of our form—our vehicle so to speak—but it's not who we are totally. Like Moondog in New York City who walks around, he's a signpost to otherness. He's a signpost to something that isn't concrete. It's that same thing.

Where did you get the idea about pointing to some new place?

We never formulated it, it just was what was happening. We were doing the Acid Test, which was our first exposure to formlessness. Formlessness and chaos lead to new forms. And new order. Closer to, probably, what the real order is. When you break down the old orders and the old forms and leave them broken and shattered, you suddenly find yourself a new space with new form and new order which are more like the way it is. More like the flow.

And we just *found* ourselves in that place. We never decided on it, we never thought it out. None of it. This is a thing that we've observed in the scientific method. We've watched what happens.

What we're really dedicated to is not so much *telling* people, but to *doing* that thing and getting high. That's the thing; that's the payoff and that's the whole reason for doing it, right there.

REICH: *Does the new culture scene seem to be falling to pieces?*

It does *seem* to be doing that, but it always seems to be doing that. It depends on what level you're looking at it. If you're looking at it on the level of what you *hear* about it, yeah, it's going to pieces. If you look at it on the level of the guys you know and what they're doin', I think that things are going pretty good. Everybody I know is doing stuff and nobody I know is on a particularly declining trip.

REICH: *That's what I see; individual people are doing fine. Then why are we being told that it's all dying and falling apart?*

I think that the people that are interested in it not dying and falling apart are probably a lot closer than we think they are. I think that's probably it. There's *always* somebody that has to say that it's *not* happening; and the people who are into saying that it's not happening are the people that aren't into stuff.

Hey, Jann, have you ever had anybody say anything to you about what you print, man? Anybody, like anybody just from the world?

Yes, indeed.

Far out. It must be weird.

What do you think of it?

I think that anytime you do something that's even remotely involved with the public that there's going to be stuff comin' at ya. If you stick your head up a little, there's stuff comin' at ya. You gotta be careful not to listen to it; you gotta be careful to follow *your* vision, 'cause it's easy for somebody to say something to you and then for you to believe that that's the absolute truth and then start fighting with yourself, twisting everything around some new little reality, something somebody tells you that you're doing wrong. It's that little bit of poison in communication that everybody has to look out for, that sense of doing something wrong.

I really think that everything that's been going on around here for a long time is super-positive and everybody should be just getting really high on it and doing it real hard. That's the way I feel about it.

Here's the thing that has to happen: as you spot an inequity as you're going along, you gotta be able to do something about it right then if you can. You gotta try to deal with stuff as real as you can and simply as you can, and as righteously as you think you should. I find that you can do it, and it's not particularly tricky or anything like that; it's just a matter of how much you think you *oughta* be doin'. That's what it comes down to, how much *you* think you oughta be doin'.

REICH: *A lot, don't you think?*

Yeah, but I don't think you should be getting crazy about it. Myself, I do a lot of stuff but a lot of times I don't think I should be; a lot of times I think that I'm just working for the sake of being working; but the thing that happens—a real neat thing that happens—is that if you're working along on energy that's weird, coming from a weird place, you go a certain amount of way but you don't accomplish anything and that's the way you know that you're doing something wrong, just by that sense of non-acccomplishment, or the stuff not clicking. But as long as you're doing the right kind of stuff, it's a gonna just keep working.

I'm not looking to say something to everybody, or do something that could accomplish anything for everybody, dig? That's a big danger in the thing of focusing on individuals. Then it becomes that thing of *that's* the truth or *that's* right or any of that. That's what I run into with somebody who says, "Hey, man, I read in an interview where you said blah blah and so because you said that everybody should take twenty caps of acid a day back in 1963, I've been living like that all this time."

I always want to say something like, "Wow, man, I didn't mean for you to go on a trip like that," or "I wasn't really serious in that particular interview." It's like, "Who can you believe? Who can you trust?" Everybody's lookin' to believe something or somebody. In fact, two people hit on me the other night at that benefit about Jesus, Jesus people. There's a lot of Jesus talk going around in certain worlds.

REICH: *Well, Jesus himself wasn't such a bad cat, it's the Christian Church that's not such a great thing.*

Those of you who know Jesus, don't turn him in.

I don't know, man, I really don't know what's happening. Do you know that? I *wonder* what's happening.

REICH: *Everything is growing, if you observe carefully, that's what I see.*

A guy had an idea the other night that was good . . . an idea for hippie money.

MOUNTAIN GIRL: Hippie money?

Yeah, right, and the rate of exchange would be something like $1000 hippie dollars to $1.00. But then there would be a black market rate which would be like one-to-one so that you could have a huge income and then convert it the regular straight way not getting taxed and all.

REICH: *That's pretty good.*

It's a good idea. It's just a matter of having everybody go for it. If you can get everybody to agree to do it, you've got it. That's where it's really at in terms of making changes: getting everybody to agree to something because if we all agree to one thing, everybody on the planet, then we can make the next step and that's what everybody is waiting around for. The news has to get out, because that's the next step, that everybody has to agree to *one* thing, *just one, one little thing.* Everything is going slow—although it's going faster now than it has ever before—it's still going painfully and incredibly at a snail-like rate.

That is to say that the news that there has been a change of consciousness on the planet and that everybody is going to get into it eventually, is slow getting out. That's essentially it. It's still trying to get out and we're still waiting back here, because nothing can happen until all that gets out. It is getting out, just here and there, just real slow.

REICH: *Yeah, and the older people don't know it yet.*

They don't know it because they're still focused on that old stuff, still focused on survival translated into "get a college education," that kind of shit.

REICH: *They haven't looked around to see all of this.*

There isn't anything to see, that's why.

REICH: *Because they're not there.*

Because there isn't anything, because nothing has changed.

REICH: *I want to ask about trying to communicate in the community of people who are seeking more space.*

Well, I don't think of it so much in terms of speaking, so I have to translate. In relating to somebody who is seeking more space, the basic thing is being able to open a window, to let them see that there is more space before you can even think about it. I think we're a first step in that whole progression and on a good night we can illustrate that there is more space.

REICH: *You really believe that people are teachable.*

Yes.

REICH: *You can show them something that they never saw before and they can learn it?*

I think so. Teaching really comes down to a matter of method. But I also think that not everybody should be out teaching. People should be out working. Teaching is one of those things that . . . that way you learn music, for example, is that you go around to where there's music and that's a good example of teaching. I would say that I was taught music, but I never had a teacher.

Essentially, I think that life is a progressive matter. Going through life you find that there aren't any true setbacks, you just continue to know more, to find more out. More stuff happens to you and more things become known to you. It's continual.

There are enough people without walls—personally in my own life—where I don't feel that I'm really alienated from anybody else because of all the walls. That experience is not happening to me. But I know that it's a thing that people talk about a lot, so I assume that it's happening somewhere. OK, it's happening somewhere and the only thing that I can even comment on is that it's just a lie. I know you don't need them.

The whole security trip that Americans are obsessed with is just a misplaced, poor understanding of death. Basically all security trips are fear of death. It's basically protecting oneself and the only thing there is to protect oneself against in life is death. And death is something that's been handled so incredibly awkwardly in society. Nobody seems to know what it is. It's nothing that you're acquainted with. Most people spend their lives without ever seeing anybody die or without ever seeing anybody dead and so it makes the whole thing weird. There's a lot of Christian weirdness about death. They've just been weird about it.

REICH: *You refuse to say that the rock music world is going through some terrible times and seems to be dying.*

I think the whole world is going through a terrible thing.

What about the new culture?

I don't see the rock and roll scene as being the new culture. I think the rock and roll scene is just the rock and roll scene. Basically it's a professional trip. It's business and stuff like that and that the music and musicians are still a whole other world really and I don't think that what the musicians are up to and what their heads are like is ever really filtered out into that world. The "rock scene" is a fabrication of media. Any time you have people doing the same thing, you have shop talk, you have a shop scene, you have a professional scene. Because music is a high-energy trip and it's important nowadays it's this thing called the rock scene. But I know an artists' scene that's at least as clannish as the rock scene—the comic book artists' scene. It's all kinds of scenes that are all doing stuff, and accomplishing stuff and creating stuff and defining culture and doing all those things that everybody says they're doing. They really are doing it but I think that what is really new and what is happening now in the post-revolutionary thing is not being focused upon. I think that it's good that it's not, because it might have a chance to develop into something that really works before the focus lays in on it.

I think that what's happening is an almost infinite number of possibilities of ways to live your life are being thought out. Ultimately people are going to be able to choose any possibility and find a scene that does it.

REICH: *How are you going to communicate between one kind of scene to another?*

Just by hanging out.

REICH: *The music scene comes to me through records. And it isn't that hard to translate. Some people think it is.*

No. I think everybody sees. Now everybody in America has had so much of the same kind of influence; communication is super easy and images and stuff are available to everybody and it's possible to really lay stuff out and have people know what it is. The problem with artists communicating is that the old avant-garde art world is doing what it was doing twenty years ago—it's dying, and it's pretty much dead now. The new stuff, which has real energy, real vitality, and really talks to people on the level of what's going on in their lives, on the level of what their personal images are and so forth, works. It's like new definitions of what has been lost in our culture in terms of where art fits in or where culture fits into people—whatever those weird terms are.

REICH: *Well it's all in the way we tell each other about what we've found out. This leads me to our ending, something that we agree about although we come from very different worlds. We both think that everybody really knows the truth underneath all their appearances. Could you just say what you think that means and then I'll say what I think it means.*

What the truth is?

REICH: *Well when we both say that everybody knows something that most people aren't letting on to.*

I don't know what it means. There is some basic premise there are some basic forces that are occurring in the universe that—in inhabiting this universe—you can't escape knowing what they are. I think of it as a universal—a cosmic conspiracy. Or, the information we're plugged into is the universe itself and everybody knows that on a cellular level. It's built in. Just superficial stuff like what happened to you in your lifetime is nothing compared to the container which holds all your information. And there's a similarity in all our containers. We are all one organism, we are all the universe, we are all doing the same thing. That's the sort of thing that everybody knows and I think that it's only weird little differences that are making it difficult. And there's been a trend among humans to try to stop everything, that we're going to stop the force called change in the universe and we're going to stay here. But it just doesn't happen. The thing that everyone should know is that *change* is the thing that's happening, all the time, and that it's okay to change your clothes, it's okay to change your face, it's okay to change anything.

You *can* change. And you can create change. And you can do it knowing that it's what you're supposed to do.

REICH: *You and I and all the others in this thing have almost a conspiracy going among us.*

There's no losing. I think the way you can have a conspiracy is to have trust. A certain kind of trust. For example, the way the old power dynasties were built was somebody would marry somebody's sister and stuff like that and it would be blood trust which is the old way of thinking it. But now it's like a new family trust—global village trust. The thing is that we're all earthlings. And in the face of the enormity of the cosmos, it's best for us to stick together as earthlings. The earthling consciousness is the one that's really trying to happen at this juncture and so far it's only a tiny little glint, but it's already over. The change has already happened, and it's a matter of swirling out.

It has already happened. We're living after the fact. It's a post-revolutionary age. The change is over. The rest of it is a clean-up action. Unfortunately it's very slow. Amazingly slow and amazingly difficult.

REICH: *But everybody knows it now?*

Well if they don't, they will.

REICH: *So the thing is to keep on . . .*

Keep it on, keep it on. Just keep on keeping on, folks.

PART 2

A
STONED SUNDAY
RAP

CHARLES: I want to talk about evolution because I've been thinking about it and I've been trying to do it and I think I've been seeing it everywhere.

JERRY: Yeah.

CHARLES: I want to compare notes on whether I'm seeing it or making it up.

JERRY: Well, I hope I'm seeing it but I might be making it up too. Oh, somebody said something to me about evolution. O yeah, we were into one of those raps about, you know, poisoned air and pollution and the concerns of the material survival unit or whatever the hell it is, and Dave Parker at the office said something about that whole Darwinian evolution thing, you know, that a species makes an evolutionary change because of some peril or some weirdness in the food cycle, you know, but it has to be a *real* thing for a change to occur and it's like if the stuff that they say is going on in the world is real, then it's time for a real change to happen, you know, and the only place for it to happen is the consciousness thing.

CHARLES: Well, for example, men are getting less competitive.

JERRY: Right.

CHARLES: That's because it doesn't serve any social purpose for people to be so competitive anymore.

JERRY: Right.

CHARLES: Maybe it did fifty years ago—had to fight with animals and Indians—but it doesn't make any sense now.

JERRY: I don't—yah right—I don't think—yeah right—well I think there's that moving into a cooperative functioning Gestalt group thing which is the survival unit rather than the basic human, you know what I mean . . . but it's hard to say whether you can see that happening or whether it's happening but the percentages are now . . . it's always been happening in some percentage margin but now because the numbers are great and communication is high that percentage is more easily visible and whether or not, you know, which of those is true is anybody's guess, it'll take fifty years to see.

CHARLES: Tell you something I'd do is, I'd watch kids play ball like outside a school or something.

JERRY: There you go.

CHARLES: And I'm convinced that they're nicer to each other and they care less about winning than they used to.

JERRY: Yeah.

CHARLES: I've watched that in a lot of places around California.

JERRY: Right, now where does that come from? Why would the kids do that? Is it because of what they see on TV?

CHARLES: No, TV is just a reflection.

JERRY: But it's a feedback situation too.

CHARLES: Yeah.

JERRY: So that it tends to reinforce anything that happens.

CHARLES: Well . . .

JERRY: Well, see, I don't know for sure.

CHARLES: I think it's got to be because there's nothing good to be gained by being so fiercely competitive, being the Wild Cats or something.

JERRY: Right, right, right. That's true, that's true. It doesn't work out too good.

CHARLES: And also because it's so much better to get good things off of people than get bad things off of people and people are waking up to it. One test of evolution is the way kids walk. Have you noticed the change in that since the Fifties?

JERRY: Sure, yeah, well, there used to be in the city anyway in the Fifties there were like several, you know, like illustrative styles of walking, you know what I mean, like, you know, "This is my turf" and you know, and there was the one where "I'm a visitor here and I'm cooling it" you know, and there's the invisible walk, you know what I mean, the sidewalk shuffle, that kind of stuff, it's ah you don't see so much of that now as you used to and you don't see so much of that kinda like ingrown . . .

CHARLES: *Prowl.*

JERRY: Yeah right, things have expanded beyond that, it seems, even on the funky level and it's like even in my old neighborhood and stuff, you know, I go back there and see what it looks like, what they're doing.

CHARLES: I see a bounce, it's one walk that I recognize, bouncing along looking happy, it's kind of a stoned walk and I see trucking in all kinds of forms, trucking is a way to walk.

JERRY: Trucking is a nice expression. But I tell you though I've observed a certain amount of that but I haven't taken note of it because I haven't been watching for it. I will now but I haven't been so far, so like I haven't gotten any verification for that one way or another.

CHARLES: If you were looking for signs of evolution where would you look?

JERRY: I'd look right around, you know.

CHARLES: I mean for what kinds of things, like homemade bread or—

JERRY: No, I'd look for whatever makes itself visible and I mean I don't look for any specific thing, but if there's more than one thing saying this is what's happening then I'd go along with it. I'd go along with it on the basis of what kind of input I've gotten from just what's going on around me, from who's doing what and how they're doing it, and I'm into a place where all those things are a little more controlled, I think, than the regular world, you know what I mean. In the Grateful Dead things look fucking great, you know what I mean, so it's like I'm concerned with that world since that's my unit.

CHARLES: One thing that I've always been curious about is how do you stay high if you're working in the Grateful Dead but you're not a guitarist but you're doing something that's, you know, like lugging the equipment around or doing the books, bookkeeping, things like that.

JERRY: Well, to find out those answers the thing to do is talk to, come and do an interview with the Grateful Dead sometime.

CHARLES: Well, I could visit you in San Rafael.

JERRY: That would be good, that would be good.

MOUNTAIN GIRL: And they'd be charmed.

CHARLES: I have a letter from Alan Trist a long time ago that asks me to come . . .

JERRY: He's a fantastic guy.

CHARLES: Bet he is.

JERRY: He's a, he's a . . . yeah right . . . our whole scene . . . I'm really just one, I'm only one component of the Grateful Dead, I'm an equal unit with everybody else in it and everybody else is really far-out, you know what I mean. Like Alan, man, Alan is fantastic, he's like some kind of cosmic diplomat. He's a guy that there isn't any-body; there's no way that you can dislike him, you know what I mean, he never disturbs any karma ever. He's fantastic, really man.

CHARLES: Well that's a high thing to say.

JERRY: Really man, what I mean I'm talking about it, you know, on the basis of how the guy moves around in a world full of people, that's it. For example, the kind of work he used to do was that he actually was a diplomat of sorts and he worked you know with like Near Eastern countries, he worked for some sheik: you know that sort of thing; there's all that complex protocol, and if you say the wrong thing to some sheik, bam, there goes your head. It's like all those things are happening and it's like being able to move gracefully through different worlds and through the world of English Classicism, which is like his academic background, it's like it really takes some considerable grace. I've known Alan since he was eighteen and he and I met down in Palo Alto in fact.

CHARLES: I thought he was an Englishman.

JERRY: He is, but he was down there with his father who was working at the behavioral sciences institute. And he and I, in fact, and Hunter and Phil were all part of that early scene that was like our early scene down there and really the Grateful Dead is a continuation of that.

CHARLES *(referring to the tape recorder)*: Now I'm uptight because I have this need to check things.

JERRY: So you want to see if this thing is recording.

CHARLES: The essence of me is you have to play along with my little worries and then I get relaxed and high.

JERRY: Right.

MOUNTAIN GIRL: Are you sure you ever get relaxed or high?

CHARLES: Well, Mountain Girl, you have like, high standards.

MOUNTAIN GIRL: Well it's easy for me to relax.

JERRY: Oh, gotcha ah, them high standards.

CHARLES: I mean high standards of relaxation. Now I do, but it's hard around people, like I do much better if I were down at the beach I'd get higher and higher and higher all day on the beach and I've been trained to have a lot of self-concern with people.

JERRY: Right. Everybody's got that. I've got it too. It's the movies, for me it was the movies but, you know, for you it was something else.

CHARLES: I tried to show a little bit of that in the introduction I wrote but I didn't do it well enough yet but I'll try some more.

JERRY: Right.

CHARLES: I feel insecure around you and Mountain Girl because you still represent that extra dimension of of of . . . doing anything you please.

JERRY: I don't see that as an extra dimension, Charles.

MOUNTAIN GIRL *(to Jerry):* You certainly don't do anything you please. You do a lot of things you please but you're stuck, man, just like all the rest of us.

JERRY: That's true but I decided . . . to be . . . I mean I decided to be, I *just* decided to be . . . like two months ago or three months ago.

CHARLES: What did you decide?

JERRY: I decided that yeah, okay, I'll do it.

CHARLES: Far out.

JERRY: That's what I decided you know and I've never decided that ever before.

CHARLES: I realize that's a profound thing.

JERRY: Yeah, it's really far-out for me . . . yeah, very far-out.

CHARLES: It happened to you but you never had a choice about it but then you suddenly said I'll do it.

JERRY: Yeah.

CHARLES: I know exactly, I know all about that.

JERRY: I've just been going along with it, I've been going with it all along but now I've decided that okay not only am I going with it but I'm fucking well, you know, like paddle and everything cuz I felt like I'd seen it long enough, I'd been watching it long enough and timing was right and given this lifetime in which to accomplish whatever and it's like there isn't anything else for me, I know it, you know what I mean, that's what I'm doing, so it's like that's been my decision. I don't know what it means but that's where my head's been at, well, like I could also develop cold feet and say, well, fuck it all, I'm leaving . . . the streets of Bombay . . .

CHARLES: No, but that's a great moment when you decide.

JERRY: Very far-out for me, like for me it was like that's . . . I've been feeling like, okay, like now I'm ready to do it . . . the Grateful Dead.

CHARLES: It's like if you'd been a doctor for fifteen years and then you decided that you were going to be a doctor. How far-out that moment would be.

JERRY: Right, right.

CHARLES: Because you'd know that you had never decided it before.

JERRY: Right, right.

CHARLES: It's an incredible thing. I *totally* understand that.

JERRY: Right, right.

CHARLES: It's just something that I've done myself. You have to do it more than one time.

JERRY: Probably, probably.

CHARLES: You do, you have to decide about each next elevation of your life. You have to get up on it and be there a while and then you'll have to choose it as the next elevation.

JERRY: Well, I don't know now, well, I've gone a lot of places not deciding and not choosing and not, and not willing in any way, you know what I mean, it's like up until like two months ago everything's been free form, I've been improvising, I've been taking it as it comes.

CHARLES: I take what I said back.

JERRY: Yeah.

CHARLES: Because I was talking on too superficial a level.

JERRY: Oh, I see, okay.

CHARLES: And I think that you're talking about the one big moment when you decide it all.

JERRY: Yeah, yeah right, well I mean, yeah right, that's the moment I'm talking about. I mean for me that was the moment so far, there may be others or there may be more.

CHARLES: I don't know, can you believe this—this is like sort of a horoscope thing—but that's what I came out here to California for, was to do that same thing.

JERRY: Well I'll be damned.

CHARLES: That's what I was doing the last . . .

JERRY: Well hang me for a toad. (*laughter*)

CHARLES: Yes, it's just happening now and I'm just starting to stay out here until I've made a choice.

JERRY: And did you make a choice?

CHARLES: Yes, it's just happening now and I'm just starting to really experience it.

JERRY: Far out! Well it's great to make a choice I guess, or at least you know if that's what's happening, that's what's happening.

CHARLES: Yeah, it unleashes so much inside of you it's like energy that always went into reserve.

JERRY: Reserve. Well, I've always been in reserve in terms of you know, whether I'm going to run full out and use it all or whether I'm going to, you know, lay back and see what happens, and I've been laying back to see what happens for a long time now I feel, like, you know, but see like the whole Grateful Dead thing has been kind of like, ah, you know, like waking up, you know what I mean, it's like ah you know, ah, ah ha, here we are, you know. It's drying out the wings and all that wrrrr you know, looking around.

MOUNTAIN GIRL: We kind of dig that together.

CHARLES: Drying out the wings.

MOUNTAIN GIRL: Although totally separate at that time it was really neat, we really did, I mean like I really did too because I finally got over being pregnant. That affects you for about two years afterwards.

CHARLES: Being pregnant affects you . . . ? Mentally?

MOUNTAIN GIRL: Mentally. Yes, your intellect. Your intellect takes a nap for about, I would say, two years per pregnancy, yeah. I've like compared notes with a lot of other chicks and they all agree two years *after* the baby was born.

CHARLES: Boy, oh boy.

MOUNTAIN GIRL: Like, it's insurance, biological insurance, if you're going to take care of your kid.

JERRY: Well, it's a huge chemical trip. Right, right, obviously, that's weird.

MOUNTAIN GIRL: It's like insect mentality, it's like caring for the egg.

JERRY: Survival—straight survival—survival device stuff, yeah, I can dig it.

MOUNTAIN GIRL: Yeah.

CHARLES: I think it's probably important to have some years like that and men don't.

JERRY: It's not something you have a choice about.

MOUNTAIN GIRL: Well, no it's certainly important.

JERRY: It's not something you have a choice about, right, I mean it's like the color of your hair or the shape of your nose or something like that, it's the framework within which whatever it is that you consider to be you can express itself through.

CHARLES: If you think and think and think you could turn it off maybe, except I couldn't.

JERRY: No, I don't think you can turn it off if it's biochemical.

CHARLES: Maybe not.

JERRY: You know, I think that it suddenly will shape and control your viewpoint and your, your everything, you know.

MOUNTAIN GIRL: There's one thing that can suspend all that and that's nitrous oxide.

JERRY: Nitrous oxide cuts through just about anything.

MOUNTAIN GIRL: Uh huh!

JERRY: It's like death.

MOUNTAIN GIRL: It's like to be actually alive from moment to moment, like the brink of death, right.

JERRY: It's death! I think it is. You know how it is, like they say when you're about to die, have you ever had an experience when you came very close to death? Like an automobile accident, a scare, a bad scare, a wound of some kind?

CHARLES: Terrible scares, but "in my head" scares.

JERRY: There you go, well see if you ever in your real life have that experience, without actually dying that is, a lot of stuff kind of falls into place and nitrous oxide is a short version of that flash. I think what it does is, it triggers your "I'm dying" mechanism; it tickles it because it's like an oxygen starvation thing.

CHARLES: Woo, yeah.

JERRY: Right, and so an opening occurs and it's far-out, the nitrous oxide place, it's synchronous and things happen super fast, lightning fast, like it's calculator space.

CHARLES: Woo.

MOUNTAIN GIRL: Right.

JERRY: And if you do it with other people and there are other people who are similarly programmed you have just a telepathic thing that's fantastic and it's unbelievable; it's just like in the old Walt Disney comic books they used to have Hewey, Dewey and Louie, the three nephews speaking sentences adjacently, so one would say the first half of the sentence, the other would say the middle half and the other would finish it. Nitrous oxide is that world, yeah.

MOUNTAIN GIRL: Of being Hewey, Dewey and Louie.

JERRY: Right, it's even got that duck rap.

MOUNTAIN GIRL: Quack, quack. Somebody invariably says quack, quack. *(laughter)* Always, always a duck.

JERRY: Always? Well, that's a gross generalization, man.

MOUNTAIN GIRL: I don't know, if I'm around . . . *(pause, then points out the window at a hawk)*

CHARLES: No, I don't see the hawk.

MOUNTAIN GIRL: He's sitting right on top of the pine tree.

CHARLES: Right on top of the tree there, watching.

MOUNTAIN GIRL: Well, you see it's foggy and they can't fly up in the fog, they have to come down below the fog to get anything to eat and they fly blind and they can't stand it.

CHARLES: Jerry, think about like consciousness and then think about how a hawk can see six times better than you can.

JERRY: Yeah right.

CHARLES: Now . . .

JERRY: Far out!

CHARLES: Now, do you realize there will be a day when our minds, when we can see six times more things than we see now.

JERRY: Yeah.

CHARLES: Like, and music will be like six times more cosmic than it is now.

JERRY: Well I'm pushing for that day. *(laughter)*

CHARLES: That's what I think is a great fantastic thing that we'll get to where we can see like, for instance, looking at another person we'll be able to see *six times more.*

JERRY: Well I think, I think LSD is that, man, and psychedelic drugs are that, you know, really, you know, because I've seen things that you know *(laughter)* there would be no other way to do it, you know, I mean . . .

CHARLES: I've got to tell you about this thing that I did. This is just about the last three weeks; I would sit in one place and I could like get back to say age seven years, and I could go through all the feelings of seven years, I mean when I was seven years old.

JERRY: Right. You better watch that stuff. You may want it when you're old. *(laughter)* You can't play those things back that much.

CHARLES: Really?

JERRY: Yeah, right, because they start to lose it after a while because you start playing back your second playback and then you play back your next playback and it's cumulative, it's like tape, there, just exactly like tapes.

CHARLES: It *is* like a tape and it went through my head. I saw some family scenes, and you mean that's like a limited play, that's . . .

JERRY: Yeah, you'll only hear it that way so many times.

CHARLES: God, what an incredible thing!

JERRY: It's just like a tape because there's an entropy thing happening, you know, with the energy and the electrical connections and the neurons and all that shit darting around in your brain, all that stuff is matrixes, you know.

CHARLES: Because you know what I did, I had a lot of it sort of scribbled as I thought of it in the note book and I tried to read it back and I couldn't experience it.

JERRY: That's great, yeah, well, of course, but now your next problem will be playing back that in addition to your commentary.

CHARLES: Yeah, I see.

JERRY: You know what I mean, you see.

CHARLES: So it's slowly covered.

JERRY: Exactly—*eventually.* So like it's like, you know that's the thing I mean, it's like go forward now, man, because someday you might want to play those memories back. *(laughter)*

CHARLES: Well, I did want to play them, this was like, but Jerry, I wanted to find out why I was so terrified.

JERRY: Oh, there you go, okay, I can dig it. Well then, in that case you *want* to play it back, in fact, you probably want to play it back so much that they're gone.

CHARLES: The terrors, because . . .

JERRY: Yeah.

CHARLES: You see, like I was a *frightened person.* You know what? You know there are some people in the world who are frightened persons and some people in the world who are like unfrightened.

JERRY: I don't believe it.

CHARLES: You think everybody is a frightened person?

JERRY: No, no, I don't believe that anybody is a frightened person. I believe that any truly frightened person would have died out thousands and thousands of years ago, because you can't survive and be frightened indefinitely. I don't think that there is an organism that's frightened, I think that there's an artificial fright energy implant that's like the horror movies.

CHARLES: Yeah.

JERRY: It's not real fear because if it was real fear you would have been afraid to live this long; you're part of a surviving strain, man.

CHARLES: Yeah, but I've had to'like put an awful lot of energy into building up safeguards against the fear.

JERRY: Oh, well, that's a drag, you know, that's a drag.

CHARLES: And if I could put that energy into positive forward motion, it would be much better.

JERRY: All you need is a positive forward . . .

MOUNTAIN GIRL: Confidence.

JERRY: No, not . . .

CHARLES: You have to keep that dragon in you which is fear.

JERRY: All you need is a form through which to be positive.

CHARLES: Right, but like if a lot of that form is dictated by fear . . .

JERRY: Oh well, whew, the old switcheroo.

CHARLES: Then you have to like go back and look at the fear, take a trip and run that tape again.

JERRY: Yeah, right.

CHARLES: And say, "What the fuck, this is all over with, forget it," and then you can come forward and you may not carry that tape again.

JERRY: Well, you could also come to the realization about the nature of ultimate fear. You can scare yourself as much as you can possibly scare yourself and find out what it is, what the fear really is.

CHARLES: Yeah.

JERRY: You can experience real fear, I mean you know *(laughter)* it's like with me for example, fear, I'm fearful, but the thing that like when I played out my fear fantasies like, you know, I was high and all of a sudden I begin to feel that feeling of "Oh oh, I'm scared," I'm afraid, and I'm afraid of something that's just back here and I know that if I turn around it's going to be the most horrible fear possible and at that moment I went into it and it was plenty scary but, you know it wasn't that bad, you know what I mean. The worst, the thing that I was afraid of was that I was afraid of dying a horrible way, in a horrible way. That's what I was afraid of. Ultimately, I didn't want to die horribly and painfully and just at that time I went through all of the horrible and painful deaths that I could possibly go through and it wasn't like I said, "Okay, now I'm going to die horrible and painful deaths," it was like all of a sudden, man, there they were, here comes the insect horrors and all my flesh was stripped clean not once but millions of times and then it's going to be the fire and now it's going to be really all of it, the whole fantasy, cccckkkk, *(laughter)* and it's like since then it's hard for me to work up a fear.

CHARLES: Well, my fear is a whole different thing. My fear is like being alive but not having your freedom.

JERRY: Oh God, I can't imagine being alive and not having your freedom.

CHARLES: Well, my freedom is . . . let's suppose you were locked in a jail or a closet, that's my fear.

JERRY: Oh.

CHARLES: It's all got to do with losing.

JERRY: Then you got that *inside* fear, the *Night of the Living Dead* fear.

CHARLES: Well . . .

JERRY: The one which goes farther and farther in, which recedes to a smaller and smaller point, and it's like claustrophobic in nature.

CHARLES: Claustrophobic fear, that is, if you said, "You're going to have to stay in this closet" I would be terrified, not of dying . . .

JERRY: Did you ever see *Night of the Living Dead?*

MOUNTAIN GIRL: A movie?

JERRY: Movie.

CHARLES: No.

JERRY: It's an illustration of the fear that you're talking about. That's so fantastic, man, you won't believe it, you'll love it. Basically, the thing in the movie starts out—don't worry about the tape; we'll get back to all that stuff.

CHARLES: Yeah, I'll change it whenever it seems like it should be changed.

JERRY: Basically, the trip of this movie is that there's this guy and his sister in a graveyard visiting mother's grave up in New England—this is all in New England—and they're up there visiting mother's grave and the guy starts playing a trick on the girl, sort of scaring her a little with "They're coming to get you," that kind of thing, and in the background you see one or two figures moving slowly and this guy comes up just out of nowhere and he has this horrible strange look about him and grabs the guy, immediately murders him and comes after the girl, the girl jumps into a car and the keys aren't in it, and this guy is beating and baying on the window.

CHARLES: Woo.

JERRY: She's in the car and releases the handbrake and it goes down the hill and she jumps out and runs for it and this thing is after her and she goes to this house and this whole thing gets into this house and these people who have come are running away from what's happening. These people are in this house and there's like fifty or sixty of them outside and they're coming and they make these attacks on the house and the people are boarding up the house from the inside and it finally descends down to one guy in the cellar, man, with the cellar door jammed shut and they're walking up there, having killed everybody else. It's like the ultimate drawing inward fear, claustrophobic fear. Ahhh! It's incredible, man, it's an amazing movie, truly horrible.

CHARLES: My worst fantasy would be like being locked in a dungeon.

JERRY: Right.

CHARLES: And if I were dead I wouldn't have that fear at all.

JERRY: Of course not, right.

CHARLES: I would be dead, so that would like *solve* my problem, being dead. Sometimes when I'm afraid I might say, well, jump off the Golden Gate Bridge because that will solve my problem of being afraid.

JERRY: Dig it, right, that's the suicide solution.

CHARLES: It's not the same as the people who commit suicide that like are angry at somebody. "I'll commit suicide and then you'll be sorry," you know what I mean. That's a whole different trip.

JERRY: Right.

CHARLES: Like I'll solve my problems.

JERRY: Right, a way out.

MOUNTAIN GIRL: I always thought that being locked in a dungeon would be kind of attractive because you could turn into a yoga.

JERRY: Yeah, there's time to do all those things that are meditative. Yeah, I thought about that.

MOUNTAIN GIRL: Right. With nobody bothering you.

CHARLES: But you're like, you've got this inner peace, you see, and I've got to *run* around all the time.

JERRY: You haven't an escape hatch somewhere? I'll tell you my escape hatch. My escape hatch is the streets of Bombay, you know.

CHARLES: In your head.

JERRY: Yeah, no, well, in the real sense that I've already decided at one time or another in my life that yeah, man, I could do it, you know, I could be a beggar on the streets of Bombay.

CHARLES: *Oh*, of course, I just didn't know what you . . . Oh.

JERRY: That's what I mean, the way out of everything that you presently know, you know, if you're looking for the way out.

CHARLES: But, Jerry, first think of this cosmic thing that you and I have a secret place in our heads that's alike! I've never discovered another person in my life that had a thing like that; that is, I too have a place, a thing I could do if everything else . . .

JERRY: Right.

CHARLES: But, do you realize what I'm trying to say, that the two of us have constructed a little place in our heads.

JERRY: Sure, sure.

CHARLES: Do you think other people do that?

JERRY: Sure. Well, of course I think that you do, you deal with the machinery you've got. So you create your own solutions to your own problems or whatever, . . . you do whatever you do.

CHARLES: So I've said I could be . . .

MOUNTAIN GIRL: You've got a box for a last resort.

CHARLES: So I've said I could be a person in the woods.

JERRY: There you go, right, and I could be a beggar on the streets of Bombay; it's like, sure, it's, to me, that's all the security I need.

CHARLES: That's right.

JERRY: If everybody made a similar decision at one time or another in their life we could all get it on together, because it would mean that everybody had made the choice at one time or another of opting, opting in, say, opting in from being a beggar on the streets of Bombay. Instead I decided to do this other thing which is like extremely forward going, involves a lot of energy, involves a lot of karma, involves a lot of stuff.

CHARLES: Well, I've done that too, but I've always said after it has a collision and collapses and that trip is over, there's this place and I'll go to there and so . . .

JERRY: Right.

CHARLES: I'll do this far-out thing only as long as it doesn't crash.

JERRY: Right, right, right, as long as it makes it, as long as it's working.

CHARLES: Yeah, and I can't control that, it has to just happen as long as it can happen and then I'll crash, if it does.

JERRY: Right. Well, see, now I've recently made my decision and it has been to go down with the ship, dig.

CHARLES: Yeah.

JERRY: That's what my decision was lately; that escape hatch was my escape hatch in essence in the fact that I could easily be nothing as easily as I could be something but I decided the decision was to be . . .

CHARLES: To choose.

JERRY: Right, that was it, that was what that choice thing was about; so like for me what that means is it's kind of like abandoning the streets of Bombay and going ahead with this game, whatever it is, since I've been so obviously drawn into it.

CHARLES: Well, you abandon the streets of Bombay until somebody takes the Grateful Dead away from you.

JERRY: Right, say, or whatever the calamity is.

CHARLES: Yeah, and then you're back and there's still this place you have built.

JERRY: Right.

CHARLES: And the thing I'm trying to deal with, like I want to talk about communication between people for a minute, like I never knew that anybody besides me—this may just tell you something about how uptight I am.

JERRY: Then you never communicated too well with anybody, that's all I can say.

CHARLES: Yes, I'm so uptight.

JERRY: Because like with everybody, like in the Grateful Dead that was our *basis*, in fact, you know, the basis of that understanding, that basic thing, that we're nowhere and we're nothing, and from nothing we can invent anything, you know what I mean, it's just that thing.

CHARLES: But you see I thought I was the only person in the world who had that construction in their minds.

JERRY: Fantastic.

CHARLES: So I haven't been communicating very well with people.

JERRY: Well, nobody else has been apparently, I mean, you know if that's the first you heard about it.

MOUNTAIN GIRL: People don't talk their brains very much.

JERRY: Yeah, people don't talk about their secrets.

CHARLES: If I like wrote that, where people could read about this place in my head, a lot of other people would have a sense of recognition.

JERRY: Of course they would.

CHARLES: That's the same as what music does.

JERRY: That's communication.

CHARLES: That's communication.

JERRY: Right, if you know what's happening in everybody's head, well, I mean if you have a rough idea of what the general outline is, I think you can make a lot of really, I think there are a lot of generalizations you can make about the western mind, expecially the English speaking.

CHARLES: But what I've been doing is like saying something else, like, "Oh, there's nothing to worry about" or "Oh, it wouldn't matter to me if it all disappeared," and I've been *lying* and nobody can communicate when they lie.

JERRY: That's true. If you lie, well, it won't go anywhere. You can communicate but the thing that will happen . . . well, see that's the thing that I worry about with things like these interviews when you're taking a piece of energy at a fast, huge, incredible, high speed. It's like physics, you know, the faster you go the rounder you get, the faster you go in the fourth dimension, you know, the bigger you get. As the thing approaches the speed of light it gains mass.

CHARLES: Right.

JERRY: Okay, well, that's it. And that's like when you're talking about energy in the history, the fast moving history stream, when you stick something out in there, it's gaining energy, it's gaining momentum at the rate of the time flow, so to speak. And now things are going fast, for example, well, consider how much weight the Beatles put out there or Bob Dylan or, you know what I mean, or Hermann Hesse or you know, anybody who stuck their head up in this last century, and bam!

CHARLES: Rolling, rolling, rolling.

JERRY: So if you put a lie out there, you know, and it accumulates energy, what you've got is, you know, we're living in a state of lies, you know, accumulating vast energy.

CHARLES: Right, right.

JERRY: And the result is the incredible chaos that faces civilization.

CHARLES: Well, but you should have like unusual confidence in me in that I have, that my strongest point is that I will be on guard against lies.

JERRY: Right. But I'm not worrying about your lies, I'm worrying about my lies, for Christ sakes.

CHARLES: I'm saying on this interview I will be aware of your lies and my lies and not let them go on either.

JERRY: Beautiful, great, fantastic, man, right.

CHARLES: I'm saying that that's my strength right there.

JERRY: That's beautiful, that's great, that's dynamite, that's perfect. Okay, good. Well, I'm not overly paranoid about it, but it's a point that I like to make clear because I'm conscious of it a *lot*, you know.

CHARLES: Well, it's a good thing to say, but I'm just saying like how the things I know I do well, and I'm really protective about . . .

JERRY: Yeah, right. Oh, beautiful, oh, great. Well yeah, right, that is good.

CHARLES: I have a motherly side and a little child side among the sides, and again I wonder if other people know the different sides that they each have.

JERRY: Sure. They have them. They probably just have different names for them, you know.

CHARLES: For instance, I have a side that would like to curl up in a little furry ball.

JERRY: Sure, I know that side, I know that guy.

CHARLES: Do people all have that side?

JERRY: Sure, man, I think so. I mean because all those things are like, heck yeah, man, that's stuff, that's built-in stuff, you know what I mean.

CHARLES: Well then people ought to admit it to each other and they should do it for each other once in a while and they should dig it.

JERRY: Well, I think that that's a lot for people to admit. I think that people should agree, make that one agreement of not kill each other, really, that's my basic theme.

CHARLES: Well, that's the first agreement.

JERRY: Well, yeah, well, that's the only one so far. That's what hasn't been made and the other things are refinements.

CHARLES: Well, Jerry, now suppose I'm at a Yale Law School faculty meeting.

JERRY: What are you doing at a Yale Law School faculty meeting, for Chrissake?

CHARLES: Well, because it might be because that is a real side of me.

JERRY: Okay, okay.

CHARLES: It is a truth, but it isn't like very much of a truth. But there is a little music I can play in that world.

JERRY: That's true, I know that.

CHARLES: Alright, now I have an even better reason to be there. That's because I'm the only person like me that either is there or can get there in the near future.

JERRY: Right. That's fantastic.

CHARLES: You have to dig it, it's like having seized some place where nobody like that is at.

JERRY: Right, a little turf, a little ground.

CHARLES: Yes.

JERRY: I understand that.

CHARLES: And they can't even see, like I really wear a lot of coloration in my head.

JERRY: Right.

CHARLES: And nobody like that can get there now because they're *on guard* against it.

JERRY: Right, far out, right.

CHARLES: But if they weren't on guard. (*Jerry laughs*) So that's a reason to be there. Now suppose I got up onto their great big table in the middle of an acrimonious argument and I curled up like a little furry ball and said, "I need a little of this now, I don't need any more bullshit from you people or your cutting each other up, please come over and pet me a little."

JERRY: Right.

CHARLES: What would happen if I did that?

JERRY: Well, I don't know, you would have to try it. But I know damn well that it wouldn't communicate jack-shit to those guys.

CHARLES: It wouldn't?

JERRY: I don't think so.

CHARLES: Wouldn't they know that they wanted to do that too?

JERRY: Not unless you were able to do it so perfectly, not unless you were able to deliver the lines with such utter conviction that they could immediately identify the reality of it.

CHARLES: They would think I was acting or playing or being phony or . . .

JERRY: And you would be unless that really happened and you really could do it.

MOUNTAIN GIRL: That's the problem with planning to do stuff.

JERRY: I've seen a couple of guys who could do it.

CHARLES: I could do it if I were stoned enough, that's what releases all of this . . .

JERRY: That's true, but if you were stoned enough you wouldn't be able to play the game enough on their side for you to have any, you know what I mean, well I don't know.

CHARLES: I would have to get there and take a pill after I was there.

JERRY: Maybe so. It might be a good idea to slip them one too.

CHARLES: But you see, they would be like cutting each other to pieces, you see, and like I would suddenly be awfully unhappy with this and saying, "Come on, let's touch each other instead."

JERRY: Right, right. Well, what you need is to be able to show them an overview that includes the continuity between armor and soft vulnerable things. Because it really is part of a continuum, which is a circle, which is itself, which is the all, I mean it goes on blah blah blah.

CHARLES: And you've got to like get it together in some way.

JERRY: Well, it is together in some way and all you have to do is see the part that, well, . . . I don't see any inconsistency with being a furry ball and having teeth, for example.

CHARLES: Yeah.

JERRY: It's all the same stuff, you know. If you were talking about that thing really, which is an interesting thing to be talking about, like actually doing that at one of those meetings, it would be, if you are talking about the game part of it, you would have to be ready. That would be like your, your, trump, or whatever the fuck, your big move. It would be the only time you would be able to pull that, really, in the real world there.

CHARLES: Only once.

JERRY: Right, it would be a one-time-only thing. So you might want to use a different incarnation, or you know, it's hard to say. See now, what you've got is a fantastic stage set and because you're the wild card you always have the possibility of playing the off hand position—I have some other friends who have been in that position. It depends on how straight the game is.

CHARLES: That's why I think I wouldn't quite do that.

JERRY: Right.

CHARLES: Because I want to do more than one thing.

JERRY: Right, so you have to conserve your moves.

CHARLES: And I want to do them all with my real self.

JERRY: It's all your real self, man.

CHARLES: But you know what I mean.

JERRY: It really is. If you don't believe that it is, too bad, but it is.

CHARLES: No, I can put out a false self at times.

JERRY: Sure, but you know, so what? (*laughter*) You mean you can lie.

CHARLES: Well, there are like degrees where you take another curtain and pull it aside and there's still another curtain.

JERRY: Right.

CHARLES: And like getting to know me is like pulling one curtain beyond another.

(*Jerry brings out a large illustrated book of Tantric Art and opens it to a painting of a figure with many different faces and arms.*)

JERRY: See.

CHARLES: Woo!

JERRY: That's one thing that's you, that's me, that's everybody.

CHARLES: Isn't that unbelievable.

MOUNTAIN GIRL: Yeah, I love that.

JERRY: Right, they've got it all, it's all written down and illustrated clearly.

CHARLES: And this is like completely understood, isn't it?

JERRY: Totally, yeah, absolutely, I mean, you know.

CHARLES: I just never have seen anything that's so great.

JERRY: (*pointing at one face*) That's you there at the Harvard Law School, man.

CHARLES: That's right.

JERRY: You know, that's you there, you know, and you know that's all of them too, you know, that's the whole picture, you know what I mean.

CHARLES: Isn't that incredible, but . . .

JERRY: I love that stuff.

CHARLES: But it's important to start telling people and making them see the different sides, because . . .

JERRY: You can't tell people that; either they see it or they don't. I don't think you can do it by, ah, I don't think you can do it by explaining.

CHARLES: No, no, I really don't mean that. What I mean is like what I'm trying to do now is say take a face that they haven't seen of me, see.

JERRY: Right, and that's bad.

CHARLES: And I'll show it to them, see.

JERRY: Right, ooh! You know, aaahhh!

CHARLES: And that's what I'm getting into now, is make more and more faces to more and more people and I'm now like doing like letters back to the East in which I make a face that ah they've never seen before.

JERRY: I love it, great.

CHARLES: Isn't that incredible.

JERRY: I love it, man, it's fantastic.

CHARLES: And like I have a correspondence with a sort of a raspy guy, you know, back and forth and back and forth, and so I write him and I say, "I can't stand this, I need love and reinforcement and support and gentleness and not all this shit," and like you know I've completely altered the whole thing, the game between us by saying that.

JERRY: Fantastic, too much!

CHARLES: And I've like done that with each person, you know.

JERRY: Too much. What a job. That's fantastic.

CHARLES: It's fun.

JERRY: Right.

CHARLES: You said what a job . . . you meant it was good?

JERRY: Right, right, right, right, that's a good space.

CHARLES: And if you could really show it you'd like show this whole thing to another person.

JERRY: Yeah, and I'd try to get a few more different kinds of ones to show, too.

CHARLES: Wow!

JERRY: You know, I mean because there's an infinite faceted or you know, the million petal lotus or whatever. That's real, that stuff is real.

CHARLES: Oh, it's absolutely real.

JERRY: And if you can let yourself run that way, it's far-out. It is far-out, that's all I can say. It just lets you, it's just more freeing energy, you know, freeing images and all those things, and, well, personas, or whatever it is.

CHARLES: Like children free us to play. For instance, I'll tell you a whole thing about me. I could just go down to the beach and make canals in the sand all day.

JERRY: Yeah, that's nice.

CHARLES: That's a *real* part of me, that's really real.

MOUNTAIN GIRL: But you wouldn't be able to do that every day.

CHARLES: I could do it a lot, a lot—mountains in the sand—I used to make mountains in the sand every day and trails up them and roads up them and . . .

JERRY: Right, marble runs.

CHARLES: And you see that is a real face, but, you see, trying to do that like with your solemn students . . .

JERRY: Is funny!

CHARLES: It's funny, but I haven't . . .

JERRY: And it's groovy to try it.

CHARLES: That's my trip, is doing those things, you see.

JERRY: Right, I love it, yeah, I love it. That stuff's great. It's especially great if you've got a completely gullible audience.

CHARLES: Isn't that what you do in your music, the same many faces?

JERRY: Oh sure man. Hey, this is a picture of us. I could draw you, almost anybody in the Grateful Dead could draw you a picture of the Grateful Dead, man. It's got like six or seven weird legs, mismatched pairs, and one moth-eaten eagle wing and one bat wing, you know, and it snorts fire and it's cross-eyed, you know, and you know, *(laughter)* but it's . . .

MOUNTAIN GIRL: A genuine monster.

JERRY: And it jumps up and kicks around and laughs real loud. We really know that guy, man, we really know that thing.

CHARLES: Well, people are so scared of it, they're so scared of it. Well, if you ever hear of me being locked up . . .

JERRY: I'll know why.

CHARLES: You now know why.

(*Mountain Girl laughs*)

CHARLES: Don't laugh, it's very likely to happen.

JERRY: Well, that's why I'm saying don't get locked up if you can avoid it.

CHARLES: If you can possibly avoid it.

JERRY: Right, so save your moves.

CHARLES: Well, it's very good advice. I don't know if I'll succeed, because . . .

JERRY: Well, you know, you'll succeed, whether you succeed or not.

CHARLES: Yeah, but I mean, but you're always like dealing with unknowns.

JERRY: Sure.

CHARLES: And so sometimes you think it's not dangerous and you're out there at a very dangerous place.

JERRY: Well, it's the thing of having that backup. You know the thing of, "Okay, I'm going to the woods, but first I'm going to make this move."

CHARLES: Right.

MOUNTAIN GIRL: First I'm going to call my lawyer, that's what you say to yourself. *(laughter)*

CHARLES: No, but then I wouldn't do it.

JERRY: Right, right, yeah, I mean it can't be that way. For one thing because it wouldn't be fun unless you could just jump up and do it; you want to be able to do it when you want to do it.

CHARLES: If I called my lawyer before I smoked dope, you see, I would never do it: he would say not to—I don't even have a lawyer.

JERRY: You've got the wrong lawyer, man.

MOUNTAIN GIRL: No kidding.

JERRY: I mean, isn't there anybody that . . . you have law school, ha ha, there you go. What would be groovy would be if you had like one or two other allies that you could relate to who had positions similar to yours and I bet they're in existence somewhere out there.

CHARLES: I know. I don't know how to find them.

JERRY: Right.

CHARLES: I want to find them.

JERRY: Right. It would be interesting to see how you could communicate with them. If I were you I would include some kind of secret message in your next book.

CHARLES: To those people alone.

JERRY: Well, you know . . .

CHARLES: At the beginning.

JERRY: You figure it out, but I mean, you know how you'd best be able to communicate with the people that you would be able to communicate with.

CHARLES: Well, what I'm going to do in my next book is like I'm going to tell people about as many of these places as I dare to do . . .

JERRY: That's great.

CHARLES: And know about.

JERRY: Right.

CHARLES: Number one. Number two, I'm going to like take songs and movies and everything that I dig and show these same faces in the songs and movies and show that it is there, folks, it isn't just me seeing it.

JERRY: Right. Oh, you're going to put together a bibliography.

CHARLES: I'm going to put together a thing in my . . . that starts with my head.

JERRY: Out of sight.

CHARLES: And around my head will be like these other . . .

JERRY: I've always wanted to do that.

CHARLES: For instance I can say, like in Bobby McGee. When Janis sung it she said one thing, showed one face and when you did it you showed another place and . . .

JERRY: Right.

CHARLES: Two whole different places.

JERRY: And when Kris Kristofferson does it, it's a whole other face.

CHARLES: And when I tell people about that at the same time I'll be telling them about all those places in my head . . .

JERRY: Yeah.

CHARLES: . . . that they've never been able to see.

JERRY: Right.

CHARLES: And I'm going to say, "Come on people, show us everything you can show us."

JERRY: Right.

CHARLES: And that will be the book.

JERRY: *(to Annabel)* Come on people. She says come on people.

ANNABEL: Nice people.

JERRY: Nice people, yes.

ANNABEL: Nice people.

CHARLES: I wrote to a younger teacher at the law school and I said, "You know, you act years older than me and I'm really sorry you've gotten caught in this trap of dignity and solemnity and everything else," and then I said, "It makes me sad because I'd like you for a real friend."

JERRY: And?

CHARLES: That was showing him a place in me that I had never shown him. That was another of those things.

JERRY: Right. Well, I think that what happens is that the more faces you show, the more faces get shown to you.

CHARLES: In return.

JERRY: Sure.

CHARLES: I think that's right.

MOUNTAIN GIRL: *(to Annabel)* You're the noisiest little kid I've ever known.

JERRY: I've found it to be true. I mean I've experimented with this kind of stuff.

CHARLES: You go along and if you don't dare show things, other people don't dare show things.

JERRY: Right.

CHARLES: And nothing gets shown.

JERRY: And the kind of stuff you show is the kind of stuff that gets shown you.

CHARLES: Right.

JERRY: You know.

CHARLES: I think that's absolutely right. It's incredible.

JERRY: Well, it's one of those things, you know.

CHARLES: It's actually, see, it's incredible, our heads are now so together today, because this is another thing I've been actively doing the last few months and out here and like I've been, I have a different place in the City for working on each important face of mine.

JERRY: Too much.

CHARLES: Now can you dig that?

JERRY: Oh yeah, absolutely, man, absolutely.

CHARLES: And like Clement Street, which is old and ethnic—I have a whole project out there of working on my ethnic-ness, or whatever.

JERRY: Right, that's neat.

CHARLES: And like I have a place like Shattuck Street in Berkeley, the shopping center at the old Co-Op, for working on—it's just above the New Monk.

JERRY: Yeah, I know the place.

CHARLES: I work on like my sense of a community there because the people there are so diverse and so together.

JERRY: Right.

CHARLES: And like Polk Street is a great kind of cruising, pickup street.

JERRY: Right.

CHARLES: And I can stand there and people look at me and I realize that they're looking me over as a piece of flesh.

JERRY: Right. The meat street.

CHARLES: And rejecting me.

(*Jerry laughs*)

CHARLES: But it's my experience of being a piece of flesh instead of being like looked at so and so.

JERRY: Right.

CHARLES: Like it's so far-out.

JERRY: It's another space, sure; it is far-out, right.

CHARLES: It's incredibly far-out.

JERRY: All of that stuff is far-out man, all that stuff. You ought to cruise the Tenderloin sometime. That's one of my places.

CHARLES: The Tenderloin is another side of it.

JERRY: Yeah, I like, I go to those kind of places.

CHARLES: It has that thing you sung about in "Wharf Rat." "Down, down, down and dirty."

JERRY: It's real, man, it's fucking real and everybody knows it too.

CHARLES: Yeah.

JERRY: That guy's in there somewhere.

CHARLES: That's really the way that people do feel.

JERRY: Sure.

CHARLES: That other isn't real. Like pretending it isn't there isn't real.

JERRY: Right, oh yeah, man, ridiculous. I mean why pretend anyway?

CHARLES: Well, alright now, you got to like just dig this one place of mine. I go out to the reflecting pool of the Palace of Fine Arts and I bring along like bread or other stuff for the birds.

JERRY: The duckies.

CHARLES: And I become an eccentric old person . . .

JERRY: That's a good spot too.

CHARLES: . . . who feeds the birds.

JERRY: Yeah, I like that spot too.

CHARLES: And I get into things with these birds—I become like this eccentric person and in that guise I can like develop rapport with children because I say, "Do you want to feed the birds?" and the mother will say, "Oh, the nice man is going to give you some bread, Billy." You know.

JERRY: Right, right.

CHARLES: And then this eccentric person does that whole thing.

JERRY: Right, that's a good space.

CHARLES: And so those are things, that's what I want to write about.

JERRY: Right.

CHARLES: It's like all of those places.

JERRY: It's like saying okay, here's some places you could be, here's some people you could be, here's something you could do. Right, models.

CHARLES: And there are things that give you so much to communicate with other eccentric people like yourself.

JERRY: Who's everybody, I mean, you know, really, I mean like for example in England everybody is eccentric, I mean, you know what I mean, it's kind of like a national . . .

CHARLES: That's what we've always needed, what we don't have in this country.

JERRY: Exactly. That's what America needs is crazies.

CHARLES: Crazies.

JERRY: Yeah, and that's one of Kantner's lines, man, he's right.

CHARLES: He's right about that.

JERRY: Right, really.

CHARLES: Incredibly right.

JERRY: Totally right. You know, I used to know a guy who used to dress, who used to wear old man's clothes—those old vests like the old Mission Streeters wear?

CHARLES: Yeah.

JERRY: And an old hat and all that and he used to make the rounds with the old guys—and he was just a young guy, he was under thirty at the time and freakin' out good, you know, pretty hard—and he used to make the rounds with them, man, and do that thing and walk real slow and do the whole thing just like an old man and really getting into it. It's fantastic.

CHARLES: See, there again I don't think people have talked very much about doing these things.

JERRY: No, I know.

CHARLES: See, what people do is they play prescribed roles . . .

JERRY: Right.

CHARLES: Like the young executive and then he becomes a mod swinger and then he becomes the skier.

JERRY: All bullshit.

CHARLES: It's all bullshit.

JERRY: Yeah, Hunter once wore eye patches on his eyes for a couple of weeks to be blind, you know, was blind, like spent a couple of weeks blind, as a blind man.

CHARLES: Well, the point is you have to find these places in yourself and not the bullshit places that they're giving you in the advertising media.

JERRY: Right, right, try out the possibilities.

CHARLES: And you have to find whatever personality . . .

JERRY: Well, it would be groovy to get media so that it describes more of it, you know what I mean.

CHARLES: That told you about these places.

JERRY: Sure.

CHARLES: Well, for example, like "Mannix" is on Wednesday nights—he's a private eye. They had a whole program of Mannix just being paranoid. And you know it's so amazing for a tough guy like that to be paranoid and he had been hit on the head was the excuse.

JERRY: Ah. Right.

CHARLES: But like you went through a whole hour and said, "This guy, Mannix, who is so cool and tough, is just as paranoid as I am," you know. I mean, in other words it's happening on television.

JERRY: Oh yeah, if it happens on television, it's happening. Oh well, you know it's just a matter of time, the more of those things that come out. *(Looks at the book again)* I love these things, man, God, I could stare at them for hours. There are so many of them and they're all different, you know, and it's so right on, you know. It is *right on.* Let's see.

CHARLES: The name of this book is *Tantra Art* by Mukerjee published by Ravi Kumar.

JERRY: Right.

(Garcia shows the album cover from Anthem of the Sun*)*

CHARLES: But . . . oh, you have one of those.

JERRY: Right. See now that's the Grateful Dead there.

CHARLES: I confess that this completely escaped me, totally escaped me.

JERRY: See, that's us. See, that's us.

CHARLES: And I never knew what it was.

JERRY: And it's us. The guy who painted this picture is a guy who is obviously into this kind of art and he worked on this thing for six months and only worked on it when he was high. This thing is really that big, you know, it's huge, it's immense.

CHARLES: Unbelievable.

JERRY: The color they screwed up because this shouldn't have been purple, it should have been white and you could see really what this does.

CHARLES: I just never understood what that was.

JERRY: That's the Grateful Dead, man. That's a guy's true real vision of the Grateful Dead. There's the lotus and everything, there's the eyes, there's the fire, . . . the guy . . . that's pretty far-out.

CHARLES: That's incredible.

JERRY: That's a straight nervous system painting.

CHARLES: Here's a place that I would know about.

JERRY: Yeah.

CHARLES: An enchanted garden.

JERRY: Sure, you know that place. There's the universe back in here.

CHARLES: In and in and in . . . the universe is back there.

JERRY: Right . . . love it.

CHARLES: The thing is I . . . this day is blowing my mind because I didn't know that other people know about all these places . . . I thought I was some kind of fucking lunatic.

JERRY: Well, you know, I mean you've been out of touch or something. Out here this stuff has been going on for a long time, obviously, because hell, this is from when? 1966 or 67.

CHARLES: Yeah, I thought that I was a lunatic. I've been out of touch with all the people who are like this, I suppose.

JERRY: Right.

CHARLES: But, let me tell you, nobody has like written it down.

JERRY: There you go. That's right because nobody writes.

CHARLES: Well . . .

JERRY: And there are guys that have written it down, it just hasn't been published.

CHARLES: It certainly hasn't been. It's not been available.

JERRY: There's a couple of people I think that write the way I see it. I think Gary Snyder does a lot of times.

CHARLES: But he doesn't spell it out like this, he's as obscure as the rest of you guys.

JERRY: That's true.

CHARLES: You say it in weird language.

JERRY: In jokes. *(laughter)*

CHARLES: Well, it's necessary to protect oneself in a way.

JERRY: When you say spell 'it' out, what exactly is the 'it' that you're talking about spelling out?

CHARLES: Well, I can't . . .

JERRY: You tell me because you're talking about spelling it out now, so spell it out.

CHARLES: Alright. If I wrote something I would say, "Look, each person is an infinite number of faces like this and an infinite number of ways to act and is that, whether they act that way or know it or not."

JERRY: Well, I would take it a step or two further than that.

CHARLES: Alright.

JERRY: If you're really going to spell it out.

CHARLES: Well, but I was going to.

JERRY: Okay.

CHARLES: I mean I was just starting.

JERRY: You're just warming up. Okay, go ahead. Okay, I'm sorry.

CHARLES: However, they are so imprisoned in roles that they must play—one, two, three or four roles—that they sometimes never show even one true face; but they never show all these faces and they're trained to be incredibly afraid of showing it or having it shown.

JERRY: Also a good many of them are illegal.

CHARLES: Illegal. Of course. Of course they're illegal.

JERRY: So you have that restriction which is certainly real.

CHARLES: All right, getting high is against the law and so over and over again you have these bummers, these paranoid things that keep you from doing it.

JERRY: Right. But there are other considerations as well. I mean obviously certain faces are destructive.

CHARLES: Yeah.

JERRY: And not necessarily, but those are real too.

CHARLES: Right.

JERRY: See, I would go for letting every face manifest itself when it's time for it to do so. And I think in a properly orderly universe that's exactly what's happening.

CHARLES: Right. Now the importance of this lies in each person acquiring a control over his own life. Now the advantage of my telling about this is to liberate each person.

JERRY: But it's only liberating them in the sense of . . . Don't you think there has to be an experience there, at the root of that, I mean, in the sense of . . . how would you become aware of your faces, of the possibilities unless you had something which gave you a view where that idea seemed at all pertinent.

CHARLES: Right. There has to be all these things around.

JERRY: Right, exactly.

CHARLES: And some use for them, and so . . .

JERRY: Yeah. But I think there has to be a basic experience. I think that a human being has to undergo a basic experience in order to be able to appreciate the possibility of manifesting an infinite number of faces.

CHARLES: Yeah, maybe that's right. But now you two do appreciate that and, uh, maybe lots of people do. Now for instance, I've always had a face. Why are you holding your nose? Because of odd . . .

JERRY: No, because you have all kinds of nasal passages and capillaries and all that stuff in there and it gets it into your blood stream.

CHARLES: Oh, alright. No, I just wondered if it was a comment on the conversation.

JERRY: No, no, no, no no, not at all.

CHARLES: Well, I was just going to say that I have a face—let's say this one, who is Captain Charles.

MOUNTAIN GIRL: Right. I can see him now with white tennis shoes on.

CHARLES: Can you dig that?

JERRY: Yeah, I know Captain Charles, sure, hell yes, man.

CHARLES: Right. The whole thing, you know.

JERRY: Admiral of the fleet or whatever.

CHARLES: But now you remember like you were Captain Trips.

JERRY: Right.

CHARLES: You see . . .

JERRY: That was my guy like that.

CHARLES: Captain Charles is like the ruler of the rocket ship, right?

JERRY: Sure, Captain Charles, man, Captain Charles and the space patrol.

CHARLES: Right. And the thing is I want to tell other people about that but I feel, ah . . .

JERRY: But you need a rocket ship and a uniform and a bunch of stuff like that to really do it right.

CHARLES: And I feel foolish and ashamed and ridiculous.

JERRY: Really, God.

CHARLES: And that's my problem.

JERRY: You ought to meet Babbs.

CHARLES: You said that he was like a good leader.

JERRY: He's got his Captain Babbs thing together, man. *(laughter)*

CHARLES: Yeah, right.

JERRY: I mean he's Captain Babbs with absolutely . . . I mean he knows how to become that guy, how to just turn it on.

MOUNTAIN GIRL: He has it.

JERRY: He really can do it good.

MOUNTAIN GIRL: He really . . .

JERRY: Oh God, he's good at it.

MOUNTAIN GIRL: You'd like him. You guys are physical equivalents.

CHARLES: That's good.

JERRY: He's straight ahead.

CHARLES: Because if the interaction is tightening up, then it just goes that way and people get more and more with-drawn.

JERRY: Right. No, it's this guy . . .

CHARLES: Yeah.

JERRY: The guy with the vise or whatever.

MOUNTAIN GIRL: Is there a guy in there with a vise?

JERRY: I don't know, but if there isn't, there should be.

CHARLES: Yeah.

JERRY: It's like, it's one of those guys with a tool, tightening it up, putting the clamps on. That's okay too; it's okay to be uptight, you know.

CHARLES: Yeah.

JERRY: If you're willing to, if you've done it out of . . . if you've chosen to play that game, what the fuck.

CHARLES: There's some times when it's necessary and desirable.

JERRY: Right, yeah.

CHARLES: Well, just to tell you a couple more . . .

JERRY: Lay 'em on me, I love 'em.

CHARLES: I get up in the morning and I go to the Mark Hopkins and I order breakfast.

JERRY: Out of sight.

MOUNTAIN GIRL: The Mark Hopkins.

JERRY: The Top of the Mark.

CHARLES: No, down in . . . where the people are.

JERRY: Ah, right, right.

CHARLES: And I know I'm a little odd-looking by their standards, so I experience oddness; whereas like when I'm with you, I feel very conventional compared to you.

JERRY: Right.

CHARLES: So I experience my conventionality.

JERRY: Right. There you go.

CHARLES: But there in the Mark Hopkins I am there experiencing my weirdness.

JERRY: Right.

CHARLES: And I'm the weirdest freak that's ever had breakfast there. And I do have money for breakfast so they can't throw me out, and then I go and I go to the Fairmont and sit in a chair. You know, the Fairmont has the grandest lobby. Have you ever seen the lobby?

JERRY: Yeah, I've seen it. Yeah, marvelous.

CHARLES: All gold and everything like that, and I sit there and I become my European expatriate intellectual self, sitting in the corridors of this European hotel.

JERRY: Right on.

CHARLES: Another whole person.

JERRY: Sure, I know that guy. I read that novel.

CHARLES: It's *Death in Venice*.

JERRY: *Death in Venice*, right.

CHARLES: Decadent, decadent, decadent.

JERRY: Right, yeah.

CHARLES: And like that's a fantasy, that whole . . .

JERRY: I love it, man.

CHARLES: It's unbelievable. And you can, like you can go all day with these real . . .

JERRY: For years, man, you can go for an eternity.

CHARLES: But they're all real.

JERRY: Ah, yeah, man. They're, they're . . . I mean they're real enough so, if you just manifest a little of that guy, man, you'll find a space that's exactly like that and where that world is happening, yeah, I love it.

CHARLES: But tell me, that's what you've been playing about all these years, isn't it, really?

JERRY: Ah.

CHARLES: Playing about like this kind of . . . all these places.

JERRY: Oh yeah, and more and others and other things and other viewpoints, I mean, you know, because we're not, you know, it's an elemental thing rather than a conscious . . .

CHARLES: You mean it's not . . . it's something deeper than faces, it's like for instance . . .

JERRY: It's something more elemental, it's more . . .

CHARLES: It's got more body than . . .

JERRY: Yeah, and it's fire and water and that kind of stuff.

CHARLES: Yeah.

JERRY: I don't think of it as being quite so specific except we get into those specific places, but I think of it as being more . . .

CHARLES: Wind and sun, rocks and sea.

JERRY: Yeah.

CHARLES: And sea urchins.

JERRY: Yeah, elements.

CHARLES: Yeah, that's right and I've always known that.

JERRY: Yup.

CHARLES: See, and you're not so much like into person-to-person personal like Janis sung about in "Bobby McGee."

JERRY: Right, we haven't been, but we're getting into that space.

CHARLES: Well . . .

JERRY: We're starting to throw a little of that out, as well, although that's not our regular place.

CHARLES: When she sang "Bobby McGee," she was singing about loving one man.

JERRY: Yeah.

CHARLES: That was what the song was about. When you sing it, it's like the whole thing of being in a truck and traveling across the country . . .

JERRY: . . . is incidental. And it's really the freedom is just another blah, blah, blah part. That's the part that we punch.

CHARLES: You're talking about what it feels like to be free and she's talking about loving a guy.

JERRY: Right.

CHARLES: It's like two different songs and that's what I've been trying to like tell people. It's two songs about two different subjects, having nothing to do with each other.

JERRY: Right, and it's only a vehicle, it's all in the same words.

CHARLES: Right, and I've always known that!

JERRY: And the same melody.

CHARLES: Right.

JERRY: But it's not the same song.

CHARLES: There's no resemblance except that using the form.

JERRY: Right. Same with "El Paso." We do "El Paso" but you couldn't in a million years compare it to Marty Robbins.

CHARLES: Totally in another place.

JERRY: Yeah, right, it's another place.

CHARLES: See, I've always known that and so, for instance, when like Newman does this film, *Sometimes a Great Notion*, it has nothing to do with the book.

JERRY: Right, nothing at all, right, absolutely nothing.

CHARLES: It has only to do with like Newman's head.

JERRY: Right.

CHARLES: Which is the right thing for it to have to do with.

JERRY: What else could it have to do with?

CHARLES: Well, people go there and think that they're going like to get into *Sometimes a Great Notion* by Ken Kesey.

JERRY: I know, but that's because people don't sufficiently understand what directors and movies are . . .

CHARLES: That's right.

JERRY: . . . as opposed to books and writers. It's a different universe or whatever, people just don't understand enough about . . . it's like the magician thing. If everybody knew how to make a movie, if everybody knew how to make music, there wouldn't be any musicians or moviemakers.

(laughter)

CHARLES: There wouldn't be any music?

JERRY: I don't know. The thing I feel sometimes is the thing of being specialized. It could be like all wrong, I don't know.

CHARLES: Now, let me play that one again.

JERRY: Here it is.

CHARLES: That's so important, this one.

JERRY: I mean you can play it back again on the tape.

CHARLES: No, no, no. I remember. I want to go back to it. If everyone could play music . . .

JERRY: Yeah.

CHARLES: . . . there wouldn't be any reason to do it?

JERRY: That might be an error. No, no, I meant . . .

CHARLES: That's what you said.

JERRY: . . . there would be no reason for there to be a professional musician.

CHARLES: Now, I wouldn't like erase it from the tape because it's not the truth, but it's, it's the pursuit of a truth. It's not a truth yet.

JERRY: Right, that's right.

CHARLES: Because my belief is that each person's music would be different.

JERRY: Right, right, right, there you go.

CHARLES: And that it would just be an incredibly better world. And you'd only listen to a musician for the special thing he plays.

JERRY: Right.

CHARLES: Not for the fact he's a musician.

JERRY: Right, that's the way it is in the band.

CHARLES: But now people do it for both reasons. Now they say, "Wow, what a guitarist" you see, without listening to what you play or something like that.

JERRY: Uh huh.

CHARLES: Whereas if everyone was such a good guitarist they would listen mainly to your thoughts. And the more profound the consciousness becomes, the more we're all going to play music and all going to dig on things and the entertainer will disappear and we'll be like our own entertainers.

JERRY: Exactly, right, that's where it's at.

CHARLES: And everyone will just have friends that they specially dig.

JERRY: Right, well, that's the way it is with us.

CHARLES: That's far-out. That's incredible.

JERRY: That's the way it is in our scene. It's like we entertain ourselves, I mean what else is there except entertaining.

CHARLES: No, but what I'm trying to tell you is that I couldn't have this conversation that I'm having with you, with any other person that I know.

JERRY: Oh man, you know all the wrong people.

CHARLES: You're right, you're right.

JERRY: That's all I can say. *(laughter)*

CHARLES: I do. I know them *all*—that's another funny thing.

JERRY: That's incredible.

CHARLES: Like students of mine would think I was out of my fucking mind.

JERRY: Far out.

CHARLES: Yeah, it is far-out.

JERRY: Far out.

CHARLES: Yeah, it is far-out.

JERRY: Almost anybody you could stop on the street right around here, for example . . .

CHARLES: Can do this.

JERRY: Right. (laughter)

CHARLES: I just know the wrong people, that's all there is to it.

JERRY: Right, it's almost supernatural.

CHARLES: It's almost supernatural how I know all the wrong people.

JERRY: Yeah, or how you know so few people you can get it on with. I mean there's a lot of people who are . . . who are, well, you know . . . God, everybody I know just about.

CHARLES: Well, I think you're sort of in a specially good spot.

JERRY: That's why I'm here and that's why all those people are.

CHARLES: Yeah.

JERRY: But the energy here is very strange in terms of . . . it seems as though it's all very close.

CHARLES: Yeah.

JERRY: You know, I don't know what that means but it just seems like it's very close and it seems like you can't hardly do something without immediately knowing what its effects are. And it's like your actions have . . . there's a karma; the karma wheel is moving very fast, we're close to the center of it.

CHARLES: Right.

JERRY: It's spinning around real fast so that things *are*; I don't know why that is or why it seems that way or anything; it's just, it is.

CHARLES: Yeah. I just know so many people that you couldn't do anything like this with. I mean they couldn't begin with you, you know, not only could they not go anywhere.

JERRY: God, I know very few people like that, very few.

CHARLES: I tried to tell you about that last summer and you kept ... I said, "There were people with walls up" and you said, "It isn't happening to me."

JERRY: Right, that's right.

CHARLES: And, you know, well that's great if it isn't, but it is happening with so many other people, but maybe it's my fault for showing walls to people instead of those faces.

JERRY: That's true. The more energy you put into the game ...

CHARLES: Well, let's get that rule that you said, that like when you show faces, you get faces back.

JERRY: Yeah, and they're usually faces like the ones you show.

CHARLES: Yeah, that's like a profound rule.

JERRY: I think it's, well, it's, yeah, but it's not mine, you know what I mean, it's everywhere.

CHARLES: Yeah.

JERRY: It's everywhere, it's standard information. The thing, see, in my opinion all the information, the stuff that we're talking about is hard data.

CHARLES: Right, right.

JERRY: It's like facts.

CHARLES: Right.

JERRY: And it's all like so heavily documented but it's just like there's been ...

CHARLES: It's all hard scientific information.

JERRY: There you go, man, and you know it's just a matter of like making the source, the material, the source material available and understandable and puttin' it out as much as you can.

CHARLES: You said like we learned this in the scientific method.

JERRY: Right.

CHARLES: Somewhere in that interview. And that's like another thing that I have always understood, is that I've always known all these things and they were available and they're factual.

JERRY: Right.

CHARLES: And what's the matter with the damn people that deny them all the time?

JERRY: *(laughter)* Who are these people? We want their names.

CHARLES: Yeah, I mean I'll have to go back to them in the fall and . . .

JERRY: Well, see, you know them. I don't know them. If I knew those people I would talk to them, you know, I would do what I could, I mean.

CHARLES: You'd try to show them these places.

JERRY: I wouldn't try to, man, I would. I could do it. We could do it. The Grateful Dead can do it, man, *en masse.*

CHARLES: That's, oh, yeah, because you're such a group.

JERRY: We *can,* and also because there are people who are not afraid to do whatever kind of weird tricks are necessary, and it's nothing that anybody means to do, it just happens.

CHARLES: Right.

JERRY: Like we haven't rehearsed it or anything, it just happens, but we don't want to telegraph the punch. That's what I'm saying.

CHARLES: Yeah, I don't think I'd want to print exactly what tricks you do, because . . .

JERRY: Well, you know, that's up to you.

CHARLES: That would be, no, because of prudence.

JERRY: Right. There you go. Prudence. I like that one.

CHARLES: Look at my face.

JERRY: *(laughter)* There you go, very prudent.

CHARLES: Prudence, man.

JERRY: Extremely prudent. *(laughter)*

CHARLES: Right, if I only showed that face I'd never do anything, would I?

JERRY: Right, but you know . . .

CHARLES: But, I'm very . . .

JERRY: But it would be extremely prudent.

CHARLES: I could say to you, "Jerry, you could do it but it wouldn't be prudent."

JERRY: (*laughter*) I love it.

CHARLES: It's just as well to have that once in a while.

JERRY: It's handy.

CHARLES: It's handy.

JERRY: Well, all those things are, you know, that's flexibility; that stuff means that stuff is survival shit.

CHARLES: Shit, but it's survival kit.

JERRY: It's survival stuff, man.

CHARLES: It's your survival kit.

JERRY: That's it, that's it.

CHARLES: And another piece of survival kit. Oh, let's talk about survival kits for a minute.

JERRY: Sure.

CHARLES: Because these are really important things to talk about, now. I have a survival thing called overload.

JERRY: Uh huh.

CHARLES: And like if I get into too heavy a scene, I go on to overload.

JERRY: Overload, right.

CHARLES: Overload means—eeerrr—it won't work anymore and I've got to get out.

JERRY: It'll all go tilt.

CHARLES: Right. You're into that, aren't you?

JERRY: We in the pinball world call that tilt.

CHARLES: Right.

JERRY: But I very seldom hit it.

CHARLES: Yeah, that's really fine.

JERRY: I mean I've got a pretty high tilt tolerance.

CHARLES: That's pretty fine.

JERRY: But I have tilted.

CHARLES: Yeah.

JERRY: (*laughter*) Yes.

CHARLES: I'll accept that word tilt for that instead of overload, it's better.

JERRY: Overload is good, but it's the same thing.

CHARLES: A better word.

JERRY: Overload for those of an engineering bent, tilt for those on the street.

CHARLES: (*pointing to cat*) Now, I have a thing that's like what this cat has, namely a kind of innate sense of judgment or balance.

JERRY: Yeah.

CHARLES: About what you can do and what you can't do.

JERRY: Uh huh.

CHARLES: And that's like a funny, tippy gyroscope.

JERRY: Right, right right, absolutely.

CHARLES: Now, that one, I bet you I have to an unusual degree.

JERRY: What makes you think you have it to an unusual degree?

CHARLES: Because, ah, because I keep being a gyroscope for other people. That's like one of my functions.

JERRY: Other people use you for a gyroscope.

CHARLES: That's one of my functions in life, is helping people restore their center balance.

JERRY: Oh, dig it. I see, that's great.

CHARLES: I don't do it so well with myself. (*Jerry laughs*) You see, and I'm always doing that with people, with people and with students and with people and everything.

JERRY: That's a fantastic ability, man.

CHARLES: I think it's a good thing.

JERRY: Really. Really, I've run into a few people that have that ability.

CHARLES: It's like a thing like music, you can play and learn.

JERRY: That's right, that's right. It's a gift.

CHARLES: But it's like you should play it if you have it.

JERRY: Absolutely. You should play anything you've got.

CHARLES: Another thing that I know about you so completely is that you . . . it's so important that you play all the time because the things that you have to say any particular day you never have to say any other day and so they'd be lost.

JERRY: True.

CHARLES: And that's why you have to play a lot. *(Jerry laughs)* Because otherwise, like so much of what you play would never be said. But so much of what you said to yourself would never be said out loud.

JERRY: That's true. But is it all that important to say what you're saying to yourself out loud?

CHARLES: Hmmm?

JERRY: See, I doubt the value of what I'm doing a lot of times.

CHARLES: No, it's very important.

JERRY: So I go through changes.

CHARLES: No, no, but it's very important to say what you have to say *all* the time because it's important to communicate with other people.

JERRY: Yeah.

CHARLES: And it's important to help other people with their communication. And so like the greatest service that I could make in the world would be to constantly tell people . . .

JERRY: What's on your mind.

CHARLES: . . . where my head was going, yeah. As long as a lot was happening.

JERRY: Right.

CHARLES: But if I was just being boring, or in one place, or not saying anything I should shut up and stop making other people uptight and all that.

JERRY: Right. Of course they'll leave if it's too boring.

CHARLES: Yeah, that's probably right.

JERRY: There's the Doris Day rule working in there somewhere.

CHARLES: Yeah, they will leave and like they'll discourage you.

JERRY: Or fall asleep or something.

CHARLES: Or say shut up.

JERRY: Right.

CHARLES: Yeah, but like it is important to play a lot and you can judge whether you should be playing by whether anybody plays your records or listens to them.

JERRY: Yeah.

CHARLES: Now, you want an image to make you really see how this is. And I'll give you like three images. Image number one: balmy beautiful day in the Yale courtyard with all the kids' rooms around it. What they do on a day like that is everybody lies outside and takes in the sun and there's got to be some communal agreement about which kind of music is to come out of which kind of window, because, you know, like bedlam and the tower of Babel . . .

JERRY: Right. *(laughter)* Right.

CHARLES: And so somebody will put up two big speakers, like stereo speakers, outside, but there's got to be agreement.

If there was like cacophony it would be awful. So the image is that it's always the Grateful Dead.

JERRY: Whew! Too weird.

CHARLES: And that's what's so far out.

JERRY: Well, I humbly apologize to those people for my errors on those records.

CHARLES: No, I mean it's just so fine. It's like, and anyway did you know that in a certain part of their head, you're not the Grateful Dead but you're Uncle John's Band.

JERRY: Uh huh, sure.

CHARLES: Because . . .

JERRY: Yeah, a lot of people think that.

CHARLES: Well, let me tell you why. The Grateful Dead is like . . . stretch your mind, right. Sometimes I might be in a tight place and I don't want my mind stretched.

JERRY: Right.

CHARLES: Then I will listen to Uncle John's Band.

JERRY: *(laughter)* Right, I understand perfectly. There's the music you can live with—the music for Saturday, or Halloween, or whatever.

CHARLES: The second thing that is, like if people are in an incredibly good place on dope they want to play the Grateful Dead. The Grateful Dead is for being in a real . . . you know, it's the only music to play. Other things might take you off this. It's like when the place you're at is so good that nothing should be allowed to disturb it. That's when you play the Grateful Dead.

JERRY: Yeah, we'd like to play about that place too.

CHARLES: Yeah, and that's like a very high far-out good thing.

JERRY: Makes it. Definitely makes it.

CHARLES: Now the third image is only just me—I've given you one of the whole courtyard and so forth—and that is that when you play the song about opening windows. The name of it is "Box of Rain."

JERRY: Right.

CHARLES: Now, really dig on this. It's the song that I've used since it came out to accompany me when I didn't have any people in this whole exploration that we have been talking about.

JERRY: Uh huh.

CHARLES: In other words, it was my company.

JERRY: Oh. Too much. Good company, man, good company.

CHARLES: Yeah, it was like the thing that told me that somebody else believed it was so.

JERRY: Yeah, right, well Hunter will tell you.

CHARLES: And think about like having, being able to play music that people can use for company and things like that.

JERRY: Right. Right, and company in those places where, right.

CHARLES: Well, a good way to talk about music is like that it's company. Did you ever think about that?

JERRY: Yeah, always, because it's company for me for sure, all the time.

CHARLES: Yeah, it's company and like so . . .

JERRY: An accompaniment!

CHARLES: Yeah, but sometimes you're using it for one, and sometimes the other. Now if I want to sit down—and this is another me—I keep . . . like it's fun to tell about these me's. I've never told anybody about them. This is me in my *chair*, do you like him? (*Mountain Girl laughs. Jerry laughs.*) And I have a drink and I have a plate of maybe like olives and cheese, you know, and it's five o'clock and I don't know if you do this, but it's a good thing for a person to do. I'm in my *chair* with my drink and my hors d'oeuvres and like I have a newspaper, and it's me in my chair and for that I would only like want music to *accompany* me.

JERRY: Right.

CHARLES: Right. Alright, but then later, maybe it's late at night and it's a whole other person who's feeling like this, you know . . .

JERRY: Right.

CHARLES: Badly, you know, and in need, and then I might go downstairs for *company* and I might play the New Riders' "Portland Women."

JERRY: Ah, yeah, that's nice.

CHARLES: Because that's a song that is company.

JERRY: Yeah.

CHARLES: And you no longer have an accompaniment, but you would be saying, "That's a song about somebody else who needs somebody."

JERRY: Right.

CHARLES: And so it's company for me now.

JERRY: Right, right, I getcha, I getcha, I never thought about it that way before.

CHARLES: Alright, now . . .

JERRY: But I know exactly what you mean.

CHARLES: The thing is the Grateful Dead are company for an extraordinary number of important things that are happening to people today. That's the point. Not accompaniment, but they're like company during these changes.

JERRY: Right.

CHARLES: You play music that's the company for what's happening in me, which is also happening to many other people. But you don't play like company for a love affair . . .

JERRY: Right.

CHARLES: Somebody else plays that music.

JERRY: Right.

CHARLES: And it's company for that.

JERRY: Right.

CHARLES: I think Janis did to some degree, you know, heavy love affairs. But you play like company for very, very important places that are happening now.

JERRY: I've never realized, I mean I've never been aware of that, but I know that place from the other end of it because I've had that kind of company.

CHARLES: That's right, and like there were certain kinds like Chuck Berry.

JERRY: Right, he was some of my company.

CHARLES: You knew something of the truth from him.

JERRY: Yeah, man, right on. *(laughter. Jerry sings)* "Up in the morning and off to school."

MOUNTAIN GIRL: Yeah, right.

CHARLES: When he told you that, you knew that somebody else thought about school.

JERRY: I don't think Chuck Berry probably ever thought about it that way either.

CHARLES: Yeah, but you see I have to think about it. It's like my trip to think about it because so many people say, "It's just the music I dig," or, "It's just the music that's happening to me, that's why I want to listen." But my trip is, my whole reason for existing is that I can take a feeling that that kid has listening to you play, and I can put it into an idea, like the idea of company.

JERRY: And explain it to somebody.

CHARLES: Yes, and present it so that people can see the idea itself.

JERRY: I know, but is that . . .

CHARLES: And that's my gift.

JERRY: Doesn't it make you feel a little weird?

CHARLES: Yeah, very weird.

JERRY: It seems a little weird.

CHARLES: I think it's like really weird because it's like sorcery.

JERRY: Yeah, it's like transmutation or something.

CHARLES: Yes, you know who I am, is an alchemist.

JERRY: Yeah, right, Owsley's an alchemist too.

CHARLES: Okay, like with chemicals.

JERRY: I dig it.

CHARLES: And the point is like you don't need to know the idea of company when you listen to music.

JERRY: That's true, because I think that's the thing that a lot of people experience, most people, I guess.

CHARLES: Right, and you don't need to know it to play.

JERRY: That's true.

CHARLES: And so it's just my trip. That's what I do is I make pictures of ideas, you see.

JERRY: Far out, yeah, I do understand.

CHARLES: It's just a thing I manufacture.

JERRY: Right.

CHARLES: And the same way, like you may want to have like a thing hanging in the window, like a piece of stained glass, or you might want to have something manufactured, is my idea of company.

JERRY: Right. Gotcha.

CHARLES: And that's what I do for a living.

JERRY: *(laughter)* That's incredible. *(laughter)* That's fantastic. I love it.

CHARLES: But music . . .

JERRY: There's somebody else I know that does . . .

CHARLES: It's good for you to know, like that's what you do in music.

JERRY: Yah, I guess it is. Well, I don't know whether it is or not.

CHARLES: Sure it is.

JERRY: Because now I might be conscious of it.

CHARLES: Oh, you shouldn't be afraid of consciousness. That's the last thing to be afraid of.

MOUNTAIN GIRL: Yeah, not if it means you have to put up with millions of screaming fans.

CHARLES: Oooh! Oh, no, because he's not going to . . .

JERRY: I'm not going to appeal to millions of people.

CHARLES: Do you know why he isn't? Because he is not in the place where they're at and he can't play from that place. You can't play from the place they're at.

JERRY: That's true. I've never been able to. I've never had any million sellers.

CHARLES: Right, you see he never could, no matter what, he couldn't do it.

MOUNTAIN GIRL: Yeah, but the fans may catch up with him, you know, like they caught up with Bob Dylan.

CHARLES: But that's nothing you can do anything about, and then you'd have a lot of friends . . .

MOUNTAIN GIRL: Oh, man.

CHARLES: If everybody caught up with you.

JERRY: Yeah. Incomprehensible. It's a double-edged sword, suffice it to say.

CHARLES: Well, all I can tell you is like what we were talking about, you make a choice in your life.

JERRY: Yeah.

CHARLES: And I have totally chosen consciousness.

JERRY: Yeah, right.

CHARLES: I don't think it's a double-edged sword.

JERRY: Right, no, I don't mean consciousness. I'm talking about the other thing. I'm talking about the thing she's talking about, which is the more attention equals more, you know, whatever . . .

CHARLES: Yeah.

JERRY: That's the thing she's talking about, not consciousness, consciousness I'm all for, I'll put in my vote for consciousness as long as it doesn't come and get me.

MOUNTAIN GIRL: *(laughs)* Or your other half.

CHARLES: No, you had momentarily sort of been not so sure about the consciousness.

JERRY: Oh, yeah, right.

CHARLES: That I was putting you on.

JERRY: Right, right, right, right you are. And I was going to continue that but we got off into . . .

CHARLES: I was afraid you were going to say I was making you too conscious and . . .

JERRY: No, I would be more afraid of being made not conscious enough.

CHARLES: That's what I believe, I hoped you'd say that.

JERRY: Yeah, because that's, you know, that's the thing I'm afraid of. Because I know that it's dangerous to have not enough knowledge.

CHARLES: Right. But do you see where you had a momentary reaction, or you said maybe I shouldn't know this.

JERRY: That's right, right, strike me dead.

CHARLES: No, no, the lightning won't strike you dead. I have those moments. I constantly have these drawbacks too.

JERRY: Right. *(laughter)*

CHARLES: Holdbacks.

JERRY: Well, I think that a certain amount of them you should respect. I think there are some things you should pull back from, you know what I mean. I mean, I've had at least one or two experiences where I've been warned by something.

CHARLES: Yeah.

JERRY: To not go into certain areas of certain kinds of information, certain kinds of knowledge which . . . whether it happened or not isn't important but it happened in my head and I've learned to respect that.

CHARLES: And you've survived.

JERRY: Right, exactly, you know.

CHARLES: But my feeling is . . . see . . . (*slowly*) . . . here I am, me, like if you read that I had jumped off a cliff or been sentenced to prison or like, picked up, drunk on the street or any number of other things like that, I would like you two to know that it was because I stepped into some other place.

JERRY: Right, right.

CHARLES: And didn't have enough warning, or wanted to do it, anyway.

JERRY: Right.

CHARLES: And I'd like you two to totally recognize . . .

JERRY: Right, well you either made your move or you fucked up.

CHARLES: But whatever it is, you would know why I was there. It was just one more face.

JERRY: Yeah.

CHARLES: And you understand it as an effort to go one step further.

JERRY: Sure, sure. That's where . . . yeah.

CHARLES: What I'm trying to tell you is how incredibly important to me it is to think that some other people can understand that, because I get very paranoid as I keep trying to do this thing and then I shrink back in fear.

JERRY: Right, right, because you're afraid you're doing it all by yourself.

CHARLES: And I'll think no one will ever know why I did this.

JERRY: Boogieman in the dark.

CHARLES: No one will ever understand why I did this weird thing that I just did.

JERRY: Right.

CHARLES: And it's good to know that two people understand.

JERRY: Well, I think a good many more than two.

CHARLES: Well, I'll . . .

JERRY: I mean, I think there are probably a lot of people who understand perfectly.

CHARLES: But it's tricky, it's very tricky.

JERRY: Not if you telegraph your punches. Not if you say who you are, you know.

CHARLES: And say this isn't my trip, this whole thing?

JERRY: Or say this *is* my trip, you know, or that, you know what, I mean if you put it out, if you say what you mean and say who you are and all that stuff.

CHARLES: Then everybody knows it.

JERRY: Pretty much. I mean the kind of feedback that we get, the Grateful Dead gets, excluding the crazy percentage, is like pretty much like the way we are, you know what I mean.

CHARLES: Right.

JERRY: When we get letters it's as though they were from people who had known us for a long time.

CHARLES: Alright, now let me just get . . . here's where I just want to say it again to be sure I understand. If I were arrested robbing a record store or a supermarket, I should . . .

MOUNTAIN GIRL: I can't imagine . . . *(laughs)*

CHARLES: But Mountain Girl, now you're making me uptight.

JERRY: We will be shocked, outraged. *(laughs)*

CHARLES: Now you're freaking me out.

JERRY: Outraged.

MOUNTAIN GIRL: I'm afraid, Charles, it would have to be a case of mistaken identity.

CHARLES: Now you're really freaking me out. *(laughter)*

JERRY: Upstate New York.

CHARLES: You were going to say upper middle class.

JERRY: Same trip. Well, upstate New York.

CHARLES: Uptight middle class.

JERRY: I wasn't going to say that. You're putting words in my mouth.

CHARLES: Mountain Girl . . .

MOUNTAIN GIRL: Robbing a supermarket. Good heavens. *(Jerry laughs)*

CHARLES: No but, is it, does it mean that I'm really far-out? No, I don't think I'm . . .

MOUNTAIN GIRL: Yeah, right.

JERRY: What else could you possibly do?

CHARLES: Right, and I've done that. That's like how I live my life, and . . .

MOUNTAIN GIRL: Oh! Robbing supermarkets!

CHARLES: And if I have that reaction from you . . .

JERRY: What can you expect from those straight people?

CHARLES: Yeah, my God.

JERRY: She's straight.

MOUNTAIN GIRL: I'm straight, yeah, I'm real straight. *(laughs)*

CHARLES: No but, is it, does it mean that I'm really far-out? No, I don't think I'm . . .

MOUNTAIN GIRL: I don't know, you might be over the hill, senile. *(laughs)*

JERRY: Well, what do you mean by really far-out? Suppose we were to say to you, you're absolutely the weirdest person we've ever met. I mean, you know, so what?

CHARLES: So what? It's ridiculous.

JERRY: Well, as a matter of fact, well, it's not ridiculous, but I know people who are a lot weirder than you.

CHARLES: Right.

JERRY: And who are still communicating clearly.

CHARLES: Alright.

JERRY: So you've got a lot of margin.

CHARLES: Alright, so you're like reassuring.

JERRY: You've got a lot of margin, man, you've got a long way up. You can push it a lot farther.

CHARLES: Okay.

JERRY: Definitely.

CHARLES: But I can't . . .

JERRY: You're definitely not too weird.

CHARLES: But I've already shocked Mountain Girl.

MOUNTAIN GIRL: Oh, not really.

CHARLES: Alright. *(everyone laughs)*

JERRY: You've got to watch her, man, she doesn't mind lying to you, you know. *(laughs)*

CHARLES: Oh, I'm relieved. I thought, here I've done one timid move and I've gone beyond you already, oh, and that's like nowhere compared to where I could go, you see, already I've lost, that's very bad.

MOUNTAIN GIRL: It's just the image of you robbing a supermarket, holding up this guy.

JERRY: I could see you doing it.

MOUNTAIN GIRL: I think it'd be neat. I'd get a big laugh out of it.

CHARLES: Just, this—the heavy—inside of everybody.

JERRY: Sure, I've got my guns in the closet.

CHARLES: Anyway, the point is that when people react with disbelief, they tighten you up from making that next move.

JERRY: Right, but then somewhere along the line you've agreed to be tightened up, if they can do that to you.

CHARLES: I think that's right.

JERRY: If you create space around you enough, you can be awfully crazy. I've known a couple of people who were really far out, but they always had plenty of room. Cassady always had a lot of room and he was really pushing it, and Paul Foster, shit, you know.

CHARLES: Now let me ask you . . .

JERRY: You know, walking down the street with ice skates on is pretty far-out.

MOUNTAIN GIRL: Everywhere with ice skates on.

JERRY: And right, you know.

CHARLES: What I think is that, what you were going to say before is, if I said if they caught me robbing a supermarket and I said to the cameras, this is my trip, it would be alright.

JERRY: Sure.

CHARLES: The thing I shouldn't say is this is an awful mistake.

JERRY: It would be funny to boot, right?

CHARLES: Right, and so Muskie's fuck-up was that when he cried he didn't say this is my trip.

JERRY: Right.

CHARLES: Right?

JERRY: He didn't put it out.

CHARLES: And so he fucked it up and so everybody saw the lie.

JERRY: Right.

CHARLES: And that's why he fucked up.

JERRY: Right, the lie.

CHARLES: It's a good example of that.

JERRY: Right.

CHARLES: He should have said I'm a cry-baby.

JERRY: Television always shows the lie, yeah, right.

CHARLES: Wow, I'm a cry-baby and this is my trip.

MOUNTAIN GIRL: God, what a tough thing for a candidate to have to do.

CHARLES: Well, if . . .

JERRY: Nixon said it.

MOUNTAIN GIRL: He did, kinda, didn't he?

JERRY: He pulled it off with that Checkers trip, sure.

CHARLES: And then other people who like cry-babies would vote for him.

MOUNTAIN GIRL: Why did he cry? Because Checkers got run over or something?

JERRY: No, no, no, because he, because there was some doubt about campaign funds or something.

CHARLES: Hanky panky. Isn't that a great word?

JERRY: Hanky panky. Right, hanky panky with money. Some money trip, you know, some question as to where it came from or something and he was there explaining how Pat was wearing a cotton coat.

MOUNTAIN GIRL: Oh. God, I can't imagine that. You've gotta be kidding.

JERRY: It was a beautiful piece of political theatre.

CHARLES: Businessmen when they go out of town and want to show another face of theirs, they go down to like Broadway in San Francisco, places like that.

MOUNTAIN GIRL: Right.

CHARLES: Carol Doda, and all of that kind of thing and that's a hanky panky face, and there's music for it, Jerry, you know.

JERRY: Hanky panky music.

CHARLES: There's music for it and it's like nothing that appeals to me at all, but it's like real. It's a thing to go to see.

MOUNTAIN GIRL: It's going on down there all the time.

JERRY: The circus is in town.

CHARLES: Convention face, the people, most of those aren't real. Most of those are like put on roles. They don't count as real faces.

JERRY: Well, none of them. Not many of them are conscious unfortunately, that's the thing wrong with all that stuff.

CHARLES: Unconscious bad roles are things you should get rid of and go to your real good role.

JERRY: Right, go to your immediate self.

CHARLES: You said you were more or less rehearsed in the role of Jerry Garcia.

JERRY: Yeah, I've had a lot of experience in that role.

CHARLES: Right, but he is real.

JERRY: It's a pretty wide open role.

CHARLES: He's a face, he's not a role.

JERRY: Well, there's lots of shading in there.

CHARLES: Yeah.

JERRY: Because I play a lot in that, in that space.

CHARLES: But that's how I believe you got so much space for yourself.

JERRY: Yeah.

CHARLES: Now, my Charles Reich thing . . .

MOUNTAIN GIRL: Oh. Yeah.

CHARLES: . . . doesn't give me much space. *(pause)* You know that like in Marin County there must be more communication. They should install super-thick cables here to represent the degree of communication around here.

JERRY: Super-thick tables?

MOUNTAIN GIRL: Cables. Telephone cables.

JERRY: Cables, cables.

CHARLES: Yeah, because there's so much communication compared to other . . .

JERRY: There is a lot.

CHARLES: . . . parts of the world.

MOUNTAIN GIRL: We were thinking of getting short-wave radio at one time.

JERRY: Yeah, we wanted to set up our own communication system . . .

MOUNTAIN GIRL: I think we, we could still do it.

JERRY: Independent of Ma Bell, we could. Matthews is still thinking about it.

MOUNTAIN GIRL: It wouldn't be hard.

JERRY: Not too hard.

MOUNTAIN GIRL: Get them from Japan.

CHARLES: How would you key into the right people?

MOUNTAIN GIRL: We'd all have our own frequency.

JERRY: We all know each other.

CHARLES: Ah, and then you just wait for people . . .

JERRY: To say something. *(laughter)*

MOUNTAIN GIRL: You'd just . . .

JERRY: Hot flash! Blah blah.

MOUNTAIN GIRL: No, no. You see your radio could be activated by a coded signal, you know, just like a television.

CHARLES: Well, here's the thing . . .

MOUNTAIN GIRL: And it'll only come from our set.

CHARLES: Now see the frequency we're all on now, right.

MOUNTAIN GIRL: I was talking about the physical plane. I was talking about radios.

CHARLES: But I'm talking about like . . .

JERRY: Communication units?

CHARLES: Communication frequency, like, we're on a frequency.

JERRY: But it's a language one, I mean, outside from being basically a friendly vibes one as well.

CHARLES: It's a frequency on the same mental frequency. A very profound frequency, it's not only got to do with good vibes, or friendships, or those things.

JERRY: Well, around here we call this a stoned rap.

CHARLES: Yeah, but it's on a subject that we both understand.

JERRY: That's true, but I've had this rap with a lot of people.

CHARLES: I haven't, because the people I know . . .

JERRY: Ah, right.

CHARLES: Because even though they get stoned . . .

JERRY: That's what I got to keep remembering. I can't believe it. It's almost incomprehensible, you know what I mean?

CHARLES: The people that I get stoned with don't think this way even when they're stoned.

JERRY: God, what do they think about?

CHARLES: Very little, I mean like about these things, so that's why I get such a sense of recognition today, "Wow, there are other people like me," you know, "I'm not like, you know, dropped from another planet."

JERRY: Well, that's a possibility too, but there are probably more of us than you know.

CHARLES: Yeah!

JERRY: There used to be people going around saying there's 4,000 of us and there was others saying well, the Bible says that there's 40,000, and the other is like they're . . . I've heard a lot connected with this thing that you're talking about, in terms of finite numbers, it's . . . remember when those kind of people were talking that kind of talk?

MOUNTAIN GIRL: Kind of, yeah, distantly.

JERRY: Yeah, there was a time when all that kind of stuff was happening. It was like who was going to leave when the flying saucers landed and that kind of stuff. All of that somewhere back in there. These discussions were discussed in much greater detail than we're discussing them now but I've sort of lost touch with it, you know what I mean.

CHARLES: It didn't ever get to where it was ever put down.

JERRY: Well, that's right, and everybody went off into their trip.

CHARLES: Alright, but then you'll see another place with me . . .

JERRY: Everybody's gone off into their trips.

CHARLES: . . . where I'm a scribe.

JERRY: Uh huh, I see that face.

CHARLES: Dig it, I write down what is already known.

JERRY: Right.

CHARLES: But in writing it down, making like a parchment out of it, is not, I mean it's not a wholly plagiaristic art, I mean it's not, it is not like simply ripping off, is what I mean.

JERRY: No, no, no.

CHARLES: Because writing it down . . .

JERRY: There's a lot more of a craft to that.

CHARLES: When I think I'm unworthy, it's because I think that writing down what everybody else has thought is a minor, trivial activity.

JERRY: Uh huh.

CHARLES: That's when I think I'm unworthy.

JERRY: Right, I get yah.

CHARLES: But, I then try to think, but it is an art too, like you could play it in music—in other words, the writing it down is an art.

JERRY: Right, right.

CHARLES: But it's what I do again, is like write down all of the things that people have in their heads and if a lot of people did that it would be like overlap.

JERRY: Right, which would be good.

CHARLES: But, as a matter of fact . . .

JERRY: In a way.

CHARLES: . . . too few people do it.

JERRY: Right. That's probably more like it.

CHARLES: And it's the same as music.

JERRY: But not that many people read either.

CHARLES: No, people do read, some people.

JERRY: That's true.

MOUNTAIN GIRL: But not as many as . . .

JERRY: Right, as a form, it's definitely receding.

CHARLES: That's right, music is coming . . .

JERRY: Yeah, music is getting a lot of attention, but I think music is the one that always steps in because something happens to all the other forms or something or another. As time changes they go through some sort of cataclysm and bam, there's a new step and I think that music is like something that takes in those changes at time, you know what I mean. I don't think that music is a form that civilizations are built on, for example.

CHARLES: No, no no.

JERRY: But I think that it's one that . . .

CHARLES: And it's a very elemental . . .

JERRY: Right, that's the thing.

CHARLES: And sometimes civilizations have to be built on more than elements.

JERRY: Right, absolutely, but the elements have to be there as well.

CHARLES: Right. So, for instance, the written word is a thing you build civilizations on.

JERRY: But it's also one of the things that make civilizations fuck up.

CHARLES: When it gets frozen.

JERRY: Yeah, right.

CHARLES: It's like, so like what you hope to write about is the thing that has infinite meanings when people read it.

JERRY: Right, and that means it has to be, uh . . .

CHARLES: Therefore . . .

MOUNTAIN GIRL: Kind of like the *I Ching*.

JERRY: A friend of mine just did a translation of the four Gospels into movies, you know, a script, a shooting script, and it's got as much integrity as like the King James translation into definitive English.

CHARLES: That's incredible, that's unbelievable.

JERRY: Yeah, right, and it's like that is the kind of thing that's fantastically challenging.

CHARLES: And beautiful.

JERRY: Right, and it represents that translation into new forms of old but important thoughts, but that's like, that's the news in that world.

CHARLES: That's the news.

JERRY: That's the latest, that's the news I know about this guy who's like a real good friend of ours.

CHARLES: That's so incredible.

JERRY: It is, and man, it's, God, it's fantastic too, it's whewww!

CHARLES: It's really wonderful.

JERRY: Right. I mean it's really like scholarly, you know, in terms of his approach has been total. He's taken advantage of all of everything that's available concerning place and time and what's known about all those things, the whole thing, even parts of it are even dated.

CHARLES: Wow.

JERRY: The day and the date like when Christ was here and at this point what day it was, what day, what the date was.

CHARLES: Far out.

JERRY: I mean he's really like whewwww, what a job. It's really imposing and beautiful. And it's like waiting for somebody. Now it needs like a director to complete the translation.

CHARLES: I just totally dig that.

JERRY: Right, right, because you can see that starting to happen now with all thought.

CHARLES: Right.

JERRY: And it like becomes a greater and greater, you know, I mean, that blew my mind, that blew my mind just real hard.

CHARLES: Well, now . . .

JERRY: But that's that same thing you're talking about. I mean it's just a different form.

CHARLES: I want to try and blow your mind with another . . .

JERRY: Okay.

CHARLES: The idea simply is that the more the thing that you do is use a metaphor, the more truth you can get into a statement in any field. So for instance, if for a metaphor I used the idea of first going to Clement Street and then going to Berkeley . . .

JERRY: Right.

CHARLES: There's a lot of truth in that and a lot of people can dig on it and so forth. But suppose I say, instead of the truth, instead of the metaphor, suppose I use a very narrow kind of a phrase like "free elections in South Vietnam" and I leave out all the blood and the killing and all the things that are happening besides the free elections . . . then I use unmetaphorical language and I distort the truth and something bad might happen because of terrific limitation, squeezing it all into one idea.

JERRY: Gotcha.

CHARLES: There's nothing worse than a monomaniac, a person that has only a single idea.

JERRY: Right.

CHARLES: And so artists are like the enemies of monomania, because artists are always telling you more and more and more.

JERRY: Right.

CHARLES: And monomaniacs are people like politicians and lawyers who are always squeezing it and making it less and less and less. *(Jerry laughs)* And like all of civilization lie is fought between the squeezers and the people that are broadening the thing out.

JERRY: I wonder why?

CHARLES: Because if only you artists were around with your metaphors, there'd be no form, like the fish would have no backbone, there'd be nothing on which to hang it all.

JERRY: Right, gotcha. No firm reality in that way.

CHARLES: It needs some prudent prunes (*Jerry laughs*) to come in and squeeze some backbone rigidity. We need some rigid compulsive people to come along and take some of that and make it into something solid to hang on to.

JERRY: Uh huh.

CHARLES: But, it needs a proportion between the two, and what it must not have is like we have all squeezers now and hardly any artists.

JERRY: Right, right, right you are.

CHARLES: And so you're like at a moment in time when you're restoring art and restoring metaphor. But the primitive man, with all of his gods and his flowers and his animals and smells, he in a way needed more structure.

JERRY: Well, it turns out he probably didn't.

(*Pause. Both laugh*)

CHARLES: It turns out it was a fucking mistake.

JERRY: (*laughter*) Right. Too bad.

CHARLES: Too bad, but now wait a minute, let's just think a minute. Yes. That's right.

JERRY: Well, the thing is, the mistake has been made. It's not a question of whether it was a good mistake or a bad mistake, it's just been made and that's it.

CHARLES: But that's right, isn't it? That's just what happened.

JERRY: Sure, that's what happened, right, right, it's a big error. So now, what we need is more balance in the other direction because balances are continuous in the universe.

CHARLES: What an inconceivable mistake, I'm just thinking about it.

JERRY: Incredible. *(laughter)* It's a terrible bummer.

CHARLES: Man is open to everything, can you imagine, like he could smell as well as a dog or a cat.

JERRY: Right.

CHARLES: What a fuck-up.

JERRY: (*laughter*) Right, right, really unfortunate, yeah, bad news.

CHARLES: And like man could see a god in every tree and plant.

JERRY: Yup.

CHARLES: And now we can't and what did we get for it?

JERRY: A little more room.

CHARLES: A little more life, we live longer, we don't get eaten by diseases.

JERRY: Right, and we also have the capacity to get off this planet. But, see, there's two versions of us. There's man as earthling. There's man as consciousness in the universe. Now if man occupies a place of consciousness in the universe, we're supposed to eat this planet and evolution is supposed to squeeze us off it.

CHARLES: Well, what does it mean to you if you say that you're really religious or spiritual? Because we're right at the point where I think I become religious.

JERRY: It doesn't mean religious. Religious and spiritual don't mean anything to me, what means something to me is the fact that I know that I am in line with the atoms and universes game in this universe. That I'm not inconsistent with them.

CHARLES: Right. That's religion.

JERRY: Well, yeah.

CHARLES: It's a sense of a particle.

JERRY: That's it, or a whole. I don't see me as any different from you or the planet or the garbage or the pollution.

CHARLES: Right, alright. Well, the other things that is religious for me is like the blinding light of all these different truths.

JERRY: Right.

CHARLES: Like religion to me is just total truth.

JERRY: I can dig that.

CHARLES: It's everything that we could ever say if we talked for infinity.

JERRY: It's every lie we could ever tell.

CHARLES: Yes, and that's what religion is and that's why I can't relate to what they call religion.

JERRY: No, well, it's all messed up.

CHARLES: It's so fucked up.

JERRY: It's all weird, you know.

CHARLES: Like too narrow a metaphor. Total truth is total religion. If you know everything about the sea and everything about like air . . .

JERRY: Right.

CHARLES: . . . it's religion. So like a totally wise man would be a most religious man. But, you see, like in America they train you to be dumb. Well, I'll show why. Like suppose you're a vice-president and I'm a vice-president and we're trained to try to get to be president of the company. There's only going to be one of us president so I've got to deny that you're like me in order to fight my way against you to the top. Otherwise I might say, "If you are just like me it wouldn't make any difference."

JERRY: That competition would be okay provided you first spent three years in total silence and went through a long ritual where you cut off all your hair and you met the guy that you were going to compete with. And said, "We are going to enter this game officially," and it's going to be, "I'm going to win or you're going to win."

CHARLES: That's right. I can dig it.

JERRY: And if it was done with that kind of consciousness . . .

CHARLES: It would be far-out.

JERRY: Great, yeah, and if wars were fought that way and all things . . .

CHARLES: That would be a completely human experience.

JERRY: Heck, yeah, man, those things are okay. It's only being a victim, being a pawn or being an unconscious tool, you know, that's a drag. That's the impingement on freedom, the thing of not knowing that you can do it or not, you know, that's the thing, man. (*pause*)

CHARLES: You were talking about being a channel of energy and I see you do that and I do it too.

JERRY: Right.

CHARLES: I wondered how it works, like how does it happen?

JERRY: Ah . . .

CHARLES: It's what I do sometimes when I'm high.

JERRY: You know somebody that knows something and somebody comes to you who wants to know something and you say,
"Well, here's the connection you want to make." It's just that simple,
that's the most . . .

CHARLES: It's being a connector.

JERRY: Right. Just connect him and that's just the thing of communicating and getting down to it. I think that that's what the new
human is.

CHARLES: Is a communicator.

JERRY: Right. You know, people make connections and do it and
like in our scene it's kind of like regular, almost regular standard operating procedure. It's the thing that we do.

CHARLES: Well, this may sound like coming down from the cosmic to the ridiculous, but I've told you that I've clung to a little corner of the power structure world as a professor of law.

JERRY: Right, that's quite a large corner.

CHARLES: Now my goal in clinging there is to tell the lawyer that
he should be a communicator between what people feel are the limits
that they need and the law. Could you stand for a person to like stand
right here and scream at you all day? Terrible threats? No, at least
Mountain Girl couldn't stand it; you told me you didn't . . .

MOUNTAIN GIRL: I don't think anybody could stand it, not if you
could call the cops.

CHARLES: Right, now you communicate that to my hypothetical
lawyer, the communicator, then he makes a law that says that it's
against the law to stand there and scream at people who don't dig it.
And so laws become a reflection of peoples' real needs instead of
being total fuck-up laws.

JERRY: The Zorro hall of mirrors style of reflection.

CHARLES: And so my goal would be to maintain that niche there
until I could teach lawyers how to listen to what people really want
and what they don't want.

JERRY: Gotcha. Right, because lawyers should be able communi-
cators first.

CHARLES: But they like . . .

MOUNTAIN GIRL: Anybody want a peanut butter and jelly sandwich?

JERRY: No thanks, too dry.

CHARLES: Oh, but, but, I'm raising my hand, Mountain Girl, because . . .

JERRY: Here's one.

CHARLES: My hand is up because I'm like a kid in school when you ask me a question like that. Can you see it?

JERRY: He wants to be called on, he wants to be called on.

CHARLES: Right.

JERRY: You have to call on him.

CHARLES: I always like to be called on, because I want attention paid to me.

JERRY: Right, gotcha.

CHARLES: Especially.

JERRY: You don't want a peanut butter and jelly sandwich. Right. Can I have a cup of tea or something like that?

MOUNTAIN GIRL: Yes.

CHARLES: That would be good too.

JERRY: Delightful, delightful.

CHARLES: Isn't playing music a form of attention getting?

JERRY: Oh sure.

CHARLES: Sure, well then you dig it. It's like, but sometimes I just do it like this.

JERRY: Right, that's a good way to do it. I do it that way too sometimes: *Me, me. (laughter)*

CHARLES: See, if you see one of these ugly hideous things happening in this country and that is, let's say a person is sent to jail for something that we all know he should be doing . . .

JERRY: Right, well, Owsley is still doing time.

CHARLES: Yeah, that wouldn't happen in a country where there was better communication.

JERRY: No, it shouldn't, right, right you are, right you are.

CHARLES: Dig? That's what I've been trying to talk about.

JERRY: In any hip country, for example, they would have Owsley up there in the environmental control thing thinking up ways. He's too brilliant to lock up. He's a natural resource.

CHARLES: Yeah, they wouldn't have these people in jail.

JERRY: And it's stupid. They wouldn't be hounding him. *(The cat jumps on the table, almost upsetting the tea cups)*

CHARLES: I'm just protecting this book.

MOUNTAIN GIRL: Come on, Scratch, get down. Here's the honey, Honey.

JERRY: The cat has a right to that book.

MOUNTAIN GIRL: He's so dirty.

CHARLES: Oh, well, I didn't think the tea . . .

JERRY: There you go.

CHARLES: . . . would be good for it.

JERRY: Well, whatever.

CHARLES: Didn't you see Mr. Prudence there for a minute.

JERRY: Right. *(laughter)* Oh my, look out.

CHARLES: Well, it's good for the book to be that prudent.

JERRY: Right, but you know . . .

CHARLES: Hmmm, it's really good tea.

MOUNTAIN GIRL: Quit hogging the honey spoon.

JERRY: I'm playing with it, I'm playing with it. What's this green thing on the honey spoon?

MOUNTAIN GIRL: It's probably a piece of jasmine leaf.

JERRY: Oh, too much. It's a lot like an onion.

CHARLES: I've focused my mind on this peanut butter and jelly.

MOUNTAIN GIRL: Oh, oh, I thought it was all a joke.

CHARLES: Well, I was afraid . . .

MOUNTAIN GIRL: I'll run in there and make it in just a second.

CHARLES: We almost had a communications breakdown.

JERRY: Well, you have to be able to discern the difference between a joke and something serious.

CHARLES: Yeah, I can't always do that because I'm so solemn and serious.

JERRY: Well, our scene is pretty jokey.

MOUNTAIN GIRL: Now wait a minute, you have to know . . . you mustn't care so much whether it's a joke or not.

JERRY: Right, that's true.

MOUNTAIN GIRL: You know, if in doubt, take it as a joke.

JERRY: Right.

CHARLES: Yeah, that's a different scene than I'm used to. *(Mountain Girl laughs)*

JERRY: Right. I can't imagine it, you know, because man, it's like, God, I don't know, you ought to hang around in our scene sometime if you, you know, it's pretty hilarious. There's a lot of joking.

MOUNTAIN GIRL: There's a lot of jokesters.

JERRY: Right.

CHARLES: Can you imagine how serious like faculty members . . .

JERRY: Hey, man, I couldn't live in a world, I mean, I left that world because it was that serious and it was too serious. And that was back in high school, you know, it was too serious for me then.

MOUNTAIN GIRL: I can't imagine being a teacher, man, it would be the dullest, uuuh! Hate it, sittin' in some room all day talking to a bunch of idiots. You could be home reading books.

JERRY: That's not being a teacher, that's not teaching.

MOUNTAIN GIRL: Shit, yeah, the fuck it isn't. Who don't want to be there in the first place.

CHARLES: Well, if that's what you're doing, you shouldn't be a teacher.

MOUNTAIN GIRL: Right, and I'd never be a fucking teacher. Oh, school.

CHARLES: I'm going to try to justify being a teacher.

MOUNTAIN GIRL: Well then, you're going to have to do something for changing the schools, man.

JERRY: You just have to be a super-good teacher. You have to be able to be a teacher in spite of the bullshit.

CHARLES: I think that when I can really get it on, which isn't all the time, that I can like . . .

JERRY: Nobody always plays perfect sets.

CHARLES: They certainly don't.

JERRY: Nobody.

CHARLES: I think I can be cosmic and I can open up cosmicness in the kids' minds.

JERRY: Out of sight, man. Then you should be a teacher.

CHARLES: But I can't do it all the time or every day or . . .

JERRY: Nobody bats a thousand, you know.

CHARLES: But like there was a woman teacher that you spoke of that like did that with you.

JERRY: Yeah, a couple . . . I had a good string of teachers. I was lucky and you know those counted, those counted because they gave me an education, you that, that really, that made it.

(Peanut butter and jelly sandwich arrives)

CHARLES: Thank you. See, that's when it wouldn't be dull to be a teacher if you have it . . .

MOUNTAIN GIRL: Right, yeah but, I was thinking in terms of elementary . . .

JERRY: But it's all percentages because when you're a teacher and you deal with whatever, thirty or forty random people, or fifty or sixty or seventy, or however many you have to deal with, it's like percentages are not always in your favor. Because I remember that those teachers were into really like jumping on anybody who was bright in a sense of that they were hungry too, the good teachers were hungry for bright kids.

CHARLES: Yeah.

JERRY: And it depended on what was happening because not all the kids could dig it, and I mean a couple of those teachers even got into trouble, in terms of, they got too, I mean it got too advanced or whatever for somebody and they went home and complained to Ma, you know, and it all came down.

MOUNTAIN GIRL: The teachers I had always got into trouble for indecent exposure and molesting and . . .

CHARLES: I would do all those things . . .

MOUNTAIN GIRL: Being drunk in class and stuff.

CHARLES: I would do that at Yale if I could get away with it.

JERRY: What would you do?

CHARLES: Indecent exposure. *(Mountain Girl laughs)* You see, I mean that would be a totally real part of me, *(Mountain Girl laughs)* but my protective devices are up. I won't do it. But like, you see, like I'm constantly being thwarted.

JERRY: Thwarted. *(laughter)*

CHARLES: Thwarted, isn't that a great word.

JERRY: I've always liked that one, that's a good one. Goes well with the whole Oil Can Harry trip.

MOUNTAIN GIRL: I wonder what the etymology of that word is?

JERRY: Thwarted?

MOUNTAIN GIRL: Yeah.

JERRY: I don't know, but it sure is nice.

MOUNTAIN GIRL: Thwart is part of a canoe, isn't it?

CHARLES: Not the same kind of thwart.

JERRY: It's a different kind of thwart. I don't think that thwarted . . . I think that thwarted came before thwart in a canoe. "Thwart" is a peculiar word, to say the least . . . "thwart."

MOUNTAIN GIRL: It must be some kind of weird Norse word.

JERRY: Saxon-anglo, something like that.

CHARLES: What a struggle it is to close it down, is what I would have said.

MOUNTAIN GIRL: It is a struggle to close it down, but then once it's closed . . .

CHARLES: Yeah, once the lid is closed . . .

MOUNTAIN GIRL: Or closing or almost closed . . .

CHARLES: Isn't that a horrible thing that that's what you do with a kid.

JERRY: Hah, it's not horrible, nah.

CHARLES: You don't do that.

JERRY: Sure I do, but it's not horrible.

CHARLES: Well, you have this whole unprotected little kid . . .

MOUNTAIN GIRL: Well, that's what they are.

CHARLES: And you build up all these walls around him.

MOUNTAIN GIRL: Walls?

CHARLES: I mean you tell it no, don't, mustn't.

MOUNTAIN GIRL: Only when it's a matter of life and limb.

CHARLES: And look out and watch out. And that's what I was told when I grew up. I mean like you have to dig this incredible idea because you didn't have it happen to you, maybe but . . .

JERRY: There's even weirder ones, you know.

CHARLES: I'd be like in a car with the family. We'd be going out for a drive and the whole trip would be them telling me stay away from the door, don't fall out the window, don't crawl over the seat, don't make too much noise, don't hit your brother, don't, don't, you know, stay away from that door. In other words, that's what they worked on all that time was all those don't things.

JERRY: Right, but that was just overprotectiveness.

CHARLES: Yeah.

JERRY: You know what I mean, and it's like . . . what can I say about it?

CHARLES: Well, you become overprotective of yourself as a result.

JERRY: Maybe, I don't know, I mean, I don't know. I don't think that I was overprotected myself, particularly so, I can't really tell. I don't have that kind of perspective.

CHARLES: No, I'm telling you about a different experience that happened to me than happened to you.

JERRY: Uh huh.

CHARLES: A profoundly different one that is like . . .

JERRY: Right.

CHARLES: That is like, that represents maybe the biggest difference between us as people and you're even more that way.

MOUNTAIN GIRL: I'm even more what way? Different?

CHARLES: Yeah.

MOUNTAIN GIRL: That's probably because I'm a girl.

CHARLES: No, you don't have that figure over you saying no.

MOUNTAIN GIRL: How do you know?

CHARLES: Isn't that right?

JERRY: No, I say no to her all the time.

CHARLES: Oh.

MOUNTAIN GIRL: Sure.

CHARLES: No, but it isn't over, you didn't put it over yourself.

MOUNTAIN GIRL: Did I?

CHARLES: No.

MOUNTAIN GIRL: I'm not sure.

JERRY: Did your brothers tell you no a lot?

MOUNTAIN GIRL: No, they just, they just split, that's all, you know.

JERRY: Right.

MOUNTAIN GIRL: No.

CHARLES: I'm trying to say the difference between a person who has the no inside of them like me.

JERRY: Oh, right, well it's obvious that you overreact to it.

CHARLES: Yeah, right.

JERRY: Right, because, yeah right, I see that, yeah, I can dig it. I can dig it. Well, what you need to do is to be able to go and freak freely for a year or so.

CHARLES: Right, but I can't do it.

JERRY: Lose it completely. Yeah, I've seen that happen. I've run into a couple of people who I've seen make a transition from a totally straight thing to, and usually it's characterized in fact by a year or so of off the wall, total craziness.

CHARLES: Hm, hmmm. Right.

JERRY: Right. Just because it's, you know, it's that thing, free at last, you know.

CHARLES: Right, free from . . .

MOUNTAIN GIRL: Rah, Rah.

CHARLES: It's hard . . .

JERRY: I guess it must be, yeah.

MOUNTAIN GIRL: I don't know, I don't see why it has to be. It's only hard if you're hung up about it.

JERRY: Well, that's what he's talking about.

MOUNTAIN GIRL: Stuck in all those little places. Yeah, I know.

JERRY: It seems really weird from the outside though, because, just looking around, you can't tell any difference from one person to another.

CHARLES: No, but . . .

JERRY: And I don't see any walls.

CHARLES: Well, when it gets to where more people see these things than not, then comes my political image.

JERRY: Dum da dum.

CHARLES: There's this huge balance, like this, and there's two hundred million people on it, like, you know.

JERRY: The political world game.

CHARLES: Right, and it's all this way. This is like Nixon's whole world and the cops and jails and everything like that, you know. It's just all up there. They're up and this side is down.

JERRY: Right.

CHARLES: Then one day, one 87-pound weakling freak will walk across this balance.

JERRY: And the whole thing will tilt. Of course, yeah, but it will be weird, I mean the way I see it, we can't get high unless they continue on that miserable bummer. We're a reaction to it. Our highness is the polarity.

CHARLES: Wow.

JERRY: I like riding on it, you know, so as weird as it gets over there is as high as we'll get, and it's kind of like that thing of getting the thrust. Because it's a balance thing, man.

CHARLES: Why is it? I don't understand that.

JERRY: It's just the thing going through its changes, it's the wheel making its turns, it's the pendulum swinging, you know, it's the universe . . . it's a ripple in the universe, it's like . . .

MOUNTAIN GIRL: Right.

JERRY: It's cycles, the *I Ching*, you know.

CHARLES: Why, why couldn't . . . you're saying like everybody couldn't be high.

JERRY: Ah, yeah, I don't think so, I don't think all at the same time unless say persons are miserable all at the same time.

CHARLES: Oh.

JERRY: But I think things have to get worse before they get better, blah, blah, blah. I'm of that school of thought, you know, the one where one side balances out another, one way or another, and you don't ever enjoy total equilibrium, because total equilibrium means stand still, man.

CHARLES: Nowhere.

JERRY: And stand still means die.

CHARLES: So you think that like we're getting so high off the incredible, unbelievable bad things like crisis and . . .

JERRY: Incidentally, no, no, I don't think of it as that direct but . . .

CHARLES: Bad consciousness.

JERRY: I think that those things are kicking consciousness forward. Even so, I think that one extreme necessitates the other. If you have extremes over here, you have extremes over here. I mean that's the way it looks, because it never used to be, I mean, you remember in the Fifties when things were kind of in the center. And I think that there's a scale that goes probably that long, however long that is. The Second World War represented, man, it's swinging over this way. And in the Fifties it's in the middle somewhere.

CHARLES: Yeah.

JERRY: Sixties, swinging over this way. Yeah, you know, you know what I mean, it's, you know what I mean. And it has its counter-spin inside it and all that stuff, you know. I see it as very complex but, physically, it's operating in unison with the universe.

CHARLES: Well then, what a person should do is develop some extremes in themself.

JERRY: And the ability to be able to balance themselves internally that way, because that's how you keep your momentum, man.

CHARLES: So, I'll work on both my prudence and my weirdness.

JERRY: Sure, sure, keep them both running.

CHARLES: Each one getting more extreme.

JERRY: Right, right, exactly, so that you can balance one out with the other.

CHARLES: And like I'll work on my feeding the birds old gentlemen. At the same time like working on some far-out thing, you see.

MOUNTAIN GIRL: Or, right, that's right, that's what you should do.

CHARLES: Keep on expanding them.

JERRY: Why not? Right.

CHARLES: Wow.

JERRY: Because it's the distance of the travel that counts.

CHARLES: It's the distance that's so incredible. *(Jerry laughs)*

CHARLES: The distance that describes how much of you there is.

JERRY: Right, that's how much space there is. That's your, those are your boundaries.

CHARLES: So that's like making space.

JERRY: Yeah, that's making space. That's "a" way to make space, yeah, that's "a" way. Well, that's alchemy, see. Have you ever read that? Do we have that book around here? Is that around here anywhere anymore?

MOUNTAIN GIRL: Somebody must have borrowed it.

CHARLES: Alchemy is what I'm talking about.

JERRY: Right. The twelve principles of information that's the whole basis of alchemy and one of the things is polarity. There's another that's "as above, so below." So like what's happening here is happening in the universe. Polarity means you go this way, you're going to come back this way. There's gender, that's another one of the principles.

CHARLES: I didn't think about the fact that I was doing that, but like that's . . . when you go from the Mark Hopkins in the same day, you know, let's say . . .

JERRY: When you go from Yale Law School to San Francisco.

CHARLES: Yeah, I'm doing that but I'm like really working hard on it more than most people.

JERRY: Right, right.

CHARLES: I'm keeping each world.

JERRY: You're into it.

CHARLES: And I'm appreciating the waves of it.

JERRY: Out of sight.

CHARLES: And that's like amazing, you know, like you can swing back and forth.

MOUNTAIN GIRL: You know, well, law schools are worth saving, all that stuff.

JERRY: All the good stuff, all of it is actually potentially certainly useable. It's only misconceptions in the human mind, because a tool is just a tool. Shit, a system is just, it's just, I mean, it's . . .

CHARLES: That's why I believe 100% in technology.

JERRY: So do I now, because you don't have a choice. I mean it's too late to object to it, right.

CHARLES: Because every tool has some use if you can use it in a good way.

JERRY: Sure, well, this one . . . it's a matter of necessity. Technology and all these things, expanded consciousness, all that shit, man, if those things weren't happening, there would be no hope. If this was still a Fifties state of mind, at the rate of consumption and growth and all that, man, forget it, man, because two decades wouldn't be enough to be able to pull it together and it's going to be close as it is, if everything works out.

CHARLES: That's right. I'm not so sure. Well . . .

JERRY: Oh, yeah.

CHARLES: I think it'll work out.

JERRY: One way or another, man, whether it works out or not, it's all perfectly cool.

CHARLES: It's very interesting.

JERRY: Right. *(laughter)*

CHARLES: That's the word I use.

JERRY: Very interesting.

CHARLES: Fun to watch.

JERRY: Fantastic, man.

CHARLES: Like I read the *New York Times* every day, and I know that that is completely unreal, but it doesn't matter, it's reality to some people that I enjoy getting into.

JERRY: Right, some people really are into it.

CHARLES: I like the idea that I can read that in the same day that I listen to some far-out music.

JERRY: There you go.

CHARLES: I read the one with the like *New York Times* look, the financial page, yeah.

JERRY: Too much. *(laughter)* The financial page.

MOUNTAIN GIRL: Right.

JERRY: Stocks.

MOUNTAIN GIRL: You know it's what, it's the little comments. They have these little articles in here about who's doing what, you know, what companies are going out of business and why.

JERRY: Right. That kind of . . .

MOUNTAIN GIRL: Who fired who.

JERRY: Big shake-up and . . .

CHARLES: Shake-up. Can you think of that? You have to think of it stoned. The boss comes along and he takes all these guys and their desks and it's just like, you know . . .

JERRY: Shakes them up like a can of beans.

CHARLES: Yeah, it's unconstructive, you know. It's not like good music to . . . I walk around the financial district in San Francisco and try and keep my mouth the same way that people's mouths are down there. Really, it tires your muscles to do it.

MOUNTAIN GIRL: Yeah, tight. Right, those are weirdos. The sterile peril.

JERRY: The sterile peril!

MOUNTAIN GIRL: That's what Herb Caen called it.

CHARLES: Isn't that amazing? He's stoned to say that.

JERRY: Yeah, Herb Caen's alright, by God, he's alright.

MOUNTAIN GIRL: Tremendous capacity and turns that shit out every day.

JERRY: Yeah man, he's good, he's really good, and I've been reading him ever since I was a kid, because I've lived here all my life and he's been in columns ever since, you know, I can remember.

MOUNTAIN GIRL: Far out.

JERRY: And he's been always right close to it, you know what I mean, he's never been late, you know, or anything. When the beatnik thing and all that stuff was happening, *(finger snap)* he was right on it, man, he was right on all that shit. Yeah, he's always been pretty good, alright.

CHARLES: It's a high consciousness city, did you ever think of that?

JERRY: That's it, it's the geographical location.

CHARLES: It's the geographical location.

JERRY: It really definitely is.

CHARLES: You go to other places and your consciousness stands still.

JERRY: That was another thing that they were saying there a few years back that they're saying now in India or Tibet. The guy from Tibet says that the Bay Area, right around here, is where the spiritual vortex is. There were a lot of stories in that connection.

CHARLES: But it's like living on a mountain instead of living in a valley.

JERRY: Yeah.

CHARLES: It's only recently that I've come into this spiritual thing, that we're all the same.

JERRY: Right.

CHARLES: That's like a new world for me.

JERRY: Right, I can dig that. Well, you've got to get into the questions of who is it, that's the thing, that's the thing they say. Who is it that's looking out of your eyes, or who is your you, or what's, where does the basic viewpoint come from, you know, and my feeling is that everybody is kind of like tapped into a consciousness, or consciousness is a situation and it occurs somewhere in time and that we represent the physical manifestation of it, and that time is one of the co-ordinates.

CHARLES: But there is a consciousness there.

JERRY: That's true, but I think that we're all it.

CHARLES: But each person is a different creature.

JERRY: A different creature, obviously.

CHARLES: Yeah.

JERRY: A different buzzard.

CHARLES: Well, coming back to Yale in the fall, *(Jerry laughs)* I'd like to be the person that I am.

JERRY: Well, aren't you?

CHARLES: No, that's my goal.

JERRY: Oh.

CHARLES: I mean it would be like a great triumph.

JERRY: They won't be ready for it.

CHARLES: Well, I mean I'd go further than you'd imagine.

JERRY: Too much. Be sure and get somebody to get it on film.

CHARLES: Wooow, wooow.

JERRY: It's going to be incredible. That should be good. I'll be anxious to hear what the reactions are like.

CHARLES: Sometimes I think I can't do it.

JERRY: Yeah right.

CHARLES: But there are days when I think it's possible.

JERRY: It's definitely possible, man, I know people who have done it. But also it can be a burn-your-bridges trip, too.

CHARLES: Yeah.

JERRY: It depends on how extremely you want to do it. I know people who go around operating with just a touch of weird . . . inserting it here and there, you know what I mean. Right, just enough to keep themselves amused, and then there are the other people who, like, used it that one time and went in there and *(laughs)* totally laid it out.

CHARLES: That was it.

JERRY: Nobody ever saw them again.

MOUNTAIN GIRL: They wouldn't let them in again.

CHARLES: Wow.

JERRY: I mean, it depends on how you want to play it.

CHARLES: That's pretty amazing.

JERRY: Well, look at Tim Leary, he's an example.

CHARLES: Yeah.

JERRY: A guy who was in a scene similar to yours in a way.

CHARLES: He went too far.

JERRY: He definitely burnt his bridges.

CHARLES: He went . . . did you get the letter from him? It was a nice thing he said about the interview.

JERRY: Yeah, it's laying around here somewhere.

CHARLES: Yeah, I got a copy from some copying machine. It made me very happy because I had no real hopes that I could get on a level that he could dig.

JERRY: Really? Tim Leary is just another guy, man, he's just hung up.

CHARLES: Really?

JERRY: Oh sure, man, he's just like anybody, man, he's just, you know.

MOUNTAIN GIRL: He has a lot of identity crisis.

JERRY: Everybody does. Everybody does and he's like an old-timer and he had it done to him too, that Catholic thing and all that shit. That's one of the reasons he reacted so extremely.

CHARLES: Yeah, to get out of that.

JERRY: Yeah, right. Otherwise he would have been more temperate.

CHARLES: Yeah, I feel that need for extremes too.

JERRY: Well, then you can get an idea of where it could lead for you.

CHARLES: Yeah.

JERRY: It depends on how far you want to take it.

CHARLES: Yeah.

JERRY: But see now the thing is he did it with dope, which was definitely sticking your neck out, and you don't necessarily have to have that in the sense that you don't have to go in there and turn everybody on to dope, and that doesn't necessarily have to be your identification either.

CHARLES: But he went through something at Harvard when I knew he was going to get fired and everything. That was really something I could dig, I could understand that whole thing he was up to.

JERRY: I can imagine.

CHARLES: And maybe for him it was the time to do it.

JERRY: Oh certainly, certainly.

CHARLES: Like, you shouldn't feel sorry.

JERRY: Right.

CHARLES: If he'd stayed there and not done this . . .

JERRY: Oh, I don't feel sorry, I think it's great.

CHARLES: Hm, hmmm.

JERRY: I mean, he's gone from being like a faculty member at Harvard to like a world hero. In some circles, and what the hell, and right, yeah, it's a pretty far-out figure for him. It's groovy. I think it's great.

MOUNTAIN GIRL: Well he had to do a lot of hiding out.

JERRY: But that's all adventure, man, you know, a life of adventure. Shit, you know that's alright, that isn't bad.

CHARLES: That's our adventure side. Our homey side gets to be upset about that.

MOUNTAIN GIRL: Right, poor guy.

JERRY: Oh, he's had it both ways. He probably had like thirty or forty years of standard stuff. He probably got good and tired of it. What the hell.

CHARLES: Oh, sure, forty years of that is enough for a life-time.

JERRY: Sure, right, sure.

CHARLES: It's another of those things about stepping back to your . . . or you know, he must have said he could live in Switzerland.

JERRY: Yeah, sure, I mean, you . . .

CHARLES: If it comes to that, Tim said, "I could live in Switzerland."

JERRY: Right, right. "I could live on the run." *(laughter)* Too much. I'm out of smokes.

MOUNTAIN GIRL: Oh, *no*, what are you going to do?

JERRY: And all I had were these fucking Kool filters.

MOUNTAIN GIRL: Oh shit. How'd you get, how come you, what were they, all out of the other kind of cigarettes down there?

JERRY: Yeah.

MOUNTAIN GIRL: You're kidding, Garcia. You want me to go get you some smokes?

JERRY: Shooore!

CHARLES: Down to town?

MOUNTAIN GIRL: Yeah.

CHARLES: Maybe Mountain Girl can drive, but I don't know . . . I should be put to sleep eventually, for an hour on the couch or something.

JERRY: Any time you feel like falling out, feel free to do so.

CHARLES: Then I'll wake up and drive away. I fell asleep the first time I was out here, remember?

JERRY: Yeah, it happens to me a lot.

CHARLES: And Jann went driving off.

JERRY: He's more used to it, probably.

CHARLES: Probably.

JERRY: And he's also got the kind of car that sort of takes care of you, you know what I mean. You can sort of nod and disappear and it'll drive pretty nicely. Cars, oil, money, help help.

CHARLES: I don't know why you say that.

JERRY: Well, I mean, you know, I don't but I do. Because I can look out here and see it. Get brown out here. And that's the ocean side with the westerly wind and everything and I mean it's . . . the fact is that no matter how high I am and no matter how good I feel or anything like that, that stuff is all real and it's really happening and I feel like . . . that was part of the thing about feeling like committed in the sense . . . or that part of the thing of saying, okay, I'll do it is the thing of that. I think that the stuff we're talking about is the only way.

CHARLES: The only way.

JERRY: Really. And that I'm committed in the sense that yeah, I feel that life is what's happening so I want to do what I can on the life side of the whole life-death cycle.

CHARLES: And this is your best way of doing it and that's what you mean by committed.

JERRY: Right, right.

CHARLES: And that's the same with me. I've absolutely, I've chosen that's what I'm going to do with my life.

JERRY: Right. Normally I would never make that commitment. In a normal lifetime, I don't think I would do it, but I think this time is special. I think this time is dire.

CHARLES: Well, I would do it in any lifetime, because I think it's also the best way to be alive, because the most . . . what I see in other people is that they sink back into doing nothing when they're not very alive, so I don't see any conflict.

JERRY: Oh, right, right. Well, I do, because I resent having to use what I could use for tripping out, you know, to work on stuff, you know what I mean.

CHARLES: I don't think that tripping out . . .

JERRY: I mean that's my artistic freedom resentment.

CHARLES: Yeah, but . . .

JERRY: It's not real. I feel it's an infringement. Because I'd like to be free to be able to say, "Well, fuck it all man, I'm going to blow my brains out" and step outside and do it. You know, that kind of freedom.

CHARLES: Yeah.

JERRY: And I feel that, now that I've made the commitment, I've done it. The only reason I've done it is because I really feel that if everybody doesn't get on it, it ain't going to happen, man, and that's going to be the end of life here. And I figure, what the hell. But, basically, I'm not that moral. And like I say, cause it was only two months ago and also none of this stuff is news, and all along I've been thinking, well, it's cool with me whether it lasts or not lasts. It's cool with me for life or death, either one is okay. And basically that's how I feel emotionally, but I've made my pitch, I've put my stand in for the life side of the cycle, that's the thing. Which I think, in my opinion is overbalancing it a little on that side, but I think that it's overbalanced on the other side; it's another reaction.

CHARLES: What would you do if you didn't do it?

JERRY: Well, nothing, because I wouldn't be able, I wouldn't be ... I don't believe that I would be ... don't believe that I would be going through this lifetime if I wasn't supposed to do it.

CHARLES: No, so you'd be doing nothing.

JERRY: Right.

CHARLES: But I just consider nothing to be the intake part.

JERRY: Right, right, exactly, and I would go in that direction. That's why I say the streets of Bombay and a mountainside in Tibet.

CHARLES: You must not have more output than intake or you won't keep on.

JERRY: That's true.

CHARLES: And so, that's something I've tried to cycle myself into.

JERRY: Pace!

CHARLES: Well, enough sitting and just being out in the green.

JERRY: Right, right.

CHARLES: To take in enough to put out the energy.

JERRY: Right.

CHARLES: And for years I was going on what I call battery power, using up energy, my own energy.

JERRY: Right, right.

CHARLES: But it gets to a point where you need to plug in to the cosmos.

JERRY: I can't imagine running on my own energy. I don't have any energy, you know what I mean.

CHARLES: Yeah, well that's another profound thing that we could say for a minute is that most guys—young lawyers or businessmen—run on battery power in the sense that they have this fantastic store-up of ambition and motivation and all this shit.

JERRY: Right.

CHARLES: To get good grades, and they'll run on that until they run down.

JERRY: Succeed—goals and energy.

CHARLES: They succeed and succeed and succeed and then they die.

JERRY: Right.

CHARLES: And they can't let go, they can't. They've got to either keep on—it's called an escalator—they either have to keep on going up or they're off.

JERRY: Right.

CHARLES: But the other energy . . .

JERRY: Or else they keep going up and *then* they're off. *(laughs)*

CHARLES: Right, because it comes up and then boom.

JERRY: I mean, right, that's it, I mean that's the nature of that energy.

CHARLES: Right.

JERRY: Yeah, I've seen that energy. I know that energy real well.

CHARLES: Then one day they jump down an elevator shaft.

JERRY: Yeah right.

CHARLES: And that's the end of them. And divine energy or cosmic energy, which is the source that you're hooked into . . .

JERRY: Right, it's not enervating.

CHARLES: It's just like getting high and playing music.

JERRY: That's right.

CHARLES: Well, the thing that I'm into is the switchover that I'm making of one to the other and that's sort of what has me totally involved now.

JERRY: Of course, because that's the nature of it.

CHARLES: Pulling a switch.

JERRY: You plug in, man, and you're totally involved.

CHARLES: Right.

JERRY: Instantaneously and totally.

CHARLES: And that's what's happening in this country now is people are . . .

JERRY: Plugging in.

CHARLES: And you see, like it's ecology that's at stake, because people are plugged into the cosmos, they won't destroy everything.

JERRY: Right, exactly, like I mean they'll begin to see the beginning and the end of it.

CHARLES: That's right.

JERRY: If you can see that, if you can see the cycle, you can perceive where you are in it and so on and so forth.

CHARLES: Stop.

JERRY: Right. Well, not stop, but you can alter the course. Or you can, you know, the rapids are just ahead, the big rocks, the dragons, the end of the world, whatever, you know, there it is.

CHARLES: So it's people's inability to perceive where they are in the cycle that leads to all this crap like dumping stuff in the river.

JERRY: Right, and that's been because of the policy of obscuring ancient information, like each succeeding new civilization has done.

CHARLES: If I throw a paper cup in the river, it's because I just can't think about anything before or since.

JERRY: Right, right, right.

CHARLES: It's like low consciousness.

JERRY: Right, exactly.

CHARLES: I have a test of consciousness that goes like this. If you're driving along and there are twelve cars behind you on that road, you're unconscious of the twelve cars. That's one kind of consciousness, or else you think it's a game.

JERRY: Right.

CHARLES: And then several people are types that think it's a game and they're just going to show everybody how they can fuck 'em. You know, and they say, "If you want to pass me," you know, "you can, you know, pass me." You know, and the other people are unconscious.

JERRY: Right, right.

CHARLES: And like super-consciousness would say that you'd never want to be keeping anybody behind you from going the way they wanted to go.

JERRY: Yeah, right.

CHARLES: And you would have to never let that situation arise.

JERRY: Right, right.

CHARLES: Well, that's like my little picture of growing consciousness.

JERRY: That's great. I like it, it's good, it's good, real good, real good. It's one that's easy to understand.

CHARLES: Yeah, it's like, that's what I want to sort of try to put out, is simple easy things.

JERRY: That's beautiful, that's beautiful. That really, I mean it's really, yeah, like the obvious one, like you know, if you were super-conscious, you would either be going right, you wouldn't have any twelve people behind you, you wouldn't be in that situation.

CHARLES: No, you could not have it.

JERRY: You would either be pulling over and letting them go or something, right.

CHARLES: You couldn't have it because you'd like sense each one of their own feelings . . .

JERRY: Right.

CHARLES: . . . and you couldn't stand it.

JERRY: Well, you sense the "you" in their position.

CHARLES: Yeah, and you want to remove the "you" from . . .

JERRY: Right, right, or like you know what it's like to be behind a guy, so you don't want to be keeping anybody behind you.

CHARLES: No, it's really simple. And so you can just see all the degrees of learning.

JERRY: Right, right, right, right.

CHARLES: And young kids, like in a van, will always pull over, always.

JERRY: Right.

CHARLES: Always. And like then there's the question, do you give them a toot to say thanks, or . . .

JERRY: Arm out the window.

CHARLES: Or do you like do nothing because you think it's your due.

JERRY: It's a whole complex thing. That's part of highway chess.

CHARLES: The real gamesmanship is the bad consciousness, where they say are you man enough to pass me? If you're not, stay back there. And that's like this manhood thing, like a curvy road and they're saying, well, if you're not man enough to pass me on this road, then stay behind me. That's the macho of driving.

JERRY: Oh, right, macho driving. Right. But usually you can tell by the car, in California you can.

CHARLES: And the people in it?

JERRY: Well, the kind of car. You can tell by the like brand of car how it's set up. Usually the macho cars have big wheels and weird suspension.

CHARLES: Oh, oh, I want to tell you about the righteous driver.

JERRY: Ah.

CHARLES: The righteous driver says, I'm going at the right rate of speed and . . .

JERRY: Oh, right, right, right.

CHARLES: And if you want to go fast you're immoral.

JERRY: That's the lawabiding driver, right.

CHARLES: But you see what I mean, if your urge is to pass him, you ought to stay behind him because it's immoral.

JERRY: Right.

CHARLES: It's more than law-abiding, it's self-righteous.

JERRY: Well, then at what point is it when you're going way too fast for the thing that's happening. See there's the thing.

CHARLES: And there's still people behind you?

JERRY: No, not still people behind you, but you're causing them to pull off the road at a greater speed than they might normally want to do.

CHARLES: You're bearing down.

JERRY: Right.

CHARLES: Woow. Let me think about that.

JERRY: Yeah, because that's a position that I find myself in a lot, and that's like that's one of the ones, the thing where you have to soft-pedal your own trip, your own energy. That's the thing about being able to show the faces that you're talking about, it's another version of it. Suppose you want to go as fast as you could possibly fucking go. You want to get into your car and floor it. 120 miles per hour.

CHARLES: I do that to a lot to people and they don't like it.

JERRY: Right.

CHARLES: Wooow.

JERRY: See, so that's your limit, man; I mean, there is a limit, there are limits. And if you're in a position of leading, where you play yourself leading now and again, the only way you can lead is to have, is to be able to know where it is that people are willing to be led to.

CHARLES: Right, and there's like oh, pushing people is like not respecting them.

JERRY: Bad news. Right.

CHARLES: It's a lack of respect.

JERRY: Right. But at the same time at what point does it become, is it personal freedom versus personal freedom? There comes a time in there where some decision has to be made concerning the value of one person's personal freedom over another's.

CHARLES: Right, and there's another time when you know that you can lead and that it's being asked of you.

JERRY: Right, right, right, right.

CHARLES: And that's like sometimes that happens to me and I know that somebody wants me to lead them to the next place and it's a very delicate thing to know that and not read it into your own life.

JERRY: That's true.

CHARLES: Got to know the truth.

JERRY: Well, that's one of the things about functioning in a group again, where you have that kind of balance where like in our group everybody is a leader at one time or another.

CHARLES: Yeah.

JERRY: It depends on what the situation is.

CHARLES: So you know a lot about it.

JERRY: Exactly, right. It depends on what the situation is because each person has a talent and in a completely organic fluid situation, the right guy will do it when it's time to do it.

CHARLES: But how do you like have a business made up like . . .

JERRY: We're doing that too, we're trying to do it, we're trying trying to solve these problems.

CHARLES: But how can a business be done with people like that?

JERRY: We don't know yet, we're trying to find out, we're seeing if it can be done.

CHARLES: But is it like, do you have a boss?

JERRY: No.

CHARLES: A man at a desk.

JERRY: We have guys in charge of various trips.

CHARLES: Yeah.

JERRY: Yeah, we do have people at desks.

CHARLES: Do you have board meetings?

JERRY: You'll have to come down and look.

CHARLES: I'm going to come down and look. Do you have like a room with chairs that everybody sits in?

JERRY: Yeah, right, we all get together.

CHARLES: Far out.

JERRY: Smoke dope and rap.

CHARLES: Yeah, well that's a business.

JERRY: We do exactly everything that businesses do, every single thing, we pay our taxes.

CHARLES: You do, and you have like accounts and things.

JERRY: We do all that shit, the whole thing.

CHARLES: Incredible.

JERRY: Yeah, you've got to come down and see it because what we've got, you know, this could be a working model for the new businesses.

CHARLES: It's incredible, incredible.

JERRY: Because everybody stays stoned at the time too.

CHARLES: But how do they do these business things, like . . .

JERRY: With a lot of love.

CHARLES: Why not, no, right, it sounds like it's perfectly possible, now that I think of it.

JERRY: Yeah.

CHARLES: And how do you deal with straight people, I guess that's . . .

JERRY: We just deal with them.

CHARLES: With love.

JERRY: We deal with them on their terms; we are good at what we do; our books are good; all the stuff is good, and they can respect that, dig, so as soon as there is a basis for mutual respect.

CHARLES: Right, it doesn't matter that they're not on your trip.

JERRY: Right. Because it's possible for us to go over to their trip, easy, no problem.

CHARLES: In other words, you always maintain the freedom to move onto somebody else's trip for the necessary . . .

JERRY: Sure, in fact that's one of the things that we pride ourselves on the ability to do. To be able to move into somebody else's space and work out in it. You know, that's why the trip to Europe is going to be such a gas.

CHARLES: Far out.

JERRY: You know . . .

(Mountain Girl returns with cigarettes, and sunflower seeds in a long strip of small packages)

CHARLES: Ooooooh.

MOUNTAIN GIRL: That's how they're packaging sunflower seeds now.

JERRY: Far out.

CHARLES: Oh.

MOUNTAIN GIRL: That's nice.

CHARLES: Look at that.

MOUNTAIN GIRL: I really like that. Much better than candy but it's that attractive trip going for it.

JERRY: Give me some of them seeds.

(Charles wears the long strip like a chancellor's necklace)

CHARLES: This, I want to show you what this is. It's like the gleaming, and then here it's like the chancellor's . . .

JERRY: The pope.

MOUNTAIN GIRL: Give one to Annabel, I'm sure she'd like one. Come on, Pope.

CHARLES: Annabel, here. That's one for over there.

MOUNTAIN GIRL: *(to Annabel)* Open it yourself with your little teeth. That's right, there you got 'em, whoops. Put them up on the table, there you are.

CHARLES: We've been pretty stoned, haven't we?

MOUNTAIN GIRL: Hm hmmm. I think so.

CHARLES: Far out.

(Jerry pokes the fire)

MOUNTAIN GIRL: The fire . . . dark days even the fire don't burn good.

CHARLES: I love days like this, absolutely love days.

MOUNTAIN GIRL: Like being under water, or being in an aquarium.

CHARLES: I like a day that you don't have to respond to.

(Jerry and Mountain Girl discuss some mail concerning Babbs)

JERRY: Ha, ha. Beautiful. Far out. New journalism. These guys here are working on the new journalism. Babbs.

CHARLES: Babbs?

JERRY: And they're doing a paper up there and now Babbs has always got a notebook and he's always doing lay-outs and he's got photographs and he's always cutting and pasting.

CHARLES: A newspaper?

JERRY: Yeah, and what they're doing is the whole thing as it's going on, you know. They're putting it together as things are happening. Then they become part, yeah well, it's . . .

CHARLES: Oh, you mean they almost are in the paper.

JERRY: Well, yeah, but I mean I can't possibly explain it. *(laughs)*

CHARLES: No, I don't understand it.

MOUNTAIN GIRL: Does he have one of those cameras to take pictures?

JERRY: Yeah, he has a graphic, like a press, old time press camera, you know, a big old graphic with the accordion thing and the big light.

MOUNTAIN GIRL: Far out.

JERRY: It's beautiful, man.

CHARLES: Don't you sort of mean that they're *making* it happen, besides reporting.

MOUNTAIN GIRL: He does, but that's part of his fantasy.

JERRY: Oh, yeah, I mean they're doing it all at once so like you're sitting there talking with him; for example, he'll be writing bits and pieces of what's going on.

CHARLES: In other words, he's like making the news.

MOUNTAIN GIRL: Yeah, Babbs is amazing, boy.

JERRY: Right. *(laughter)* Right, it's great, man, it's great.

CHARLES: Well, that makes sense, doesn't it?

JERRY: Total.

MOUNTAIN GIRL: It does make sense.

JERRY: Total sense, total sense. And it's like bringing in all the elements of performance and music and all these other improvisational aspects and things from all kinds of things and doing it, you know, applying it all to a newspaper. Fantastic, man, just unbelievable.

CHARLES: Of course, that's what any newspaper does, is make up the news.

JERRY: Right, right.

CHARLES: I mean, what do you think is going on, with like Hubert Humphrey. They're making up the news.

JERRY: Once again they're doing it unconsciously.

MOUNTAIN GIRL: Oh, Hubert Humphrey.

JERRY: They're doing it because they're buying it, you know. They buy it.

MOUNTAIN GIRL: He's so square.

JERRY: All those guys, man, all the guys.

MOUNTAIN GIRL: He'll never get it together. If only old Shirley Chisholm would get it, then there'd be some hope.

JERRY: Shirley Chisholm is the most . . .

MOUNTAIN GIRL: Dynamic.

JERRY: The most straight ahead, out front . . .

MOUNTAIN GIRL: She's the only one with any energy.

JERRY: She's the only one with a good rap.

CHARLES: She really does have some good raps.

JERRY: She has a great rap. There's no bullshit at all in it, man. She doesn't do any of that political bullshit, you know, she just says straight forward. She's good but, you know . . .

CHARLES: She is good. Well, maybe she won't make it.

JERRY: No, but it's groovy to see that she's getting some coverage and stuff.

MOUNTAIN GIRL: She is.

JERRY: She's around. She's making a showing.

CHARLES: She makes some black people uncomfortable too.

JERRY: I know.

CHARLES: That's one of the signs of how far-out she is.

JERRY: That's great, right, that's great.

CHARLES: *(eating sunflower seeds)* These are very amazing.

MOUNTAIN GIRL: I like 'em.

ANNABEL: I like 'em.

CHARLES: You don't have a whole dimension of really loving all weird kinds of food, do you?

JERRY: Who me? I don't really care about food.

CHARLES: I noticed that.

JERRY: I'm not really into my physical self very much at all, you know.

CHARLES: It's all into music.

JERRY: Some day I'll pay for it. Yeah right.

MOUNTAIN GIRL: And raps and talking. *(laughs)*

JERRY: Yeah right and all that kind of stuff.

CHARLES: Well, that's interesting because like I have a whole side like Chinese cooking and Bulgarian cooking and everything; that's a whole side of sensuality that doesn't get expressed in any way but taste.

JERRY: Yeah.

CHARLES: And I must be like more balanced that way and much less musical sense, you see. In other words, there must be some balance of these different senses.

JERRY: Let's see, I don't know, I don't know. There's something I once saw in a hallucination of mine *(laughter)* about I don't know, see, the only thing I know is personal images. And my personal images are kind of like, the place where I'm the place where my mind's eye centralizes from, say, the ethos out of which it appears, is like someplace that's like outer space and it's like a planetoid and it's cold, but it's going extremely fast and it's kind of like the wind of space and there's infinite emptiness around it, but the kind of emptiness that you experience in that, you know, space, 360 degree stars and galaxies and shit, that's like . . .

CHARLES: Wooow.

JERRY: Okay, now the place . . . during that particular hallucination there was kind of like an evolutionary or a cycle running thing and that was one cycle and that was the cycle now, the cycle that I'm in now, say, and one of the other cycles was a place where it was really warm, and close, which is like that ethos, and there was another one that was like extremely metallic, with a lot of pointed edges.

CHARLES: Well, I can recognize all those three in your music.

JERRY: Right, and it's the associations developing from each one was like music was from the space one, sensory input was from the flesh place, kind of like warm, that thing, you know, womb thing almost, and there was, and spirituality was from the sharp place, it was like very brittle, you know what I . . .

CHARLES: Crystalline.

JERRY: It was that kind of a . . . right, crystalline, and it was those kind of constructs. See, now those were personal images, I suppose, but they were things that I experienced as truths.

CHARLES: Right.

JERRY: So, you know, whether or not those have anything to do with anything, but they're archetypes that I've experienced.

CHARLES: So your music is space. I've always known that.

JERRY: Yeah.

CHARLES: I've always known that.

JERRY: And other things are there, too. Ah ah, I can't really go into it.

CHARLES: But space is tremendously important.

JERRY: Right, right.

CHARLES: Yeah.

JERRY: Right.

CHARLES: And it's like other people might be able to visit those spaces once, a few times in a lifetime only, but like you can get there like evening after evening.

JERRY: I can remember it. I know it, yeah I mean, I know it, right.

CHARLES: You're like a space traveller.

JERRY: In a way, right. And I'm essentially singing space songs.

CHARLES: Right, that's what I've always known.

JERRY: The space blues.

CHARLES: Space blues. Space man with a space uniform.

JERRY: Tattered . . . ruined.

CHARLES: Yeah and the Grateful Dead . . . You said, "We're a bunch of space travellers who have temporarily crashed on this planet."

JERRY: Yes, I did. Take me to your . . .

CHARLES: . . . leader. We landed on this planet.

JERRY: We crashed on this planet, unable to leave, we had to stick it out.

CHARLES: That's really great. Then this space thing has like all got to do with fire and wind and rain and . . .

MOUNTAIN GIRL: No, no, aaaah, God, look at all that honey in one teeny little half a cup of tea.

JERRY: That was just, that wasn't even a full . . . oh well, heck, so what.

CHARLES: I'd like a few more of those . . . one more little baggy, baggy, baggy, baggy. That's a whole . . . that'll change people's heads when they think in terms of baggies.

MOUNTAIN GIRL: Look at Annabel.

JERRY: I beg your pardon.

CHARLES: Well, that's how technology changes consciousness.

JERRY: Oh, I'm sorry.

CHARLES: When you realize there could be hundreds and hundreds of little baggies around in your life.

JERRY: I never thought of it before. Right, right.

CHARLES: It changes your mind. Like evolution is being forced on you by the increase in baggies. I just mean all the shapes that you see and things that you see make your mind go.

JERRY: Right. The more things you see, the more things you have in your mind. The more things you have in your mind, the more there is for the random input to manifest itself in weird thought.

CHARLES: Right, right.

JERRY: I once called . . . me and Matthews were down in L.A. not too long ago and we were mastering a single of mine and we were in the airport's little coffee shop there, and we were about to order something and the waitress came bustling over in the middle of doing about three things and she was sort of taking our order, you know. We gave her our order and then some confusion, or something happened and she picked up one of the things that Matthews ordered without him ever saying it. He didn't say it, but she heard it, and she heard it because everything else was happening too, and it left, I could see the little hole, and I could see it rush in.

MOUNTAIN GIRL: "One chocolate shake."

JERRY: Right, right, just like that.

CHARLES: That's so unbelievable.

JERRY: I remember then how many times there's those things you know when you're distracted and that instant, it's like a voice or something, like you hear a thing. I mean, I know the thing is uncovering those abilities, and that stuff; it's all . . . I don't know.

MOUNTAIN GIRL: Far out. So she brought it to him without him ever having said it?

JERRY: She said it, right there, she said it and wrote it down.

MOUNTAIN GIRL: Far out.

JERRY: Just like that. And it was a chocolate shake.

MOUNTAIN GIRL: You're kidding, far out. (*laughter*) There you go, man.

JERRY: You could ask him. The next time you see him, ask him.

MOUNTAIN GIRL: I guessed it. Too much.

CHARLES: That is too much, that's incredible.

JERRY: It was a combination of effects, but it was interesting the way it happened, because . . .

MOUNTAIN GIRL: Now, there's no way that I could have known it was a chocolate shake, because I've never been eating out with Matthews.

JERRY: Except I was thinking chocolate shake.

MOUNTAIN GIRL: Right, which makes it easy for me to pick up.

JERRY: But it was interesting the way it happened. Real interesting.

CHARLES: Those things happen between a person and in nature, the same kind of thing.

JERRY: Right.

CHARLES: Nature will send you whatever you make room for kind of. You make a space in yourself the size of a flower and it'll send you . . . you know . . . there's a lot of things in this view out the window that I'm closed off to seeing that I could see if I were a hawk or whatever.

JERRY: Right.

CHARLES: That a biologist could see. And like dope makes you see many more things than you can see normally.

JERRY: For sure. Exposes you to different levels of seeing.

CHARLES: See, the Grateful Dead are like people looking at you from these different albums who are willing to join into anything that you try to do about the cosmos.

JERRY: Right, right, they'd be willing to go along.

CHARLES: And when I look at somebody else's face . . . (to Annabel) What?

MOUNTAIN GIRL: Talk to him, he's closest.

CHARLES: What would you like? Well, I can't guess what you'd like. You'll have to tell me. Do you want me to . . . you know what I'm doing? I'm pretending I can't understand you because you're not using a word. Now, she wants these.

JERRY: She wants more nuts.

CHARLES: I knew it.

JERRY: There you go.

CHARLES: I'm not as dumb as I act. (laughter) I always act dumber than I was.

JERRY: Really?

CHARLES: Yeah, man.

MOUNTAIN GIRL: Far out. Well, that's weird. That's a weird one.

CHARLES: Because they said people would hate me if they knew how smart I was.

JERRY: You're kidding.

CHARLES: No, this is true.

JERRY: That's amazing.

CHARLES: They said that most people in the world are very jealous and envious people.

MOUNTAIN GIRL: That must have been in the Forties and stuff like that.

CHARLES: Right.

MOUNTAIN GIRL: Right, when the whole Hitler trip was going down.

CHARLES: So they said always . . . yeah, Hitler was . . .

MOUNTAIN GIRL: Hitler and communism.

CHARLES: Yeah, and so my father said like always keep it a secret how smart you are, Charles, because people will hate you and so I've always kept it a secret in little ways and in big ways. And now it's been letting out a little, but it's like more and I think it's like just saying don't use your art. Like me telling you not to play music because people would hate you.

JERRY: Boy, that's horrible.

CHARLES: Yeah, but that's how scared people used to be.

JERRY: Well it's horrible for several reasons. It's horrible for making you think that you're smart and it's horrible for making you think that you should hide it.

MOUNTAIN GIRL: *(to Annabel)* Why did you have to dump that?

CHARLES: You don't mean making you think you're smart, it's making you think you're better or superior.

JERRY: Better, right, right, exactly.

CHARLES: That was their trip. Better and superior are part of the trip.

JERRY: Right, I guess so. That's interesting.

CHARLES: Well, that's what they do in the army, isn't it? They say we're all going to act even dumber than we are.

JERRY: Right, right, right, oh for sure.

CHARLES: And so that's the trip in the army is to never tell anybody you're smart.

JERRY: Right, never be smart.

CHARLES: If somebody says, do this drill, you should say, well, that's ridiculous, you know. *(laughter)* That's being a smart alec.

MOUNTAIN GIRL: Right. Drills, man, how lucky we are to have escaped forced drilling all the way through school, man, all that marching . . . carrying arms and learning how to shoot, all that kind of stuff.

CHARLES: Kill, kill, kill.

JERRY: Right.

CHARLES: There was a really cosmic stoned column by Art Hoppe, and he said, "Today I have eight hundred million friends and yesterday I had eight hundred million enemies and I'm mad because look what they were able to do to my head for twenty years and can they do it again, probably yes." It's a really amazing thing that he said that.

ANNABEL: Doggie? Doggie? *(pause)*

CHARLES: Okay, time for me to say that lots and lots and lots of people know what the Grateful Dead are doing and dig it and that's like just a little piece of communication to you from me.

JERRY: Right, that's nice.

CHARLES: A lot of people know just what you're up to. And dig it and it's important to them and . . .

JERRY: Groovy.

CHARLES: And you have like people that are close to you on that level that can never ever speak to you in real life.

JERRY: That's too bad.

CHARLES: Well, it's part of the way it has to be.

JERRY: Right, but it's okay. Right, it's okay.

CHARLES: I'll tell you one person who's Danny Peters and he's like a guy who is in Canada with his wife, but he's so incredibly American, you know, like high school basketball player and just the whole American trip and there he is far away. And he understands the Grateful Dead at a physical level, a level beyond any level that I could ever understand. He knows how to walk so that you're trucking, you know what I mean. *(Jerry laughs)* And stuff like that. But the point is like you're among his most important friends that he has.

JERRY: Far out.

CHARLES: You know?

JERRY: Yeah, I do know.

CHARLES: Like I'm a friend of his too, but I'm maybe less important than the Dead are to him and less constant and everything else and so it's like a profound thing to be able to say that, but it's like he can put on the Dead when he needs you in many different ways so that . . . just think about that, when you wonder about your worth that like you have people who consider you a really important friend.

JERRY: Right.

CHARLES: But there is some music that is like your friend.

JERRY: Right, I know that music, I've got music that's my friend.

CHARLES: Well, believe me, the Beatles have been everybody's friend.

JERRY: For sure.

CHARLES: Yeah, and that's just the difference, that's what people don't understand, between tin pan alley and this new music.

JERRY: Right, music that's your friend. That's fantastic.

CHARLES: It's so fantastic if you realize how fantastic friendship is; that is, it shares your moods and your downs and ups and everything. What an incredible thing. So these five friends, you see, have been there through all of the changes, people have lived through up and down.

JERRY: That's nice.

CHARLES: It is nice.

JERRY: That's real nice.

CHARLES: Just about nobody else has been there. Parents haven't been there, teachers haven't been there, you know, one of the good things about the Grateful Dead was that they came at a time when people didn't have other sources of friendship.

JERRY: Right.

CHARLES: The principal of the school couldn't be your friend, you know.

JERRY: Not really.

CHARLES: Or your minister or priest.

JERRY: "I'd like to be your friend, Jimmy."

CHARLES: Yeah, yeah, you've got the tone right. "Just tell me who supplied you with that LSD, I'm your friend." *(Jerry laughs)* You haven't been watching like, not "Search for Tomorrow," but . . .

JERRY: "Search for Tomorrow."

MOUNTAIN GIRL: No, we never watch that.

JERRY: "Life with Father."

CHARLES: No, I've got to tell you the right name not the wrong one.

MOUNTAIN GIRL: "Outer Limits"?

CHARLES: No, no, it's just before "The Guiding Light."

JERRY: "A Brighter Day"?

CHARLES: No, it's the one with waves crashing.

JERRY: "As the World Turns"? Hey, where did the dog go?

CHARLES: "The Secret Storm." A girl took LSD and a boy-friend gave it to her and for months now every adult has schemed to get her to betray the name of the boy that gave her the LSD. They all say, "I'm your friend now," but she hasn't told yet.

JERRY: I wonder if she'll cop out. Eventually she'll tell somebody.

CHARLES: This one lady keeps saying, "I'm only trying to help him. We'll help him. If we know who it is, we'll help him."

JERRY: "I'm only trying to help." *(Pause. Annabel talking)* Bob's album is almost done. It's beautiful.

CHARLES: What kind of music does he play?

JERRY: Well, he's written a lot of songs with his friend, John Marlow, and it's just real pretty and some of it's rock and roll and the whole band plays and everything.

CHARLES: He seems to have a lot of energy.

JERRY: Yeah, yeah, he's getting real good. You know, he's, his record is good.

MOUNTAIN GIRL: Jesus, I've got to get you to try on this shirt so I know if I can make some more the same size.

JERRY: Okay.

CHARLES: You know that shirt is so amazing, that's a completely Grateful Dead shirt.

JERRY: This is Florence's shirt. Florence made this.

MOUNTAIN GIRL: No.

JERRY: This is one of Rosey's shirts.

MOUNTAIN GIRL: Nope.

JERRY: Want to bet?

MOUNTAIN GIRL: I bought it. I know where I got it.

JERRY: Where did you get it?

MOUNTAIN GIRL: I got it at Tam Junction.

JERRY: It looks just like Rosey's shirt.

CHARLES: At Tam Junction, did you say?

MOUNTAIN GIRL: I saw it hanging out and I just thought . . .

CHARLES: Is there a place called Tam Junction?

MOUNTAIN GIRL: Tam Junction, yeah, here.

CHARLES: Because I want a shirt like that, that's for sure.

MOUNTAIN GIRL: I haven't got all the threads pulled, but it's finished. Does it fit?

JERRY: It doesn't not fit.

MOUNTAIN GIRL: I need to redo the sleeves.

JERRY: They're funny.

MOUNTAIN GIRL: They're too long. Don't they feel like they're too long?

JERRY: No.

MOUNTAIN GIRL: They don't?

JERRY: Not really. Up here they do, but down here they don't. The inner seam is the right way, but this here is . . .

MOUNTAIN GIRL: I could take some of that out.

CHARLES: How's the back?

JERRY: How's the back look?

MOUNTAIN GIRL: It looks okay, yeah, looks okay. Looks fine. Out of sight.

CHARLES: It's country western.

JERRY: Right.

MOUNTAIN GIRL: Right, I had to master that whole technique. It hasn't been ironed yet.

JERRY: It seems okay. It's nice. They feel a little weird, the cuffs do, something right in here.

MOUNTAIN GIRL: Yeah, there's a thick spot in there that I can't seem to get rid of.

JERRY: A little skillful ironing.

MOUNTAIN GIRL: Yeah, that'll help, yeah right. That hasn't been ironed yet.

CHARLES: Remember I heard your double album here for the first time?

JERRY: Right, I remember playing it for you, my test pressings.

CHARLES: I have to tell you a story. I heard it all and I knew it was all magic and then it came out and I was back in the East and everybody was down and gloomy and depressed and then we played it and there was no magic at all and I thought, "Oh, this is so awful," you know, and "How did I ever think it was magical" and everything else and it took about another month before I could hear it again.

JERRY: Right.

CHARLES: The magic. Then it was always there from then on, but like it was amazing. It was like being afraid it wasn't there and so the fear brought you down.

JERRY: Right, it's only a record, you know, it's only sounds in your ear.

CHARLES: I want to ask about Bertha. Why do you tell her you got to leave and at the same time . . .

JERRY: Well, you've got to know who Bertha is.

CHARLES: I don't know who Bertha is.

JERRY: Bertha is a big electric fan that we used to have in the office upstairs. Colossal electric fan, and you'd plug it into the wall and it would hop along on the ground. It was this huge motor and way overpowered and the fan was a little off kilter and it would bounce around and bang up and down. And it would blow this tremendous gale of wind. It was the only air conditioning that we had at the time and if you left it for a minute, it would crash into the wall and chew a big piece out of it. It was like having a big airplane propeller, you know, live, you know, running around.

CHARLES: Bertha don't come around here anymore. That's amazing. Well, everybody either thinks it's either your mother—that's what some people think.

JERRY: I like that. That's good, let them think.

MOUNTAIN GIRL: Do you want these?

CHARLES: I don't think so. Or else they think—what else besides your mother? Oh, a girl friend.

JERRY: Oh yeah, right. Well, it's all those things too, you know. It's whoever it is you don't want to come around anymore.

CHARLES: I need you, but I don't want you to come around. It's not just don't want you to come around, but I need you to. That album is like a history of the Dead.

JERRY: In a way, yeah, you could.

CHARLES: It starts when you leave home like "Momma Tried to Tell Me."

JERRY: Right.

CHARLES: Then you're playing in the band. Then you go through "The Other One" and then you come out after "The Other One" with . . .

JERRY: "Going Down the Road Feeling Bad."

CHARLES: Yeah. That's what made me just feel like it was a piece of history.

JERRY: Yeah, although it wasn't conscious. Those songs chose themselves.

CHARLES: Yeah, but they chose themselves in an order.

JERRY: That's true, that's true.

CHARLES: I mean like, first you left home and then you had the psychedelic time and then you had . . . and "Wharf Rat" is way down hoping for salvation.

JERRY: Right, well, that's like an alternate bummer. That's like a possible ending.

CHARLES: Yeah, now I understand that.

JERRY: This is the bad news and this is the good news.

CHARLES: But in a certain way maybe "Wharf Rat" was a place where you could imagine being if you had to be like Bombay.

JERRY: Sure, sure man. I know that guy.

CHARLES: Yeah, that's a thing I didn't understand. I did on one level, but I didn't on another. See, that album really works.

JERRY: Well, pure luck. Pure luck.

CHARLES: I remember you putting it together.

JERRY: Right, right.

CHARLES: Sitting there and sitting there.

JERRY: Right.

CHARLES: See, this is my conception of work. That work is going to be a thing that people feel so happy doing.

JERRY: Right on.

CHARLES: And that's the way it will be whether you're an accountant or a dentist.

JERRY: That's the Grateful Dead's theme. You can get high doing what you're doing and you can do it real good, I mean . . .

CHARLES: Right.

JERRY: That's the theme, I mean, on that level anyway.

CHARLES: Isn't that incredible that that's . . .

JERRY: Amazing. Yeah right. *(pause)*

CHARLES: Like one kid wrote me a letter, like somebody I know very well, and he said, "I just can't stand any more freedom." This is a friend of mine and he's twenty-one years old. And he said, "I want to be guided and directed. I must have limits placed on me. I know that I function best with less freedom."

JERRY: Hmmm!

CHARLES: And that blew my mind, that letter. Because that was like a statement that the world had opened up too fast, you see.

JERRY: Right.

CHARLES: And I think that's like a statement of what a lot of kids, at least, feel now, is like they feel it's too threatening.

JERRY: Right.

CHARLES: And I'd like to join them and hide out too, but . . .

JERRY: Where is there to hide out?

CHARLES: There is no place, is there?

JERRY: No, there isn't any place that . . . I mean, that's the thing of the obvious alternative for somebody like us would be to move to another country, but there's no moving away from what's happening here.

CHARLES: No.

JERRY: You know, there's no moving away from it because that's what's happening everywhere. That's part of that commitment information. I mean that's part of my input which helps me make the decision in terms of commitment.

CHARLES: You just look around you and you say, "This is what's happening in my lifetime and if I want to live in my lifetime I have to choose to do this."

JERRY: Yeah.

CHARLES: And even if it was put on you, you would still choose it.

JERRY: Yeah.

CHARLES: You know what I mean. Even if you had no choice of some other thing.

JERRY: Right.

CHARLES: You grow up in a certain way and everything happens to you and then one day you stand up and look at it all and say, "I choose it."

JERRY: Right, right. "I'll take it." Okay.

CHARLES: Yeah, I'll accept it or . . . is another word for it.

JERRY: Hm, hmmm.

CHARLES: Well, for you to do that in the last two months is so absolutely incredible.

JERRY: Yeah, it's pretty far-out.

CHARLES: Did you talk about it with other people in the band?

JERRY: No, no. Well, yeah, I've been manifesting it.

CHARLES: Yeah, so they know about it.

JERRY: Yeah, they know it, I mean.

CHARLES: They haven't necessarily reached that spot, each of them, maybe.

JERRY: I think that you know it's generally being made all around.

CHARLES: Well, what I wanted to say now—this is going to be like getting into like my broad generalization side.

JERRY: Oh, oh.

CHARLES: Oh, oh. No, I think it's the thing that is now happening across the country to people. I really think like people are saying, "Alright, this is it. I choose it and I'm going to make something really great out of it."

JERRY: Right.

CHARLES: It's like, that's the news if I were to broadcast the news.

JERRY: Yeah, if there's news, that's the news.

CHARLES: That's right. And I think that that was not happening like all those years, Country Joe and the Fish and all that.

JERRY: No, no.

CHARLES: No, it was just uncommitted, "Let it happen to me."

JERRY: Right.

CHARLES: But now, it's like there's a choice happening in me.

JERRY: Yeah, uh huh.

CHARLES: And I know it only because of what's happening in me. I just take that to be one good illustration.

JERRY: Right, there you go, right.

CHARLES: That's the news. *(Mountain Girl brings in some flowers)* Oh, those are really beautiful.

JERRY: Those guys are pretty . . .

MOUNTAIN GIRL: Yeah, really candy-striped camellias.

JERRY: Of course they're dead now.

MOUNTAIN GIRL: No, they'll last a long time in water. They'll bloom. All the buds will bloom if I keep water in here.

CHARLES: I go out and buy flowers every day. They're just a good kind of thing to have.

MOUNTAIN GIRL: Most of the flowers you get in the City are weird. Carnations . . . yuckkk!

CHARLES: Carnations . . . a white sport coat.

JERRY: And a pink carnation.

MOUNTAIN GIRL: Yeah, these guys, they don't really go in there with them other flowers, do they?

CHARLES: Neither of us ever had that in our lives, you see.

JERRY: I never had that.

CHARLES: For different reasons, we didn't have that. I because I was too much of a creep.

JERRY: *(laughter)* Too much of a creep.

MOUNTAIN GIRL: Too weird. Nobody would go out with you.

CHARLES: And you because you were too weird. Yeah, it's like the opposite sides.

MOUNTAIN GIRL: Because you were such a punk.

CHARLES: But think about that. Like you had the, you know, David Nelson.

JERRY: Right. The Nelson family.

CHARLES: David was the square.

JERRY: Right, straight guy.

CHARLES: Yeah, really straight. Just the square shoulders taking his girl to the dance.

JERRY: Right.

CHARLES: Of course, he gets left at the dance.

MOUNTAIN GIRL: Right, for his brother, Ricky, who brought his guitar.

CHARLES: Yeah.

MOUNTAIN GIRL: Really Jerry, it's just a whole big Ozzie and Harriet story.

JERRY: Right, Ozzie and Harriet consciousness.

CHARLES: I think that's exactly like this thing of choosing—that moment you choose and then you can do anything.

JERRY: It frees you.

CHARLES: Yeah, that's it. That's it, you know what you're doing.

JERRY: Right, and once you know what you're doing, you can do it full blast. I guess, I mean you can do it as full blast as, you know, how many cars will let you pass them.

CHARLES: Yeah, but for me, I still have an incredible amount of space to blast away and so do you.

JERRY: Right.

MOUNTAIN GIRL: I was going to make some dinner.

JERRY: Were you?

MOUNTAIN GIRL: Yeah!

JERRY: Okay.

MOUNTAIN GIRL: Don't you have to work tonight?

JERRY: Yup.

MOUNTAIN GIRL: What?

JERRY: Yah.

CHARLES: I've lost track of everything from time to . . .

JERRY: What, again?

CHARLES: Yeah, it always happens. But I'll look at my watch. It's twenty after four.

JERRY: Hm hmmm. Pretty close.

CHARLES: Where are you going to play?

JERRY: I'm not playing, I'm mixing.

CHARLES: Oh, great.

JERRY: Bobby's album.

CHARLES: I enjoyed watching that process. It was interesting.

JERRY: It's fun.

CHARLES: Bobby didn't say a word and I felt out of communication with him.

JERRY: Hm hmmm.

CHARLES: But I think I know Phil without much effort, but I don't think I know Bobby at all.

JERRY: Bobby's great.

CHARLES: Well, I like him from the way he sings, but I can't tell any more than that.

JERRY: You'll be able to tell more from this record.

CHARLES: Yeah. Do you know, you ought to publish a picture of Hunter. Everybody . . .

JERRY: Hunter won't have any of that.

CHARLES: Everybody wants to know what he looks like and I suspected . . .

JERRY: Well, they'll never find out. He likes to be able to maintain his own universe.

CHARLES: Yeah. Does he go around with you now?

JERRY: Oh, yeah, sure. (*pause*)

CHARLES: I was just thinking that authors autograph books and you haven't yet gotten into autographing albums, but *don't*.

JERRY: Oh, I've autographed a few.

CHARLES: But don't, it's a bunch of bullshit. It's like real bullshit. But it's a, well you know what I mean.

JERRY: I've got an autographed version of your book.

CHARLES: Oh.

JERRY: I intend to get a lot for it on the market someday. Yuk yuk.

CHARLES: Well, what can I say to that? It was an early attempt to communicate with you.

JERRY: Sure.

CHARLES: Unsuccessful compared to, or not as good as, later attempts.

JERRY: Right, it was a good start, what the hell.

CHARLES: That's what it's like it was for.

JERRY: I can dig it.

CHARLES: Yeah, well, that's all it was.

JERRY: I like it, I mean, you know, I think that that stuff is all okay.

CHARLES: Hm hmmm. But I don't even know that voice in me very well myself, now, you know.

JERRY: Right, that's why I'll get all weird when you start talking about the Grateful Dead, you know what I mean.

CHARLES: Yeah.

JERRY: You know, because sure, I mean, you know, that's a difficult thing.

CHARLES: Hm hmmm. But it's like it's good to talk about a little bit.

JERRY: Really, man, it's great to have somebody to talk to about it.

CHARLES: I'm sitting here; Mountain Girl?

MOUNTAIN GIRL: Uh?

CHARLES: You're the one that knows what I should be doing. Should I be sitting here at this point?

MOUNTAIN GIRL: I don't care. Probably. I don't know. Whatever seems right to you.

CHARLES: Well, I'm asking you a very definite question.

MOUNTAIN GIRL: Oh, it's fine for you to be sitting there.

CHARLES: Is it alright?

MOUNTAIN GIRL: Sure, go right ahead.

CHARLES: Okay. Because I can't rely on my own . . .

JERRY: Judgment.

CHARLES: Judgment.

JERRY: Yeah right, I have that difficulty a lot.

CHARLES: Alright.

JERRY: But you can't rely on anybody else's either.

CHARLES: That's right. Well, my judgment is that it is pretty nice of you, you know, long long time between times, because I'll be back being a professor and you'll be in Europe.

JERRY: Professor. *(laughter)*

CHARLES: I think it, I was spotted. I went to a Japanese restaurant, with my notebook just to sit there and write, I often do that, and the waitress said, "You're a professor, aren't you?"

MOUNTAIN GIRL: Well, you look like a professor.

CHARLES: Yeah.

MOUNTAIN GIRL: My father looks like a professor too.

JERRY: Yeah.

MOUNTAIN GIRL: That same kind of look—distinguished.

JERRY: He looks a lot tweedier, though.

MOUNTAIN GIRL: But he . . .

JERRY: You look more like a liberal arts professor.

CHARLES: Yeah, yeah, yeah. What you need to do, you see, is you like take a notebook like this notebook and you go to some place where you feel completely different. Like I might go to a Russian restaurant and order borscht and just be Russian there, or a Japanese place, and then I just sit there and I have a new setting.

JERRY: Right, that's nice.

CHARLES: I do a whole lot of that. Or you could go to a high school sports event.

JERRY: Chestnut purée.

CHARLES: Chestnut purée.

JERRY: Yeah, that's a Bulgarian dessert that's fantastic.

MOUNTAIN GIRL: Wait till we go to France.

JERRY: God, I love it.

MOUNTAIN GIRL: Wait till we go to France, Germany.

CHARLES: Oh, you're going to . . . listen, you've got to get educated about food.

JERRY: Oh, well we've got MacIntyre along and he's like a regular straight ahead by the book gourmet.

CHARLES: Okay, because . . .

MOUNTAIN GIRL: You know, I pay attention when I read all that kind of stuff.

CHARLES: If you go to this like fabulous restaurant in France and order a roast beef on rye.

JERRY: No, I'm not that lame.

CHARLES: Okay.

JERRY: You know, I mean, I admit I'm limited, but I'm certainly not, you know . . .

CHARLES: No, but I'll always think of your gourmet side of sort of being tacos out of a box.

JERRY: Right, right, well, a little bit. Well, in that I'm completely indifferent, you know what I mean.

CHARLES: Yeah, that's what I can tell.

JERRY: I'll eat anything equally and with little relish or with none at all. That's from years of smoking and, you know, beatnik living, you know, crackers and . . .

CHARLES: The big thing that people liked was the pineapple, the cans of pineapple. People talk about that and say, "I couldn't live on cans of pineapple."

JERRY: It happened, you know. I would have preferred yogurt, or a little yogurt to go with all that fucking pineapple.

MOUNTAIN GIRL: Did I hear a call for yogurt? I have some yogurt.

JERRY: No, I really don't want anything right now, I just ate, didn't I? Or was it a long time ago?

CHARLES: I think you didn't eat for a long time ago, because you turned down a peanut butter and jelly sandwich.

MOUNTAIN GIRL: He came in here and snuck one on the sly.

JERRY: Half of one.

CHARLES: Oh.

MOUNTAIN GIRL: I'll just keep making some dinner.

JERRY: Okay. *(laughter)*

MOUNTAIN GIRL: I won't worry about whether you eat it or not.

JERRY: Right.

CHARLES: Well, I might eat some.

MOUNTAIN GIRL: Well, that's alright.

CHARLES: Because I love the idea of eating.

JERRY: Then eat you shall. I wish you could come and visit sometime. It's neat.

CHARLES: Somewhere in San Rafael.

MOUNTAIN GIRL: It's like one of the main drags, the north-south main drag, the old main street.

CHARLES: Well, I've been hanging out anyway in sort of one area of Berkeley that's my place now for the last period of time.

MOUNTAIN GIRL: At the Co-Op.

CHARLES: Yeah, well I've spent a lot of time at the Co-Op. Nobody understood, nobody knew it was a place in my head when I wrote about it in the book and so they keep writing serious letters like, "I've been to the Co-Op and the Safeway, and I can't really see any objective difference between them."

MOUNTAIN GIRL: You're kidding.

CHARLES: They write me letters like that.

MOUNTAIN GIRL: God, the Safeway and the Co-Op are as far apart as Nixon and Garcia.

CHARLES: That's what I thought but, anyway the point was that it was a place in my head . . .

JERRY: Right, right.

CHARLES: What difference does it make, you know, whether it really is so.

JERRY: Well, it might make a difference to somebody because . . . It's on a level that somebody can dig. And that's the thing that you, that what you're doing is downgrading your own trip back there . . . In the sense of whether or not you communicated successfully that idea in that book because the feedback has been a little weird about it.

CHARLES: Some of it's been weird.

JERRY: Right, but you know, I would use your argument on me, on you.

CHARLES: Yeah.

JERRY: About, what the hell, man, there's somebody who's going to dig that level or write you back, you know what I mean. Don't sweat about the small stuff, what the hell, you know.

CHARLES: Now the people I'd like to get to know next are the people that I'll communicate with next.

JERRY: Right, there you go.

CHARLES: That's what's so great, you can just send out a whole new thing.

JERRY: Play a different style of music.

CHARLES: There are new groovy people.

JERRY: Put on your funny hat and your rubber nose.

MOUNTAIN GIRL: What happened to your rubber nose, Garcia?

JERRY: I got it around here somewhere. Want to hear the new New Riders of the Purple Sage?

CHARLES: Oh, yes, yes, yes.

JERRY: All reet. Change of pace and consciousness.

A SIGNPOST TO NEW SPACE

Jerry Garcia is a symbol of everything that is new and changing and rebellious in America. Yet when we read his story, we find that be is the very essence of the old American dream . . . That illumination makes a document that has real value for the history of our times, a guide to understanding some of the profound cultural changes of the sixties. I believe it has value for people who are trying to find themselves in a new and almost unrecognizable America. Jerry Garcia says that the Grateful Dead try to be a signpost to new space. I think this book can help some readers both to recognize what is happening around them and to find new space in their own lives. At least I can say it has done those things for me.

—Charles Reich

INDEX